Revie

for
At the Crest of the Tidal Wave

"There is an old Arab Proverb which says that 'When you go shopping for wisdom, visit every tent in the bazaar.' When Robert Prechter published his first book in 1978 predicting the super bull market of the 1980s, only a very few people visited his tent. I hope more people will visit his tent today, in order to understand the financial, economic and social implications of *At the Crest of the Tidal Wave*."   — Marc Faber, Faber Ltd., Hong Kong

"Recently I finished reading for the third time Charles Mackay's classic, *Extraordinary Popular Delusions and the Madness of Crowds*, first published in 1841. Not much has changed, and here we are at yet another turning point in history. Bob Prechter's *At the Crest of the Tidal Wave* probably will join Mackay's famous book as one of the most prescient of the past 175 years. After more than forty years in the stock market, and as a fellow student of market history who thoroughly enjoys Prechter's insights, I say to you...ignore Bob's book at your peril."
— Charles Allmon, President, *Growth Stock Outlook*

"The icy logic and stunning originality with which Prechter predicts the impending death of our Grand Bull Market make *At the Crest of the Tidal Wave* eminently worthy of attention. But the fact that years ago this same author stood virtually alone in prophesying the birth of this very same bull market renders his current vision absolutely indispensable to serious investors."   — Paul Macrae Montgomery, Legg Mason Wood Walker

"The scholarly discipline, ultra long-term historical perspective and topical diversity of Robert Prechter's discerning *At the Crest of the Tidal Wave* will challenge all serious investors to re-examine today's 'buy and hold' mantra."   — Henry Van der Eb, Chairman, Mathers Fund

"Prechter reveals the Elliott Wave 'big picture' in compelling detail in a book that belongs in every investor's library. It could help save your investment future."   — Peter Eliades, Editor, *Stockmarket Cycles*

"*At the Crest of the Tidal Wave* is a brilliant and important piece of long wave research with potentially devastating investment implications for the future."   — Paul Tudor Jones II, President, Tudor Investment Corp.

"I have been fortunate to count Bob Prechter among my close friends for many years. As such, I have been elated by his astonishing record of eerily accurate market calls over more than two decades. (But as a consummate gold bug with a bullish bias toward the yellow metal, I have often wished that Bob's success wouldn't come at my expense!) Bob has done it again with *At the Crest of the Tidal Wave*. In his typically clear style, he makes the complex seem simple, and explains what the Elliott Wave Principle predicts for each major market. *At the Crest of the Tidal Wave* is the closest thing to a crystal ball that we could hope for. It is a road map to the future that no investor should be without."
          — James U. Blanchard III, Chairman, Jefferson Financial

"Based on his data and revealing multi-century charts, Mr. Prechter has arrived at a spectacularly bearish conclusion whose very specificity deserves consideration by all serious market students. It will be a long time before this convincing case for a Major Bear Market turns out to have been correct, as is always true for farsighted predictions. But all of Mr. Prechter's very readable books deserve a place in investors' libraries because if his haruspications turn out to have been correct, he will be a historic figure. His positions are always worth considering and the marvelous long-term charts are a bonus."   — James Dines, Editor, *The Dines Letter*

"Human nature includes 'the madness of crowds.' Current financial excesses are destined to collapse in overreaction and Bob Prechter explains why. *At the Crest of the Tidal Wave* is required reading if one wants to prepare for a coming rare and tragic event."
          — Ron Paul, Congressman from Texas 1976-1984

"Read this book. You may not agree, but you must understand Prechter's argument. Ignorance may not be bliss — it may mean bankruptcy. Ignore the message at your risk."   — Richard D. Lamm, Dartmouth College Fellow, Governor of Colorado 1975-1987

"This is a must read not only for serious investors but for those who are interested in the financial future of our world and the quality of their lives."   — Anthony Robbins, Author, *Awaken the Giant Within*; *Unlimited Power*

"In his first book, *Elliott Wave Principle*, Bob provided insights to the stock market for the last 15 years. In *At the Crest of the Tidal Wave*, Bob provides the road map for the next 15 years."
— Tom Joseph, President, Trading Techniques and Developer of GET Elliott Wave software

"This is no conventional and easy-to-dismiss work. Rather, *At the Crest of the Tidal Wave* is an analysis of both the past and a possible future based on the most clear-sighted and dispassionate intellectual rigour. Prechter demonstrates that the Wave Principle is an analytical tool that no serious historian should ignore." — Dr. George Herring, Senior Lecturer, Historical Studies University College of Ripon & York, St. John (U.K.)

"Seeking market truth is more important than following market fictions. If you believe in life insurance, burglar alarms, vaccinations and preventive medicine — and you are an investor — *At the Crest of the Tidal Wave* is a must read for you." —Julian Snyder, Editor, *International Moneyline*

"Robert Prechter is one of the sharpest financial minds I've ever met. *At the Crest of the Tidal Wave* is must reading for every investor. This book is a strong dose of reality for a world that increasingly bases investment decisions on fantasy." —Richard Maybury, President, Henry-Madison Research

"For *any* investor whose net worth exceeds the price of this current masterpiece, *At the Crest of the Tidal Wave* is an absolute BUY and HOLD. It is the convergence and epitome of courage, experience, fact, analysis, reflection and the knowledge of history, applied to preparing for one's future. Agree or disagree, Bob's work is to be respected, absorbed, and constantly reflected upon."
— Guy N. Dacon, Jr., V.P. Investments, Dean Witter Reynolds

"Once in a great while you come across a book you know you should listen to. This is one of them. If fact, it was gripping; I couldn't put it down. My own area of expertise, chaos and complexity theory, also suggests we are on the cusp of a tidal wave, but the obviousness of Prechter's argument and the clarity of his numbers — those amazing numbers — made me a believer for the first time. Put aside all those optimistic economic fairy tales, look at the evidence and face the implications of the change that lies ahead."
— Dr. S. J. Goerner, Director, Triangle Center for the Study of Complex Systems

"This latest masterpiece from Elliott Wave expert Robert Prechter will go down in history as an investment classic if his analysis is correct. Just as the majority did not believe his forecast of a quadrupling of the Dow in the 1980s, so the skeptics now reject this latest forecast. In my opinion, every investor owes it to himself to read this book, then judge whether the analysis and predictions for a devastating bear market sometime in the 1990s should at least be considered as a possibility. Robert cannot be described as the typical 'perpetual gloom and doomer.' In fact, for most of the time that I have known him, he was the greatest optimist. Therefore, his analysis should not be taken lightly. This book is thought provoking, not only for the expert investor, but even for the novice." — Bert Dohmen, President, Dohmen Capital Research Institute

"The feeling in the land today is that all investments always go up long term. *At the Crest* reminds us that there have been times in history when they actually go down for protracted periods, and explains why we may be on the verge of another such time. Today's wildly bullish money mangers need to be aware of Bob Prechter and his arguments, whether they agree with him or not." — Jim Rogers, professional investor and author of *Investment Biker: On the Road With Jim Rogers*

"In his new book, Robert Prechter does a complete analysis of the current economic situation and its implications for the future. He clearly points, in a step-by-step fashion, to the unfolding of the Elliott Waves that will impact the investor in the next generation. Prechter's research is complete and formidable. Anyone who has read any of his previous books knows the depths he goes to understand history and its relationship to the present and the future. There can be no doubt that the tide is turning, and upon reading the research and insights in this new book there is little doubt about the effects. This is a must read book for anyone who is serious about understanding and adapting to the future." — Richard Mogey, Executive Director, The Foundation for the Study of Cycles

"This is the most useful book on investing since the 1841 publication of Mackay's *Extraordinary Popular Delusions and the Madness of Crowds*. In fact, it is the best study of the market I've ever read. Robert Prechter and R.N. Elliott will be remembered as the two greatest social scientists of this century for their understanding of mass psychology, markets, and the economy." — Donald N. Evans, President, FX500 Money Management

"*At the Crest of the Tidal Wave* is a provocative and well-written book. Even readers who disagree with the author's methods will thoroughly enjoy this challenge to the current widespread optimism about the future direction of stock prices." — Professor Robert I. Webb,
McIntire School of Commerce, University of Virginia

"Prechter's in-depth analysis of the secular ebbs and flows in global financial markets is must reading for any serious investor. Knowing long term risks and opportunities in financial markets ahead of time is absolutely the key to consistent investment success."
— Felix Zulauf, Zulauf Asset Management, Zurich

"As Robert Prechter demonstrated in his prescient forecast of the 1982 mega-bull market, he's not afraid to stand apart from the crowd. This book presents a convincing point-by-point case for a deflationary 'accident' that could turn financial markets upside down and destroy the portfolio of an unprepared investor." — James B. Stack, President, InvesTech Research

"Your book is truly a monumental achievement that refines and perfects the original ideas advanced by Elliott himself who, I have come to realize, was one of the greatest (but sadly unappreciated) geniuses of the 20th century, if not of all time.

I congratulate you for the courage and integrity it took to publish such a book at this time, as well as for the outstanding quality of the research and analysis. The public and most financial professionals do not have the foggiest notion of how difficult it is to master something as complex as the Elliott Wave theory, or what dedication it takes to try to understand the cosmic forces that control, not only the markets, but the very rhythm of life itself.

The really important thing is not to be right all the time on every detail, but to understand the big picture - to recognize the grand design behind the apparent randomness of human behavior and indeed behind the whole course of history. You have seen the big picture with a greater clarity than anyone else, and have tried to share your vision with the public. You are absolutely right in comparing the current mutual fund craze to the South Seas Bubble. Unfortunately, very few will understand that fact, and even fewer still will act on it. Thanks for your splendid book."
— Donald J. Hoppe, financial historian
and editor of *Donald J. Hoppe's Analysis*

"I'll never forget the first time I heard about Bob Prechter. The Dow was in the 800s. No one dared forecast a rise to much beyond the 1000 level. Bob Prechter was forecasting Dow 3700. Wall Street said he was stark raving mad. But when they met Prechter in person, they were surprised to find a rational, analytical, and self-critical individual. His analysis, described in his 1978 book, *Elliott Wave Principle*, had a certain mathematical elegance that impressed readers and won devout followers. Slowly but surely, Wall Street discovered that Bob Prechter was probably the ONLY analyst alive who forecast, ahead of time, the bull market of the late 20th century — one of the greatest forecasting coups of our time. Now, Prechter is telling Wall Street that the party is about to come to an abrupt end. They've responded by slapping their hands over their eyes, ears, and everything else that might let this bad news in. I recommend that you delve into his forecasts — and the reasoning behind them."

— Martin Weiss, Weiss Research/*Safe Money Report*

AT THE CREST
OF THE TIDAL WAVE

A Forecast
for the Great Bear Market

ROBERT R. PRECHTER, JR.

JOHN WILEY & SONS
Chichester • New York • Weinheim • Brisbane • Singapore • Toronto

Originally published by New Classics Library, a division of Elliott Wave International, Inc. (Gainesville, GA)
Copyright © 1995, 1997 by Robert Rougelot Prechter, Jr.

This authorized abridged paperback edition published by
John Wiley & Sons Ltd,
Baffins Lane, Chichester,
West Sussex PO19 1UD, England
National   01243 779777
International   (+44) 1243 779777
e-mail (for orders and customer service enquiries): cs-books@wiley.co.uk
Visit our Home Page   on http://www.wiley.co.uk
                         or http://www.wiley.com

Other Wiley Editorial Offices

John Wiley & Sons, Inc., 605 Third Avenue,
New York, NY 10158-0012, USA

WILEY-VCH Verlag GmbH, Pappelallee 3,
D-69469 Weinheim, Germany

Jacaranda Wiley Ltd, 33 Park Road, Milton,
Queensland 4064, Australia

John Wiley & Sons (Asia) Pte Ltd, 2 Clementi Loop #02-01,
Jin Xing Distripark, Singapore 129809

John Wiley & Sons (Canada) Ltd, 22 Worcester Road,
Rexdale, Ontario M9W 1L1, Canada

Library of Congress Cataloging-in-Publication Data

Prechter, Robert Rougelot.
    At the crest of the tidal wave : a forecast for the great bear
market / by Robert R. Prechter, Jr.
        p.   cm.
        Abridged edition of the book originally published in June 1995 by
New Classics Library.
        Includes bibliographical references and index.
        ISBN 0-471-97954-6
        1. Stocks.   2. Speculation.   3. Investments.   I. Title.
HG6041.P74   1997
332.6—dc21   97-31513
                                                                    CIP

British Library Cataloguing in Publication Data

A catalogue record for this book is available from the British Library

ISBN   0-471-97954-6

Produced from camera-ready-copy supplied by the author
Printed and bound in Great Britain by Redwood Books Ltd, Trowbridge, Wilts
Printed on acid-free paper responsibly manufactured from sustainable forestation, for which at least two trees are planted for each one used

ACKNOWLEDGMENTS

The Wave Principle is best communicated visually. To that end, we required reliable long-term charts. Two of the best services for providing graphical representations of economic and market data are Ned Davis Research, Nokomis, FL and Ed Hyman's ISI Group, New York, NY. We are grateful to them, first, for meticulously tending to the record of where the markets and business conditions have been and then for graciously sharing that record with those of us who are trying to figure out where it is headed. Both services supplied several charts in this book and valuable assistance in marshaling the data. Richard Mogey of the Foundation for the Study of Cycles, Wayne, PA, dug deep into the Foundation's historical archives and offered several centuries of commodity and stock time series, as well as insights into economic and market conditions as far back as the 1720s. John Carder of Topline Investment Graphics, Boulder, CO, furnished us with a number of charts and helped us insure accuracy by double checking numerous time and price points. John's company is another excellent source of data that we highly recommend.

Additional information and assistance was contributed by the following people and companies: American Institute for Economic Research, Great Barrington, MA; Martin Armstrong, Princeton Economics Institute, Princeton, NJ; The Bank Credit Analyst, Montreal, QB; Barclays Trading Group, Fairfield, IA; Jim Bianco, Arbor Trading, Barrington, IL; Bridgewater Group, Wilton, CT; Coin World, Sydney, OH; The Conference Board, New York, NY; James Dines, The Dines Letter, San Francisco, CA; Eagledata, Indianapolis, IN; Peter Eliades, Stockmarket Cycles, Santa Rosa, CA; the Federal Reserve Board, Washington DC; Grant's Interest Rate Observer, New York, NY; Investment Co. Institute, Washington, DC; Lipper Analytical Services, New York, NY; Paul Macrae Montgomery, Legg Mason, Newport News, VA; Ian McAvity, Deliberations on World Markets, Tucson, AZ; Moody's Investor Service, New York, NY; National Association of Real Estate Investment Trusts, Washington DC; National Bureau of Economic Research, New York, NY; Numismatic News, Iola, WI; Craig Peskin, Merrill Lynch Market Analysis, New York, NY; Securities Data Corp., New York, NY; Al Sindlinger, Sindlinger & Co., Wallingford, PA; Jim Stack, InvesTech, Whitefish, MT; U.S.T. Securities, Princeton, NJ; and Geraldine Weiss, Investment Quality Trends, LaJolla, CA.

4

The physical production of this book was an exhaustive task, as it is Elliott Wave International's longest book and contains over two hundred charts. I am deeply grateful for the efforts of Jane Estes, who oversaw production at every level, Karen Latvala and Sally Webb, who flowed text, entered editing changes, and helped in proofreading, and Leigh Tipton, assisted by Betsy Forrester and Angie Barringer, who patiently attended to the countless details of graph production. Peter Kendall spent numerous hours chasing down data and finding specific passages in issues of *The Elliott Wave Theorist*. In helping produce our publication every month since 1983, Dave Allman over the years researched much of the data for the book, and then oversaw chart production. Susan Willoughby meticulously developed the book jacket from a design by the author. Thanks also to the stock market not only for teaching us patience, but for maintaining its bull trend long enough to get this book out as it continues to rise in record high territory.

CONTENTS

INSTRUCTIONS FOR CONDENSED READING

This book has value to general readers who find the technical aspects of the Wave Principle difficult and even to those who recoil at the mere mention of the Fibonacci ratio in conjunction with markets. If you are among either group, I urge you to restrict your reading to Chapters 1, 6, 7, 8, 9 and 13, which will entertain you while you learn the basics of market analysis. Maybe after reading that much of the book, you will find enough sense communicated that you will give the "Elliott" portion a try. Chapter 5 is the most difficult chapter in the book. It is also the most rewarding, so take your time and read it slowly.

Please note: *For this abridged paperback edition, chapters on the Dow Jones Transportation Index, the Dow Jones Utility Index, the broad market indexes, junk bonds, gold, commodities, collectibles and real estate have been omitted. For a complete discussion of these subjects, please refer to the hardcover edition of this book, which may be ordered from New Classics Library.*

A NOTE ON TIMING AND DATA

I could have decided to wait until after the bull market passed its peak to issue a retrospective analysis. However, the utility of an analysis after the fact would be negligible. (There will be no lack of learned analysis later on, I can assure you.) Far better it appears to release this volume into the heat of the culminating investment mania and give the readers who receive the message time to act under the most advantageous market conditions.

The graphs herein were produced as of April 30, 1995. The 1997 printing incorporated some minor edits (unrelated to forecasting) as well as Appendix C.

INTRODUCTORY NOTE

Elliott Wave Principle, by Robert R. Prechter and A. J. Frost, predicted in 1978 the great stock market boom that we have since enjoyed. This book presents a detailed analysis of its impending culmination and probable aftermath.

As *The Elliott Wave Theorist* put it, "we have been witnessing one mania, an investment mania, with various outlets." This book is being published now to announce in no uncertain terms that the multi-decade financial tidal wave, which grew to a pinnacle of power over many decades and has spent several years rounding the curl, is now ready to crash. Every market that has participated in what history should designate as the Great Asset Mania will ultimately play its part in what promises to be a bear market of historic proportion.

FOREWORD

A review of sixty years of writings by Elliott, Bolton, Collins, Frost and Prechter prompts the observation that while Elliott Wave expectations from this point forward may not come to pass, the thematic progression in long term outlook over the years has certainly been consistent. Most economists, analysts and forecasters change their views every six months, six weeks or six days. Each breaking news item has to be "factored in" to a new analysis. Market patterns, in contrast, often hint at what the next news item will be. While wave structures can at times be difficult to interpret, while scenarios must sometimes be abandoned when price behavior forces a change in the ordering of probabilities for various outcomes, overall the Wave Principle provides a stable perspective. Despite the historical consistency of that perspective, it must be understood, as *Elliott Wave Principle* stated, that "we will be the first to discard our predictions if the waves tell us we must." Any approach to assessing the future necessarily delivers only the probable, not the certain. Any changes in market reality must be acknowledged no matter what one hopes, wishes or thought in the past. The analysis in this book, then, is not a stone tablet of future history. It is simply the best set of conclusions given data available up to today.

The probabilistic aspect of forecasting does not mean that no approach can have value. While many people profess to understand that fact, most act as if only professed certainty and forecasting reflective of omniscience validate an analytic approach, as if either periods of error or the acknowledgment of uncertainty prove it invalid. Upon the first inaccuracy in anticipating market events, the average investor is off looking for another method, one that will not fail to describe the future with unerring precision. As *The Elliott Wave Theorist* says in every issue, "Be advised that the market service that never makes mistakes does not exist. Long term success demands a recognition of this fact." Believing that certainty of outlook and perfection in outcome are required for successful investing is truly a prescription for disaster. It makes one susceptible to the siren song of charlatans who promise miracles on the one hand, and on the other, the paralyzing doubt engendered by those who dismiss and deride valuable methods on the basis of imperfection. Preparing for the highest probability outcome, while reordering the probabilities and altering one's actions when necessary, *is the only way to prosper consistently over a long period of time.* The outlook presented in this book demands action, and prudent readers will take it. If that action later needs to be revised, so be it.

This book is written partly as an academic exercise in applying the Wave Principle to an exciting juncture in history. Indeed, that will be its long term value. However, it is also written with what is at the moment an equally important goal: to help you conserve your wealth and perhaps be one of the few people who prosper in a financial and social environment that will surely confound 99% of the population.

"As a wave increases in height, its mass increases exponentially, as does the energy released when it breaks."

— Jon Krakauer in "Mark Foo's Last Ride," *Outside* magazine, May 1995 issue

Chapter 1

PERSPECTIVE

There is a tide in the affairs of men
Which, taken at the flood, leads on to fortune;
Omitted, all the voyage of their life
Is bound in shallows and in miseries.
On such a full sea are we now afloat,
And we must take the current when it serves
Or lose our ventures.

— Edward deVere, 17th Earl of Oxford,
a.k.a. William Shakespeare

The Wave Principle is a detailed description of how markets behave. The description reveals that mass investor psychology swings from pessimism to optimism and back in a natural sequence, creating specific patterns in price movement. Each pattern has implications regarding the position of the market within its overall progression, past, present and future. The resulting insight makes the Wave Principle the most valuable tool ever discovered for interpreting market action and for forecasting future developments. While it provides a practical guide to business and financial decisions, it is a joy to observe in other areas of social behavior as well. "Nature's Law," said R.N. Elliott, "is a phenomenon that appears to mark the progress of all human activities."

Because the Wave Principle describes patterns of collective behavior, the accuracy of any resulting market forecast is dependent upon (1) the reliability of the investing crowd's behavioral patterns and (2) the ability of an analyst to identify the relevant ones properly. In fact, the patterns, while varied, are more than reliable; in a fundamental sense, they are inviolate, a characteristic that makes wave analysis incalculably superior to other methods. Investors form a crowd whose collective action reflects a key aspect of man's nature as a social animal: He is strongly induced to adopt the feelings and convictions of the group. In a realm such as investing, in which so few are knowledgeable, the tendency toward dependence is virtually impulsive. As a result, market trends are steered not by the rational decisions of individual minds but by the peculiar collective sensibilities of the herd. The pervasive dependence among its members produces an emotional interpersonal dynamic that, like all feedback systems, has *form*. As a result, the crowd behaves essentially the same way in every market cycle, regardless of degree. Some trends last longer than others and some travel further than others, but the psychological progression through each bull and bear market is always the same. Knowledge of this dynamic is the only reliable basis upon which an investor can rise above the crowd and think, and act, independently of it. Elliott's method for determining the stage of an up/down cycle for any degree of market trend has stood the test of time through such diverse applications as profitably trading tick-by-tick patterns from the floor of the Chicago Board Options Exchange to correctly forecasting trends lasting decades.

The ability of an analyst to identify the relevant patterns, interpret them properly, and anticipate the ones to follow is another matter. *That* task is exceedingly difficult, as the uncertainties expressed throughout this book attest. Nevertheless, even on that score, the Wave Principle provides some advantages that most forecasting methods lack. For instance, it provides a method of ranking alternative possibilities. Also important, it forces the analyst to look at the big picture. A proper long term perspective elevates the wave analyst above the cacophony of daily news. It provides the opportunity to make sense of the great trend changes in markets and the dramatic social events that accompany them. Perhaps most important, using the Wave Principle assures that the ultimate determinant of the objective analyst's opinion is the *market*, not a presumption about outside causes. It thus allows for objectively placed stops and a basis for changing one's opinion before losses mount.

There are many published examples, going back sixty years, of the utility of this perspective as interpreted by the foremost practitioners of Elliott Wave forecasting. As one example that pertains to this book, from November 1979 to April 1981, several issues of *The Elliott Wave Theorist* presented studies showing that the great era of accelerating inflation in the United States was ending. This conclusion was based solely upon the completion of long term price patterns in investment markets that portended a sea change in financial and sociological trends. When the tide changed in 1980-1982, it changed to disinflation, i.e., a sharply lower rate of inflation that was enough to reverse the ascent of interest rates and commodity prices. This transformation set the stage for three major financial events: (1) a 12-year advance in the bond market, (2) a blowoff, region by region, of the long running rise in real estate, and (3) an acceleration in the stock market boom that A.J. Frost and I had forecast in our 1978 book, *Elliott Wave Principle.* Despite six decades of on-balance success in forecasts at this magnitude of importance, the Wave Principle is ignored by most financial professionals. Why is that?

Several years ago, a friend gave me a copy of a study by a university professor of psychology. It went like this: In one room, a number of students were told to write an essay explaining why either the Zulus or the British would win a war that had presumably taken place in the 1800s in Africa. The students were given a list of the strengths and weaknesses of each side. The list had been constructed to make the two forces appear equally matched. In several trials, the number of essays supporting each side was about the same. Then one variable was introduced: The students were told that the Zulus had won the war. They were then instructed to *ignore that historical fact*, to write their essays on the balance of the adversaries' strengths and weaknesses alone. As you might guess, over 80% of the essays argued that the Zulus obviously had the superior force. After-the-fact knowledge colors one's view of the past so as to make any course of events appear inevitable, as if forecasting them was no trick at all.

It is impossible for most people to appreciate retrospectively the value of having a tool that provided the perspective necessary to understand the huge potential of the market in 1982, as the Wave Principle did. Calling for the Dow to rise 3000 points (back when 3000 points really meant something) from the 900 level was a dramatic prediction, yet *The Elliott Wave Theorist* gave the reasons for it to happen, quite without the benefit of hindsight. Today, people think a Dow in the 4000s is perfectly normal, and wonder why anyone would have doubted the prediction. The human trait that our professor discovered robs accurate forecasts of their due in the minds of most people. *After* an event, it always seems "normal," if not "obvious" to most people that it should have occurred. This human trait keeps people from ever bothering to investigate scientifically the few approaches to anticipating the future that actually work.

As valuable as that recognition of a major change in the early 1980s was to investors, it is well to keep in mind that wave analysts have been wrong on markets at times, sometimes very wrong. A few such times are mentioned in this book. In the end, you will have to judge the evidence for yourself. My own level of confidence at this juncture is high, a fact that perhaps shows too much in these pages. Yet, while reticence in the field of financial forecasting is often a virtue, when evidence mounts and the time is right, it is a vice.

I am writing this book now because I believe that another financial sea change is at hand. Although the Dow Jones Industrial Average and the World Stock Index are at all-time highs as this is written, and global economic forecasts are uniformly optimistic, long term wave patterns indicate that we will soon witness a change in financial trends that will prove to be *more* important than that of the early 1980s. *The Elliott Wave Theorist* said this in 1983:

> If our ongoing analysis is correct, the current environment is providing a once-in-a-generation money making opportunity. This opportunity takes on greater importance, however, because it may well precede not merely a business cycle downswing, but the biggest financial catastrophe since the founding of the Republic. In other words, we had better make our fortunes now just in case "Elliott" is right about the aftermath.

What is that aftermath? What will take the place of our long standing boom? According to my interpretation of the price patterns, the primary event will be a decline of historic proportion in stock prices, which will result in an economic depression. If an across-the-board deflation occurs, which has a substantial probability, then real estate, commodities and all bonds issued by other than impeccably solvent sources will fall in value as well.

The onset of the severe economic contraction will be signaled by a downturn in the stock market's blue chip averages. All other markets that can provide advance warning of such a change, including those for interest rates, real estate, and stock groups such as the Utilities and many secondary stocks, have *already turned down*, as have several foreign stock markets. The major U.S. stock market averages represent the last domino in the entire financial game, the only one that has yet to begin tipping, so that is currently the place to focus.

For sixteen years, since the very first issue of *The Elliott Wave Theorist* in April 1979, the front page table has included a box for strategy at "Grand Supercycle" (i.e., very large) degree labeled, "U.S. Survival." Some people have wondered why it is even there. The coming bear market will clarify the reason. While during the first

8½ years, the box carried the attendant notice, NO ACTION WARRANTED, the recommendation since 1987 has been the conservative entreaty that you ensure PRESERVATION OF CAPITAL. It now reads CRISIS AHEAD. Unlike the message of 1982, this is not a comfortable one to deliver. Being a spokesman for the bull market was fine; the public is more comfortable buying and making money on the "long" side. Being a spokesman for a bear market, on the other hand, will bring scant rewards, since few people know how to profit from a bear. There is little satisfaction in saying, "I told you so," and little added value in saying continually, "It's going to get worse." That is why I am writing this book now: to make one statement that will stand as a reference for the duration so I can get on to other things.

The bearish prediction in this book today arouses not merely bemused derision, but arrogant and heated dismissal. This common reaction is a sure sign that a very deeply shared social vision is being challenged. I know because I have been in this position before. 1980 was the year that the bull market in precious metals ended after 13 relentless years. Gold and silver topped out in January and mining stocks topped out in September. The true believers were in a bullish heat. Opinion was so one-sided that bears on precious metals were nearly nonexistent and bulls on common stocks could hardly get a hearing. People thought the few of us who said it was time to buy stocks on the New York Stock Exchange, and bonds from what all could see was a spendthrift government, were crazy for even suggesting such a thing. These suggestions challenged the shared social vision and were dismissed as a result.

Investor psychology is once again in exactly the same state. Today's true believers are no different from those of 1980. But this time, we are witnessing not the peak of a bull market in precious metals, but in the very markets that no one wanted to buy in the early 1980s: pieces of paper called *stocks and bonds*. Once again, it has been 13 years since the bull market took off. Once again, bears on the markets in question can hardly get a hearing. The few of us who say you should be completely out of stocks and bonds and in shortest term yield bearing instruments are considered crazy for even suggesting such a thing. This outlook challenges the new shared social vision and is being dismissed accordingly.

At both ends of the Great Asset Mania, then, the long term Elliott Wave forecast was, and is, widely considered impossible. In 1982, there was a general conviction that Dow 1000 was the upside limit for any advance, and downside risk was substantial. Indeed, one prominent economist said on national television in late 1982, "A Dow 3700 target? That Elliott Wave guy is too bullish by a decimal point!" Today, our roles are reversed. The vocal long term bears of yesteryear have long since capitulated to the bullish camp, which is fearlessly extrapolating an unending long term advance interrupted by occasional "corrections" limited to 10%. The Dow's target for year-end 2000, now given by countless analysts in newspapers, is 7000 to 10,000. This time, it is "that Elliott Wave guy" who says, "You are all too bullish by a decimal point."

Truly, the skepticism that greeted Frost's and my "super bull market" thesis 13-17 years ago was nothing compared to the current disbelief that an overall severe collapse in stock price values and an economic depression are nigh. Formerly skittish investors, following the lead of today's financial media heroes, are now stock pickers, fund buyers, long term buy-and-holders, and averagers-down who disdain market timing as both impossible and foolish. The economy is expanding at a moderate rate, they say, managed by the Fed to produce "the best of all possible worlds": steady economic expansion with a low inflation rate. Republicans have captured Congress, thereby in most people's eyes guaranteeing stable growth and low capital gains taxes such as the country enjoyed during the Reagan administration. The country's longtime nemesis, Communism, is gone from Europe and dissolving in Asia. Economists are extolling the future, predicting the opening of unlimited new markets, a new era of international cooperation, the expansion of capitalism worldwide, and a resulting nirvana of explosive economic growth, continuously rising stock markets, and global prosperity. A truly optimistic consensus has taken hold. Today, long term bullishness is not merely a widespread opinion. It has gone beyond even a philosophy. It is a mantra. As a result, the news media have been pouring forth a blizzard of smug statements that Dow 10,000 is inevitable, that all one needs to know is what stocks to own, not whether to own them at all.

As in the Zulu experiment, today people look back at the peak in precious metals fifteen years ago as obvious in retrospect and wonder how people could actually have been interested in owning them. In the same way, the upcoming bear market, which will carry the Dow at least to 1000 and probably below 400, will be referenced, after it happens, as having been "inevitable" and "the result of unforeseen circumstances that nevertheless had an obvious impact."

For now, though, investors are once again caught in the passionate dream of the time and are ignoring the message of the Wave Principle just when it is the most valuable. Ten years ago, *The Elliott Wave Theorist* assured readers that "We have been making wonderful hay while the sun shines, and the balance of indicators says that the sun is still shining brightly, at least for a few more hours." At this juncture, the investment landscape is slashed with the long, dark shadows of sunset. While in the late 1970s and early 1980s, Elliott Wave analysis indicated that a major bottoming process in financial and social trends was near an end, today it indicates the opposite. With "gloom and doom" now completely out of fashion, the Wave Principle says, "It's time."

Despite my sometimes passionate exposition, a bit of which I deem necessary to counter the prevailing state of social self-hypnosis, it is important to comprehend that this is not a "gloom and doom" book. It is simply an elaboration of the second half of a forecast that was made many years ago in *Elliott Wave Principle*, which predicted both a major advance *and* a major decline. My current expectation, then, is not a conventional forecast based upon the assumed continuation of currently visible trends and forces, but the application of a rule of social change that has proved itself time and again.

The essential problem with conventional forecasts is the premise behind them. Almost everyone thinks that extramarket conditions control the future of the stock market and that the best way to forecast the market is to extrapolate such conditions indefinitely into the future. This approach never works for long, because economic and social conditions are always worst at the bottom and best at the top. They cannot be otherwise, because it is the psychology behind the markets that creates the bottoms and tops. It is also the psychology behind the markets that creates economic and social conditions. These points are crystal clear once you grasp them, but they elude, and will always elude, the vast majority of investors, both public and professional. For instance, while the times today are historically positive, upbeat and optimistic, these facts are not harbingers of trends; they are the *result* of the trends forecasted in *Elliott Wave Principle* seventeen years ago. The reason there is a dearth of "gloom and doomers" today is that the future just feels too promising for most people to bet against, which is exactly why markets must be nearly fully valued, and therefore approaching a top.

In the midst of this environment (indeed, in a reflection of it), the wave structures of the investment markets and certain components of the economy indicate that the long, wonderful upward phases dating from 1987, 1982, 1974, 1932 and 1784 are at long last drawing to a close. A dozen years ago, while resolutely maintaining its focus on the bull market, *The Elliott Wave Theorist* painted this advance scenario of the ultimate resolution, which is what we face today:

> If all goes according to expectations, the last remaining question is, what happens after wave V tops out? The Wave Principle would recognize the 3686 top as the end of wave V of (V), the peak of a Grand Supercycle that stretches all the way back to [1784]. At that point, the most devastating stock price decline in United States history will ensue: a Grand Supercycle bear market that would then "correct" all the progress dating from the late 1700s. It is expected to be so severe that a worldwide monetary and economic collapse will most certainly follow on its heels. The downside target zone would be the price area (ideally near the low) of the previous fourth wave of lesser degree, wave (IV), which fell from 386 to 41 on the Dow. Government bonds and most corporate bonds will then be on the verge of a collapse to worthlessness as the bond market comes face to face with the reality that increasingly greater long term debt cannot be serviced at double digit interest rates, no matter what the government or the economy does. Worldwide banking failures, government bankruptcy, and eventual destruction of the paper money system might be plausible [results of] a bear phase of this magnitude. Since armed conflicts often occur after severe financial crises, one would have to consider the possibility that the collapse in value of financial assets of this magnitude would presage war between the superpowers.

The above paragraph, taken from the April 6, 1983 and April 3, 1984 issues of *The Elliott Wave Theorist*, remains a succinct summary of the Elliott Wave outlook today. You can stop reading now if you wish, as the rest of this book is simply an elaboration of that description and the reasons behind it. Nevertheless, it is *time* for this elaboration. While a dozen years ago *The Elliott Wave Theorist* said, "Let's forget the 'crash' part of our forecast and concentrate on the bull market part," *it is finally time to turn our attention fully to the crash part.*

Is the outlook originally sketched out in 1978, expanded in the summary quoted above and detailed throughout this book, too extreme? *The Elliott Wave Theorist* addressed even this question in 1983, with the Dow at 1200:

In writing a book about how to apply Elliott's Wave Principle, it was virtually impossible to avoid making a forecast, since a wave interpretation of the past almost always implies something about the future. At that time, the evidence was overwhelming that the stock market was at the dawn of a tremendous bull market. Even at that stage, the Wave Principle revealed some of the details of what the bull might look like. While our Dow 3000 figure was met with some derision at the time and a good deal of skepticism even today, Elliott Wave based forecasts (even competent ones) can often appear extreme. The reason is that the Wave Principle is one of the few tools that can help an analyst anticipate *changes* in trends, *including trends that are so long term that they have become accepted as the normal state of affairs.*

Today, the long uptrend has convinced people that this nearly unprecedented situation in terms of market behavior is a normal state of affairs. (It is just a different normal state from the last one!) The only kind of analysis that can recognize the typical but rare conditions of a *major turning point in a long term trend* says that those conditions are swiftly falling into place. Thus, though the outlook in this book is extreme, it is justified.

Regardless of all our data, analyses and conclusions, however, it is improbable that every forecast detailed in this book will work out. The science of social forecasting is virtually brand new, and its application relies on severely limited data and research. Nevertheless, it is not particularly difficult to be fearless when one considers the low level of general expectations with regard to such an endeavor. To be sure, most forecasters' expectations do not work out at all. For instance, in June 1990, 88% of economists predicted continued economic expansion for at least a year. A month later, the worst recession in a decade began. As merely the latest example, a June 1994 survey of 29 of the country's most influential money managers showed that *all* of them expected the long bond yield to remain below 8% during the rest of last year. It was above 8% three months later. Evidence of the failure of conventional forecasting methods is more than anecdotal. According to *The Wall Street Journal*, a study of its own surveys since 1982 of the country's top economists reveals that in the aggregate, these acknowledged experts predicted accurately the *direction* (forget the extent) of interest rates *only 25% of the time*, which is half the success rate that would be produced purely by guessing. (Chapters 7 and 8 will elaborate on the psychology behind conventional forecasting, revealing why it produces worse than random results.) So for whatever errors this book may contain, I hope that you will not judge them too harshly.

The Wave Principle is a law governing dynamism, motion and change; it is a law of action and reaction, *not* a law of stasis. Expect change and you will live in harmony with that law. Expect the status quo and you will be swept away by the tides of history. One clear message from the Wave Principle is that collective man will enjoy the same successes and repeat the same mistakes over and over, with minor differences in specifics, throughout eternity, although each time from a higher level of advancement. Mistakes are repeated not because people fail to learn from history, as many contend, but precisely because they *do* learn from history, from *recent* history, their own experience. Home buyers from 1949 to 1989, for instance, learned that house prices only go up. This was a mistaken conclusion, but it was due to learning not badly, but *well*. The problem is that the data was limited mostly to personal experience. Social patterns result partly from the fact that life span, and therefore the depth and breadth of individual knowledge, is limited. As an antidote to this problem, the Wave Principle provides such a powerful insight into the mechanisms of social psychology that knowledge of it is a shortcut to studying all the details of history. If you can say, "Today the stock market, and therefore the social mood trend that has been in force for so long, may be finishing wave $\underline{5}$ of v of 5 of (5) of ⑤ of V of (V) of Three," you are more attuned than most to the probabilities for the future.

Although aggregate social behavior is patterned, individuals do enjoy free will. If you have the mental fortitude to do so, you can act independently of the crowd and resist being swept along by the social pressure it exerts. Indeed, informed individuals can take advantage of a knowledge of the patterns of human sociology not only to survive, but to prosper. With such knowledge, they can ride a surfboard expertly on the curl of the tidal wave rather than sit blithely unaware inside a grass hut on the beach, oblivious to the danger of the impending wash. Unfortunately, independence is excruciatingly difficult for most people to assert in socially charged situations, because the effects of the patterns are so pervasive and powerful. Hope, fear, denial and inertia are all part of the process. A general and deep disbelief that anything like the outlook presented in this book will occur, for example, is a requirement for it to happen. Nevertheless, farsighted and motivated individuals need not fall into the pattern. Once the Wave Principle is understood, social dynamics can in fact be used to your advantage. Every age includes some people who discern a major change in trend well enough in advance to prepare, lead and thrive. You might as well be one of them. If you act in time, you can put yourself in a position to observe the crowd and avoid or even profit from its excesses rather than become a part of it.

The quote that begins this chapter is spoken by Brutus in Act IV, Scene 3 of *Julius Caesar*, to which Cassius replies, *"Then, with your will, go on."* Go on we shall.

PART I:

THE STOCK MARKET

IDEALIZED ELLIOTT WAVE PATTERNS

SUMMARY OF IMPULSIVE PATTERNS

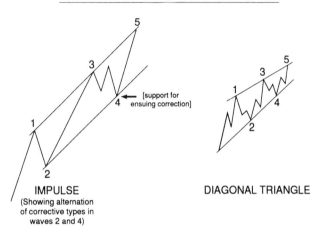

IMPULSE
(Showing alternation
of corrective types in
waves 2 and 4)

DIAGONAL TRIANGLE

SUMMARY OF CORRECTIVE PATTERNS

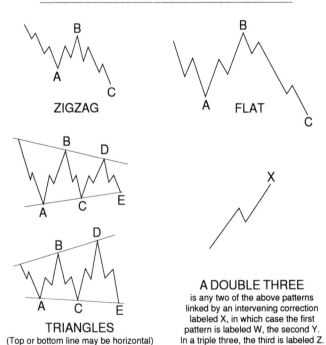

ZIGZAG

FLAT

TRIANGLES
(Top or bottom line may be horizontal)

A DOUBLE THREE
is any two of the above patterns
linked by an intervening correction
labeled X, in which case the first
pattern is labeled W, the second Y.
In a triple three, the third is labeled Z.

DEGREES OF PATTERNS (in order of relative size)	CHART LABELING
10. Millennium	ONE
9. Grand Supercycle	One
8. Supercycle	(I)
7. Cycle	I
6. Primary	①
5. Intermediate	(1)
4. Minor	1
3. Minute	i
2. Minuette	$\underline{1}$
1. Subminuette	.1

Terms used in this book, which are traditional to the Wave Principle, are summarized on these two pages and in the glossary at the end of Appendix A. Much of the presentation is technical, because there is no other way to apply a science, whether physical or social. Even without an advance understanding of these terms, readers should be able to discern their meaning from the context and the illustrations. You are welcome to jettison the traditional terms listed above and consider Supercycle degree as "degree 8," Grand Supercycle as "degree 9," etc., a convenient shorthand.

Part I is devoted to a current analysis of the stock market. To get the most out of Part I, you are advised to read *Elliott Wave Principle — Key to Market Behavior*. Each chapter in Part II takes the time to review the analytical history of the market under discussion before presenting a current analysis.

Chapter 2

PATTERNS AND THEIR IMPLICATIONS

As the authors of *Elliott Wave Principle* said with barely contained excitement seventeen years ago, "Because of the position of the Millennium wave and the pyramiding of the fives in our final composite wave picture, this decade could prove to be one of the most exciting times in world history to be writing about and studying the Elliott Wave Principle." What a time it has been! It is difficult to overstate the thrilling experience of The Exuberant Eighties and the first half of the 'nineties, which have witnessed not only a great positive social mood swing, but its results, not the least of which have been the freeing of totalitarian societies and worldwide peace agreements on a scale never before achieved. High on the thrill scale was the soaring stock market and how well it has reflected expectations based upon the Wave Principle. Before we examine that bull market, let's see how it fits into the long term picture.

THE GRAND SUPERCYCLE

In a market letter dated August 25, 1941 (see *R.N. Elliott's Masterworks*, New Classics Library, 1994), R.N. Elliott concluded that the year 1857 had marked a "wave two" bottom and 1928/1929 a "wave three" peak in a gigantic five-wave advance, the classic Elliott wave form. His labeling of waves (II) and (III) in a sequence that would ultimately be labeled (I)-(II)-(III)-(IV)-(V) was a remarkably insightful conclusion given that he had discovered the Wave Principle only five years before in smaller degree formations and that his data was limited to stock price records from 1854 to 1941.

Thirty-seven years later, A.J. Frost and I confirmed Elliott's analysis on the basis of some crucial new information. In the late 1970s, the Foundation for the Study of Cycles released a chart of U.S. stock prices dating from 1789. It was created by splicing the Dow Jones Industrial Average from 1897 to the Cowles Commission Index from 1871 to the Clement-Burgess Index from 1854 to the Cleveland Trust Company Index from 1831 to prices obtained from their independent research covering the period from 1789 to 1830. As you can see in Figure 2-1, which is updated to today, the resulting chart revealed a *clear five wave structure in progress from the late 1700s*, making it nearly certain that an advance of "Grand

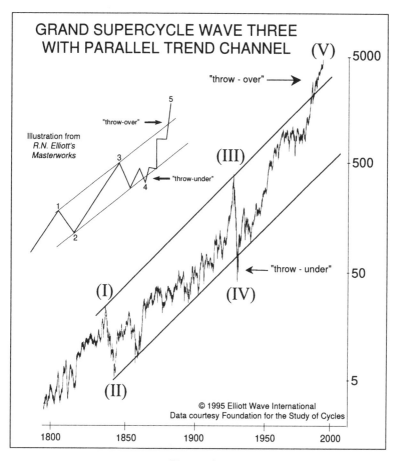

Figure 2-1

Supercycle" degree started at that time. *Elliott Wave Principle* presented the full wave count through 1977. The chart we showed then was of inflation-adjusted stock prices, which we will review in Chapter 3. Both that and the plot of actual U.S. stock prices shown in Figure 2-1 form excellent Elliott Waves.

From a low in the late 1700s, prices have risen in three distinct phases separated by two bear markets of the same degree. Usually second and fourth waves alternate in form, as you will see in all but a handful of the five-wave patterns illustrated in this book. The only aspect of this structure that is less than ideal is that both waves (II) and (IV) take the same shape, called a zigzag. Yet this *same stock price data*, when adjusted for inflation, beautifully reflect the tendency toward alternation in corrective form, as we will see in Chapter 3.

A Bit of Detective Work

What made our conclusion that a Grand Supercycle degree advance began in the late 1700s only *probably* correct, as opposed to assured, is that we lacked earlier data to prove that a bear market of the same degree had preceded it. A study of social conditions attending wave patterns uncovered some information that nevertheless supported that presumption mightily. A key characteristic of major corrective wave bottoms is that, as reflections of a deeply negative social mood, they usher in *economic depressions*, which are followed by *major wars*. The low of 1857/1859, for example, accompanied a depression and was followed by the Civil War, while the crash low of 1932 accompanied the deepest depression since the 1850s and was followed by World War II. The War of 1812 and World War I began at stock market lows of smaller degree, and were associated with recessions. Because of this correlation, the occurrence of both the Revolutionary War from 1776 to 1781 and a deep depression from 1785 to 1791 that affected the entire Western world strongly corroborated the thesis that a substantial bear market, perhaps as large as Grand Supercycle degree, had ended in the late 1700s.

A stunning confirmation of this conclusion finally arrived in the form of the record of British stock prices in the 18th century. These data were reported regularly as early as 1695 in English weekly and twice-weekly publications and were graphed in a 1981 article by Philip Mirowski in the *Journal of Economic History*. Splicing this data onto the record of the U.S. market causes the complete picture to emerge. It is clearly the case, as you can see in Figure 2-2, that a bear market in share prices was in force in England for 64 years, ending in 1784. This latter date falls neatly within, as Chapter 5 of *Elliott Wave Principle* had put it, "our presumed time period for the beginning of the Grand Supercycle in the stock market around 1770 to 1790." The bear market began in 1720 at the peak of the South Sea Bubble, a stock trading mania, and culminated with the British loss of its American colonies in the Revolutionary War. It took the classic three-wave shape, as you can see by the labels (A), (B) and (C). Corrective forces remained in effect for over six decades despite prolonged periods of vigorous economic growth in England, a fact that is consistent with a conclusion demanded by the mere fact of the Wave Principle: *stock price movements are mass psychological phenomena*, not the results of economic conditions. As market analyst Charles Kirkpatrick expressed it, "the crash from

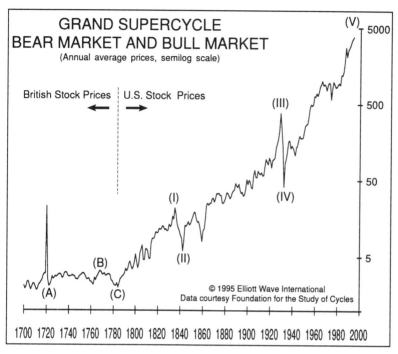

Figure 2-2

the South Sea Bubble must have really dampened enthusiasm for stock investment for a long time."

Notice that waves (II) and (IV) within the Grand Supercycle advance are smaller and far briefer than the bear market of the 1700s. This fact indicates that the correction of the 1700s is of one degree *larger* than each of those and is therefore the same degree as the ensuing rise, which is Grand Supercycle.

One may, of course, object to the idea of connecting 18th century English share prices to American stock prices to get a continuous picture, but as Americans (for the most part) *were* Britons at the time, American fortunes were closely entwined with English ones. Indeed, they still are today, as the similarities in their long term stock market trends attest. It is not unreasonable, then, to assume that British colonists shared with the British in England popular opinions on the valuation of the empire's productive enterprise, at least up until the start of the Revolutionary War. At that point, the trends diverge somewhat. Data collected by the Foundation for the Study of Cycles suggests a low in prices for the few existing American stocks either in 1788 or in or just before 1779. An earlier low in colonial stock prices makes sense in that the American market would have discounted the devastation from, and possible loss of, the Revolutionary War, while British stock prices would have reflected a probable win until the end of the war in 1781. Regardless of the exact date of the low, all available evidence supports Elliott's and our conclusion that a Grand Supercycle advance began in the late 1700s.

The Message From Two Long Term Trend Channels

The mere fact that five waves have unfolded according to the rules and guidelines of the Wave Principle for over two centuries is a strong indication that the biggest bear market since the 1700s is imminent. There are two studies that firmly support this conclusion.

First, take a look at the upper trendline drawn in Figure 2-1, which has served as a technical measure of overvaluation for over one hundred sixty years. (Some people say that technicians create trendlines, but the market creates them; we merely make them visible.) Each time in the past that the stock market advanced to meet this line, it reversed direction and suffered a bear market of historic size. It has been touched or nearly touched only three times before: at the top of wave (I) in 1835, at the top of wave (III) in 1929, and in 1966, when the inflation-adjusted DJIA (see Chapter 3) registered its orthodox (i.e., end-of-pattern) high. Those junctures were less than ideal times to be invested in stocks, as they preceded declines of 78%, 89% and 45% (74% in the Value Line index, and far more after adjusting for inflation) respectively, the three largest declines of the past two centuries. Today, for the first time ever, the Dow has *exceeded* that line. What are the implications of this feat?

The price action of most impulses (standard five-wave patterns) is bounded between parallel lines according to certain rules. The proper channel is typically drawn by connecting the lows of waves two and four, then drawing a parallel line forward from the top of wave three. One exception to this guideline is depicted by the inset in Figure 2-1, which was published by R.N. Elliott in 1946 (see *R.N. Elliott's Masterworks*, New Classics Library, 1994). It illustrates that a fifth wave will often exceed the *resistance* line of a parallel trend channel if the fourth wave, near its termination, penetrated the *support* line. As you can see, wave (IV) broke the support line, so wave (V) is ending in a break of the resistance line.

The fact that the stock market is substantially *above* this steadily rising benchmark means that stocks are more expensive than at any other time in the history of the United States. It means that stocks are more expensive than at any time since the investment manias in England and France that ended in 1720, two hundred seventy-five years ago. Chapter 6 demonstrates that this *technical* indication of overvaluation accurately reflects the overvaluation of *real assets* by all relevant measures.

To see if this conclusion is validated by wave guidelines at even larger degree, let's explore another avenue of inquiry. Because most impulse waves unfold between two parallel lines, we might be able to postulate a trend channel for the *Millennium* degree wave of which these Grand Supercycles are components. At that degree, we are certain of only two terminal years, 1720 and 1784, while being nearly certain that a third one is at hand. Figure 2-2 shows a high price in 1720 that we determined from a study of the behavior of the individual stocks traded at the time. As the graph plots annual averages, not daily extremes, we endeavored to find an equivalent figure. We took into account the majority of issues that went off the board, adjusted the average to reflect the differing times that individual stocks peak and trough, and derived an estimated aggregate decline of 91%. The resulting plot of the 1720 high may or may not be a perfect reflection of "the market," as no indexes were kept *as such* at the time, but it serves as a reasonable approximation. If you nevertheless choose to discount the analysis that this estimated top supports in the next paragraph and in Chapter 5, you are welcome to do so, as it will have no effect on this book's essential message.

The postulated peak level in 1720 provides a basis for channel analysis at the highest possible degree. It is commonly the case that subwave two within any third or fifth wave touches the support line of the larger channel. Thus, a preliminary lower line can be drawn connecting the lows of 1784 and wave (II) in 1842. This line also happens to touch perfectly the lows of 1857 and 1859, affording it further validity as a technical measure of undervaluation. We can now draw a parallel line upward from the top of 1720, as shown in Figure 2-3. The outcome is very exciting, because *the resulting line touches today's prices exactly.* This precise meeting powerfully supports both the already overwhelming case that stocks are more expensive than at any time since 1720 *and* the conclusion that the advance from 1784 is terminating. At this juncture, we are not addressing whether the rise from 1784 is wave Three or wave Five of

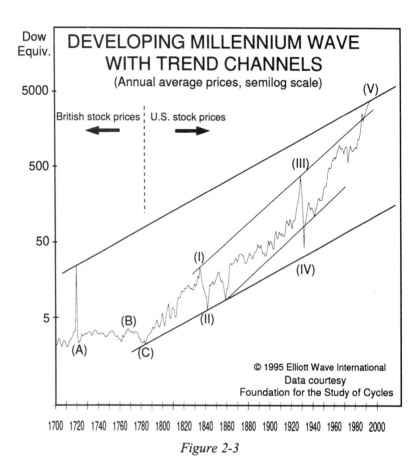

Figure 2-3

an even larger structure. The difference is of profound practical importance, though, and will be thoroughly addressed in Chapter 5.

SUPERCYCLE WAVE (V)

As you can see in Figure 2-1, Supercycle wave (V) dating from 1932 is the final component of the larger Grand Supercycle dating from 1784. Let's examine this structure in greater detail.

In 1978, *Elliott Wave Principle* argued that the pattern from the 1932 low would ultimately be labeled I-II-III-IV-V. We concluded that wave IV of that pattern had ended at the price low of December 1974, as shown at the time in Figure 2-4. As we noted then, the formation had faithfully followed all the rules and guidelines of the Wave Principle up to that point. Wave IV held above the price territory of wave I, wave III was the longest, or "extended," wave, as is most commonly the case, and the triangle pattern of wave IV alternated

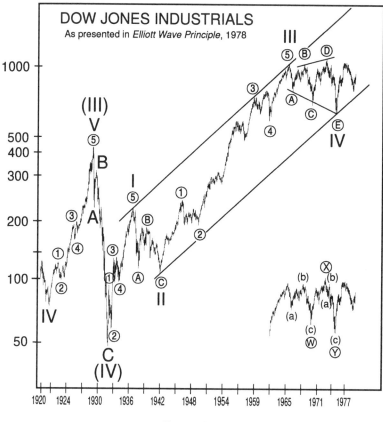

Figure 2-4

with the zigzag pattern of wave II. Subwaves I and III were well constructed also, as both sported alternation, with each Primary wave ② a zigzag and each Primary wave ④ a flat. Finally, the trend channel that resulted from connecting the highs of waves I and III, and then the lows of waves II and IV, was exactly parallel, a common characteristic of impulses.

The simple label "wave IV" implied that wave V, a great multi-year bull market of Cycle degree, lay dead ahead. Has *this* expectation been fulfilled? Figure 2-5 shows the same chart updated. As you can see, our late 1970s interpretation has proved correct in forecasting a great bull market. This rise, moreover, does appear to serve appropriately as the *fifth* wave of a five-wave formation of Supercycle degree from 1932 to the present. Now let's examine *this* structure, the great bull market forecasted in *Elliott Wave Principle*, in greater detail.

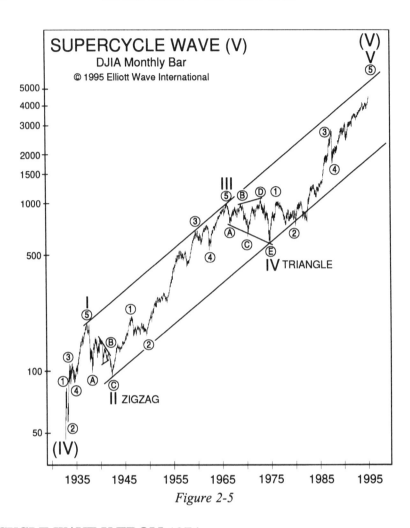

Figure 2-5

CYCLE WAVE V FROM 1974

Cycle wave V has traced out, over 21 years, the same classic Elliott Wave pattern as the Supercycle has done. As Figure 2-6 shows, the structure faithfully follows all the rules and guidelines of the Wave Principle. Wave ④ holds well above wave ①. Wave ④ is a flat, alternating with wave ②, a zigzag. Waves ③ and ⑤ are both extended, which, though otherwise rare, is characteristic of fifth waves of Cycle degree, such as the bull market of the 1920s. Finally, when the lower line of the trend channel is properly drawn by connecting the termination points of waves ② and ④ as in Figure 2-6, it precisely defines support for the pullbacks within wave ⑤.

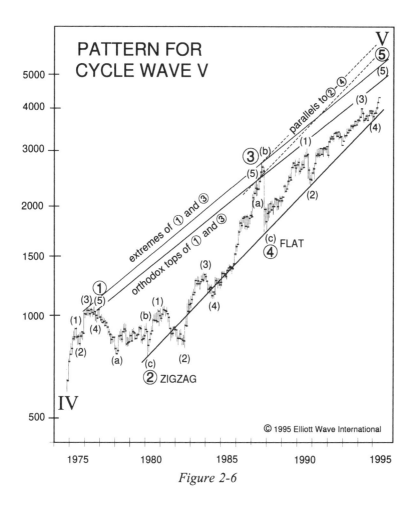

Figure 2-6

Cycle wave V is not a diagonal triangle, but connecting either the orthodox or outermost tops of waves ① and ③ (as also depicted in Figure 2-6) produces an overall wedge shape that is sometimes characteristic of fifth waves and may prove to contain subwave ⑤. The lower of these lines, by the way, is exactly parallel to one (not shown) that can be drawn from the low of wave (a) of ② to the low of wave ④. This outcome is of interest because the 1978 low, which was never broken on a closing basis, was originally marked in *Elliott Wave Principle* as the low of wave ②. The dashed lines in Figure 2-6 are discussed after the next section.

CYCLE WAVE V FROM 1982

The Elliott Wave Theorist identified the end of a sixteen year long corrective pattern in August 1982 and indicated that wave IV may have finished its pattern then rather than in 1974 (for a full presentation, see the Appendix to *Elliott Wave Principle*). This interpretation remains equally valid with that represented in Figures 2-4 through 2-6. It is therefore comforting that the two interpretations provide essentially compatible messages.

Figure 2-7 shows how Cycle wave IV labeled as ending in 1982 fits into the Supercycle. The primary difference from the standpoint

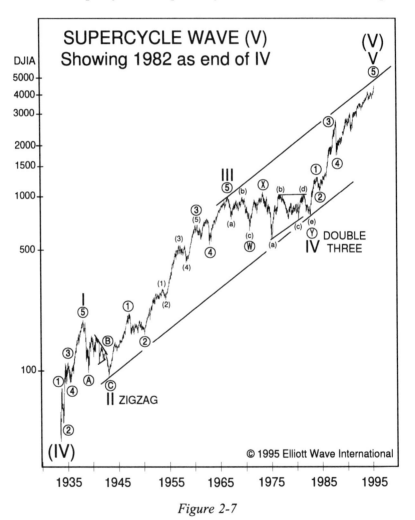

Figure 2-7

of current analysis is that the resulting upper parallel channel line is *lower* than the one in Figure 2-5. The implications of the various trendlines are covered in the next section.

Figure 2-8 displays the details of Cycle wave V and shows that it has acceptably fulfilled the guidelines for wave form. Wave ④ holds above wave ①. One of the impulse waves (wave ⑤) is an extension. There is alternation between waves ② and ④. As *Elliott Wave Principle* also states, "the usual limitation of any bear market is the travel area of the preceding fourth wave of one lesser degree."

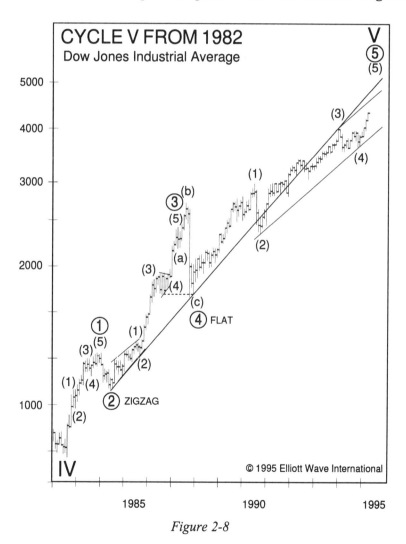

Figure 2-8

The closing low of wave ④ matched to the dollar the 1986 low of wave (4) of ③, as indicated by the dashed line.

Though wave V from 1982 is not contained within a parallel trend channel, subwave ⑤ may remain inside its own parallel channel, drawn in Figure 2-8, if it peaks soon. This channel and the labeling of wave ⑤ pertain whether Cycle wave IV bottomed in 1974 or 1982. Note that the lower line containing wave ⑤ is an extension of the support line drawn in Figure 2-6. Also of interest is the longer line connecting the lows of waves ② and ④. Normally, this line would provide the basis for an upper parallel line. In this case, it appears well positioned to provide resistance near the peak of wave ⑤.

UPSIDE POTENTIAL

The Dow Jones Industrial Average is swiftly approaching a cluster of trendlines representing resistance at three degrees of trend: Primary, Cycle and Supercycle. The resistance lines in Figures 2-7 and 2-8 and the lower resistance line in Figure 2-6 converge in the third quarter of 1995 in the 4600s-4700s, while the line in Figure 2-5 (allowing for a throw-over to balance the throw-under in 1982) and the upper line in Figure 2-6 suggest a 1995 peak in the 5200-5500 range. The Dow Jones Transports, the NASDAQ index, and the S&P Composite index are rapidly nearing long term resistance lines as well, supporting the case for an approaching stock market top. Finally, as discussed earlier in this chapter, the Grand Supercycle and Millennium degree advances are well within their ideal target ranges, bringing the number of degrees calling for an imminent top to five.

The upper parallel lines in Figure 2-6, which are drawn from the orthodox and post-orthodox tops of wave ③, are shown dashed because meeting them would force a large penetration of the highest resistance line at Supercycle degree (shown in Figure 2-5), an unlikely event. These two lines may be considered predictive only in that if the Dow were to stage an orgasmic surge above the longer term lines, one of them would probably stop the advance.

Most evidence argues that the Dow should register its final high this year, in 1995. An alternative consideration is the wave labeling shown in Figure 2-9, which implies waves (4) and (5) left to go. A delay of several years would serve to extend the lower resistance line in Figure 2-6 into the range of the resistance line in Figure 2-5. A drop below 3000 will eliminate this count from consideration.

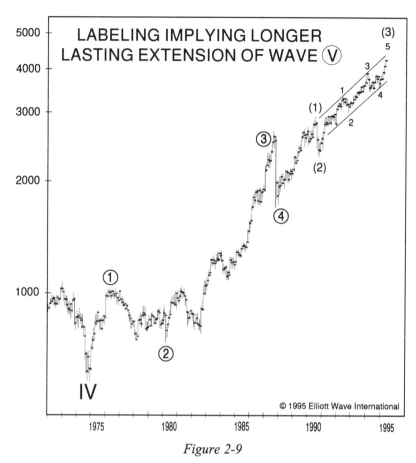

Figure 2-9

Despite the effort put into this discussion, the exact level of the ultimate top is of little importance compared to the overall message that the most important trend change in modern times is due, awaiting only a final extreme of stock market valuation and a reversal.

CONCLUSION

On November 8, 1982, *The Elliott Wave Theorist* put the kick-off to the great stock market boom in perspective:

> It has been years since the last real stock boom. In the meantime, precious metals went crazy, real estate went crazy, the Hong Kong stock market went crazy, and porcelain figurines of central African rhinoceri went crazy. Now it's time for the exploitation of the only truly undervalued asset in the world: U.S. blue chip stocks.

If the U.S. blue chip stock market has not been exploited since then, I do not know what has. As you can see by the figures in this chapter, that exploitation has taken place in such a way as to fulfill, or nearly fulfill, the requirements of a classic Elliott Wave progression of social psychological change.

Today the stock market is rapidly approaching the type of compelling juncture that comes along only two or three times in a professional analyst's career. There are times, as in 1974 and 1982, when the Wave Principle is so powerfully indicative that to the analyst who uses it, there is just no question as to the market juncture at hand and the events that are just around the corner. At such times, the patterns are perfect, the psychology is perfect, and the timing is perfect. This year presents another one of those times.

Wave forms allow for variation, to be sure, and concluding that uptrends in the Dow Jones Industrial Average lasting 8 years, 21 years, 63 years and 211 years are all terminating might appear risky. Yet market analysis is forever a task involving *probability*, not certainty, and each conclusion must be accepted on those terms, as there are no other terms available. Experience shows that the market will produce patterns such as those described herein whether or not the *current* juncture, convincing though it appears, proves to be significant. We shall proceed nevertheless under the direction of Prussian military strategist Karl von Clausewitz, who said quite rightly, "It is impossible to be too strong at the decisive point."

The market is rapidly reaching a decisive point. As the analysis in this chapter demonstrates, the Grand Supercycle has five waves: (I), (II), (III), (IV) and (V). The fifth Supercycle has five waves: I, II, III, IV and V. The fifth Cycle wave has five waves: ①, ②, ③, ④ and ⑤. The fifth Primary wave has nearly completed five waves: (1), (2), (3), (4) and (5). Never before has an Elliott Wave practitioner been alive to anticipate the termination of a structure of this magnitude. It may not happen again for centuries.

Chapter 3

THE INFLATION-ADJUSTED DOW

The actual Dow Jones Industrial Average is a stocks/dollars ratio. The plot of the stock market in "constant dollars," i.e., adjusted for inflation (as measured in these illustrations by the Producer Price Index of raw and partially processed material) is a stocks/goods ratio. The first ratio answers the question, "What quantity of *dollars* does it take to buy one share of each stock in the Dow Jones Industrial Average?" The second ratio answers the question, "What quantity of physical *goods* does it take to buy one share of each stock in the Dow Jones Industrial Average?"

One may wonder whether inflation should be considered an extramarket phenomenon that distorts the true market averages. Certainly the plot of dollar-denominated prices is *different* from the plot of inflation-adjusted prices. Yet inflation, both as cause and result, is an intimate part of the social psychology of some periods. Stock prices incorporate and reflect all aspects of the social mood, including that which both creates and tolerates, or even demands, inflation. This observation holds particularly true in societies whose finances are *credit*-based as opposed to *currency*-based. Inflation in a credit-based economy requires confidence, and confidence is the heart of a bull market in stocks. What's more, in credit-based financial systems, inflation can turn to deflation depending upon the mental state of the populace, and that is precisely what the Wave Principle tracks.

The validity of this opinion is bolstered by the fact that the *actual* DJIA appears better to reflect Fibonacci mathematics (see Appendix A) than the inflation-adjusted measure. The actual Dow is what people watch, and the feedback loop of information is therefore more intimately associated with it. The actual Dow enjoys a symbiotic relationship with the society that allows the natural laws of self-organization to reflect themselves fully. Nevertheless, the inflation-adjusted Dow is just as real in that it reflects how people value an intangible such as stock certificates against tangible things, a measure that is also a part of the social psychology of the times. Indeed, an Elliott Wave analysis of the inflation-adjusted Dow has proved so valuable, as detailed below, that there is every reason to have confidence in the validity of its message.

PERSPECTIVE

As *The Elliott Wave Theorist* has maintained for over thirteen years (see Appendix to *Elliott Wave Principle*), the proper wave count for the inflation-adjusted DJIA is that the Grand Supercycle bull market that began in 1784 ended in *February 1966*. The pattern under the Wave Principle over that period is a classic five waves. Figure 3-1 is reproduced from the January 1982 issue and shows the position of the inflation-adjusted Dow exactly as *The Elliott Wave Theorist* viewed it at the time. As you can see, the third wave is characteristically long, and the fourth wave does not overlap the first. Waves (II) and (IV) alternate in form, which is normal; specifically, wave (II) is a well constructed flat correction labeled A-B-C, and wave (IV) is an excellent contracting triangle labeled A-B-C-D-E. Validating the entire analysis, as well as that in Chapter 2, is that triangles appear *only* in the fourth wave position. We know, then, that the advance from the low of wave E to the 1966 high was a fifth wave. Accordingly, that was when the uptrend in real U.S. stock values, and therefore social mood, and therefore economic and social health, ended. As *The Elliott Wave Theorist* concluded in 1982, "This [analysis] argues eloquently that a 'Grand Supercycle' advance has ended and that a long corrective process is underway that will serve to balance the period of expansion with a period of contraction of the same large degree."

In comparing Figure 3-1 with Figure 2-1, notice that except for the deflationary 1870s and 1880s, the wave structure of the actual Dow Jones Industrial Average parallels that of the inflation-adjusted Dow very closely until about 1942, after which time a highly inflationary environment affected the patterns very differently. For instance, while the actual DJIA held above its 1974 low, the inflation-adjusted Dow continually fell to new lows for eight more years, ultimately falling 74.76%. It was making further new lows in 1982 when Figure 3-1 was published, yet the position of this measure at the time was unquestionable: The decline from the 1966 high was wave (A) of a large corrective pattern, and stocks were on the verge of a major rally for wave (B). The forecast published at the time is crucial to understanding today's situation. In January-February 1982, when wave (A) of the bear market was just months from its final low after sixteen years of decline, *The Elliott Wave Theorist* concluded as follows:

> From 1966, the constant dollar Dow Jones Industrial Average and the real standard of living of most Americans has been in

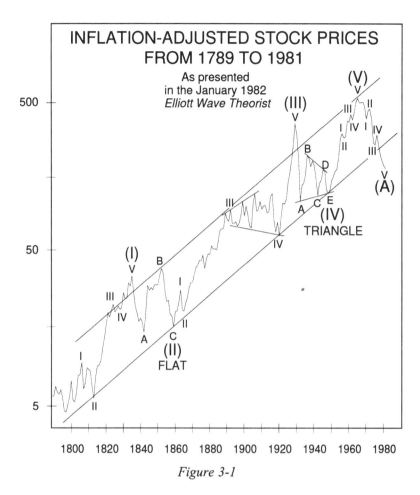

Figure 3-1

wave (A) of a large corrective process. *A clear five-wave down-ward Elliott pattern from the 1965 peak appears to be in its final stage.* Thus, the next few years could witness a countertrend three wave ("a-b-c") rally in *real* terms that should translate into a dramatic "breakout" in the Dow Industrial Average to new all-time highs in *current dollar* terms. Such an advance would satisfy the Dow's wave count from 1932 based on nominal dollars by letting it complete its fifth Cycle wave from 1974. So we still need one more dramatic new high on the Dow Jones Industrial Average, giving us wave V in current dollar terms and wave (B) in constant dollar terms. If the charts are correct, in the long run it will be a trap; in the short run, such a move would generate a tremendous euphoria and have considerable profit potential.

Wave (B) in the inflation-adjusted Dow began six months later, in August 1982, and accompanied the actual DJIA in its "dramatic breakout to new all-time highs," which has unquestionably provided "considerable profit potential" and generated "tremendous euphoria."

Targeting Wave (B)

A dozen years ago, the pattern in the inflation-adjusted DJIA even telegraphed its upside potential. As you can see in Figure 3-1, the smoothed annual figures (which were the only figures available at the time) had vaguely suggested a five-wave decline from 1966 to 1982. However, the April 1983 issue pointed out shortly thereafter (see Appendix to *Elliott Wave Principle*) that the newly available monthly range plot showed substantial overlap among waves, so the 1966-1982 decline had to be a variation of a three-wave pattern. Because wave (A) took that shape, it had to be the first wave of a *flat* correction. This was a crucial observation because "B" waves of flats always climb all the way back to the previous high and typically attain new highs by a slight margin. Figure 3-2 is reprinted from that issue. The lower graph shows the projection calling for wave B in the inflation-adjusted Dow to *exceed the 1966 peak moderately* while the actual Dow, as discussed in Chapter 2, was to soar in wave V.

The December 31, 1986 issue kept that conclusion right on track: "These charts are [still] entirely compatible and carry the same message.... Another doubling of the nominal DJIA will bring [the inflation-adjusted Dow] into the area of its 1966 high." *The Elliott Wave Theorist* added that "this compatibility suggests very little inflation during the next few years." There has certainly been "very little inflation" since then, a fact that was *required* to bring the two measures to their respective targets. It has taken a lot longer than originally expected, but as you can see in the updated Figure 3-3, the inflation-adjusted Dow is now above its 1966 high by exactly the amount that *The Elliott Wave Theorist* projected a dozen years ago.

ANALYSIS

The original upside target has been satisfied, as wave (B) has now carried slightly beyond the level of the peak of wave (V). The inflation-adjusted S&P 500 (not shown) is likewise nearing the end of its wave (B), having just edged out its 1968 high. The U.S. economy is therefore completing the topping process that it started in 1966,

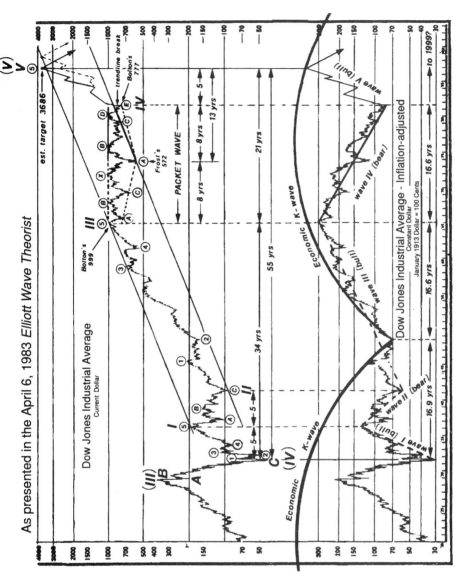

Figure 3-2

which in turn is capping a prolonged period of growth that began when the country was formed.

Because wave (B) is ending, it is finally time to consider the warning from 1982 that "in the long run, it will be a trap." That trap will be closed with wave (C), and wave (C) is imminent. Chapter 5 will discuss downside targets for wave (C) and describe how the outlook for the inflation-adjusted Dow fits that for the actual Dow.

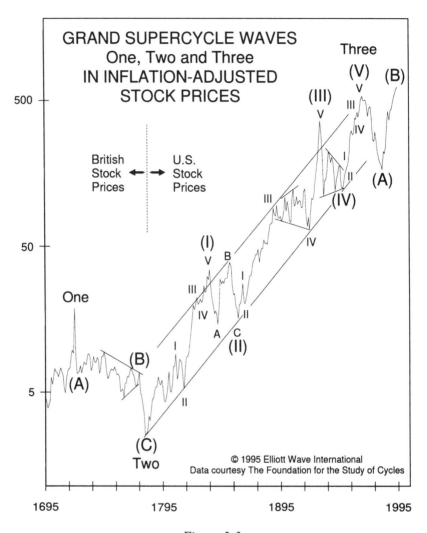

Figure 3-3

On the bigger picture, enough time has passed to confirm that the ongoing pattern reflects a correction of Grand Supercycle degree. For comparison, there are two bear markets of one degree smaller (Supercycle) over the past three hundred years. The first was wave (II), which lasted 24 years from 1835 to 1859, and the second was wave (IV), which lasted 19-20 years from 1929 to 1948/9. (For the record, wave (IV) ended in 1948 if the Dow is adjusted by the PPI and in 1949 if adjusted by the CPI.) Because the current bear market has been in progress for 29 years and is not yet over, its duration strongly supports the analysis that it is of one larger degree than the other two.

IMPLICATIONS

Perhaps the most revealing aspect of the inflation-adjusted Dow is what it says about the *economic* and *social* health of the United States. The final year of rise into the orthodox top of wave (V) was the twelve months ending in February 1966. It was the 1965-1966 session of Congress that passed most of President Lyndon Johnson's "Great Society" programs, the biggest peacetime expansion of government giveaways in the history of the country. The widespread belief that the country could afford such largesse even as it fought a war was a reflection of how boundlessly wealthy and optimistic voters felt. That collective feeling marked the peak in U.S. prosperity. We have not felt that way since.

Now let's examine the support line shown in Figures 3-1 and 3-3. For *182 years*, from 1784 to 1966, the U.S. stock market rose at a rate that allowed prices to rebound from that uptrend line, despite all the social and political difficulties encountered along the way. In 1979, 195 years after its starting point, *that line broke*. Am I just now devising an analysis that fits the thesis of this book? No, the same 1982 report quoted earlier in this chapter emphatically argued the great long term significance of that trendline break. While primarily of academic interest at the time, the analysis presented then is of utmost practical value today, so read it carefully:

> [It is] most important that in 1979, the plot of the constant-dollar price for the Dow Industrial Average sliced down through a support line that has held all downside action for over two hundred years. [This break] indicates that the brisk rate of long term upside progress from the late 1700s for the United States has come to an end. This line is statistically valid, having had four precise touch points (and five close ones). Each time the United States was experiencing or was about to experience disastrous conditions, the line defining the basic rate of economic progress held fast. It held through the early Federal governmental crises, the War of 1812, the severe depression and gloom of the late 1850s, the Civil War, World War I, the post-WWI inflation and subsequent deflation, the Great Depression and World War II. Now that the long term support line has been broken, we know that in economic terms, *the ongoing dilemma is bigger than any previous catastrophe in the history of the United States.*

The message from this chart is compelling and demonstrates clearly that an extended period of rising real value for corporate stock, which began upon the founding of the United States, *ended* [on an annual average basis] *in 1965.* A prolonged period of economic contraction has begun and in general, the quality of life will continue to deteriorate substantially before the process of correction has run its course. As I see it, U.S. markets will be experiencing an overall sideways-to-declining trend *in real value* for at least thirty years and possibly as much as ninety years from the peak in 1965.

Remember, however, that *every* trend is interrupted by countertrend movements, and it is highly likely that several years in this decade will witness a period of temporarily improving conditions that will look like the "real thing" but which will ultimately give way to another sweeping downward wave to significantly lower depths. If a three-wave advance in the real value for stock prices does get underway, the Dow Jones Industrial Average could soar in terms of current (inflated) dollars and provide a tremendous vehicle for temporary speculative profits.

Today, over thirteen years later, not a word of that analysis needs to be changed. Now that the "countertrend movement" has taken place, it is time to focus on the crucial fact that since 1966, the U.S. stock market has been in the process of discounting problems that have more ominous implications than any other event in the country's history. What could those problems be?

In my opinion, the market's first long term concern is financial. Note in Figure 3-1 that the all-time high for the annual price averages occurred in 1965. It is unlikely to have been merely coincidence that that was the year that the U.S. government stopped making coins from silver. The divorce of the U.S. dollar from its precious metal anchor meant that our "money" no longer had any intrinsic value. This one fact has had immense consequences. From that point forward, inflation edged upward, finally raging. When it slowed in the early 1980s, *borrowing*, as a natural consequence of an inflation-induced psychology, exploded to reach today's ominous levels (see Chapter 11).

Today's market patterns say that this debt buildup is about to resolve into a debt liquidation that will wreak havoc on the nation. "C" waves always expose at long last the weaknesses in the market's foundation, many of which are set in place at the pattern's outset but remain substantially hidden during the "B" wave. Besides the financial implications, which are the main focus of this book, the market's second concern ultimately will be social upheaval, which always accompanies "C" waves of this degree. Social psychology at the bottom will be the opposite of what it was at the top, and this change will have implications. For instance, the social programs that were put in place in the mid-1960s will undoubtedly be repealed at the end of the bear market. The sentiment accompanying that impulse will bring social *concern and conflict* of an intensity equal to that of the social *well-being and harmony* felt in 1965. Events resulting from social mood trends is a topic we will cover briefly in Chapters 9 and 13.

A few casual observers have remarked that since the Dow adjusted by the PPI is barely above its February 1966 high, the outlook remains bullish since there is "so much room" for stocks to go up. This assertion would be true if stocks were at low valuation levels. However, as Chapters 6 and 10 will show, the dividend yield on the Dow Industrial Average today is the lowest in its history, while the dividend yield on the Dow Transportation Average in recent years has been the lowest of *any* stock index in U.S. history.

Because of today's all-time record valuation, it is meaningful that the inflation-adjusted Dow, and therefore the real purchasing power of the Dow Jones Industrial Average, is at essentially the same level as it was in 1966. Indeed, adjusted by the *Consumer* Price Index (see Figure 3-4), it is still *below* its 1966 high, meaning that a share of the DJIA today buys less in the way of consumer goods than it did 29 years ago. For a moment, contemplate the implication of a stock market index that has made no progress in three decades and which is nevertheless historically overvalued. This event is a "first" for the entire 200 year history of the U.S. stock market and underscores the insidious and hidden regress of true value that stocks and corporations have suffered since 1966. This fact does not fit the cavalier assumption that "there is a lot of room on the upside." It rather prompts the conclusion that the business and industrial base of the United States has subtly deteriorated for three decades. These data are of utmost importance in forming conclusions about the financial, social and political health of the United States. Much looks "fine" on the outside, but on the inside, a cancer has taken hold. The outward symptoms will become increasingly manifest as the Grand Supercycle bear market wears on, and dramatically manifest at the bottom of wave (C).

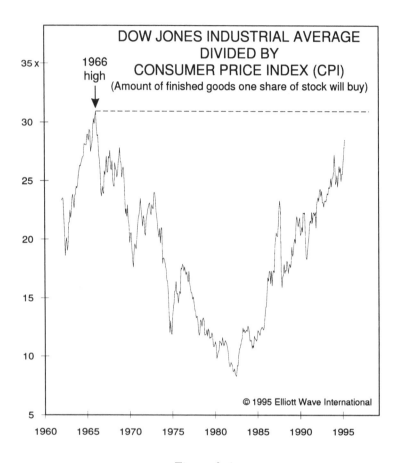

Figure 3-4

Wave (B) has served as a respite from the Grand Supercycle bear market that began in 1966. Now, however, the "temporarily improving conditions" are nearing an end, and the market is ready to "give way to another sweeping downward wave to significantly lower depths." Wave (C) will make the fact that a bear market began 29 years ago far more obvious than it is today. By the bottom, essays will be written about the "causes" of the collapse, and some of them will undoubtedly recognize in retrospect that the onset of a deterioration in the social and economic fabric of the country occurred as far back as the mid-1960s. Wave (C), then, should bring about the first culmination of the "ongoing dilemma" that should prove to be "bigger than any previous catastrophe in the history of the United States."

Chapter 4

COMMENTS ON THE
ULTIMATE PRICE PEAK

As evidenced by the published works of the foremost Elliott Wave practitioners, Fibonacci relationships among price gains attained by waves have proved invaluable numerous times in forecasting years in advance the eventual termination levels of trends in the stock market. The projection in *Elliott Wave Principle* for wave V was fulfilling in that regard, but not the final word on the subject. "Our price projection for the Dow," we said, "comes from the tenet that two of the impulse waves in a five-wave sequence, especially when the third is the extended wave, tend toward equality in time and magnitude." From the perspective of 1978, we applied the guideline in rough fashion to present a general idea of the bull market's price potential, saying that since wave I was about a 5 times multiple, wave V by the same multiple would top near 2860. In fact, the exact calculation of equality with wave I projected the 1987 high almost to the point. Wave I traveled from 41.22 to 195.15, a multiple not of 5 times, but, to be precise, of 4.716 times. Wave V began at 577.60, from which point a 4.716 multiple is **2723.96**. The actual closing high preceding the 1000-point crash of 1987 was **2722.42** on August 25, attaining a perfect equality with wave I.

Although the Dow did not budge in the four years after our 1978 projection was made, in September 1982, a month after the final low in the market's basing process, *The Elliott Wave Theorist* revised the original Elliott Wave projection and forecasted that wave V would carry to near **3885** (later **3686**) from its then-current level of 900. The forecast for an advance of three thousand points appeared outrageous. For the preceding seven years, the DJIA had meandered in the 740-1020 range, not advancing more than three *hundred* points. It was the equivalent of predicting a rise to approximately 20,000 from today's level, but without the psychological comfort provided by a preceding multi-year uptrend. At the time, bulls and bears were split, so just getting the *direction* right was considered a 50/50 proposition. That forecast was based on the same tenet of wave equality cited in our 1978 book, but measuring from the then-just-completed low of 776.92 in August 1982.

As detailed in the Appendix to *Elliott Wave Principle*, three of the four Primary degree turning points within the bull market were accurately projected by *The Elliott Wave Theorist* to within 10 Dow points, and the fourth was recognized by A.J. Frost upon termination. These precedents (as well as those set by Elliott, Collins, Bolton and Frost, as detailed in New Classics Library's other books) are convincing evidence that such accuracy is repeatedly possible using the Elliott Wave approach. The last remaining bull market turning point is the fifth one, the final high. Is the move past EWT's original upside target of analytical import?

By all modern standards, as detailed in Chapters 7 and 8, the stock market has already reached a point of record speculative fever. By Grand Supercycle standards (see the rise into 1720 in Figure 2-2), the current level of speculative insanity is entirely normal. *The Elliott Wave Theorist* communicated that thought well in advance, on September 6, 1993. As the Dow reached 3700, EWT said, "The great Cycle wave V bull market has fulfilled *all of its originally expected gains*. [Nevertheless,] do not become convinced upon any further rise that a new era has arrived. If the Dow reaches 4000+, it will not signal anything bullish, *only the extension of a top*." Whatever level marks the high in the Dow's push to maximum euphoria, it will likely coincide with one or more of the resistance lines shown in Figures 2-5 through 2-8. However, stopping at a particular level is not *required* as part of the overall thesis. Though I have always been passionate about solving every aspect of the forecasting puzzle, and while I would relish including a detailed analysis, any inaccuracy could jeopardize the overall message of this book, which is *the degree and resulting implications of the upcoming bear market*. That message is too important to risk communicating any suggestion that it hinges upon the Dow peaking at a particular level. As an example of the risk involved, R.N. Elliott concluded, even after the fact, that the ideal top for the 1920s bull market was about 300. In the heat of the time, had an Elliott Wave analyst issued an ideal target of 300, many investors might have thrown in the towel near the high at 381, convinced that the entire thesis that a great bull market was ending was wrong. An equally important reason for avoiding discussing a target is that some readers might be tempted to stay invested to squeeze out the last drops of gain. Such an attempt could prove extremely costly if an indicated level is not precisely achieved.

Regardless of how high the Dow goes, it will ultimately fall to the downside target range indicated in Chapter 5, so the only effect a continued rise will have is to increase the *percentage* that the Dow will have to decline. For instance, the extra 27% the Dow tacked on in the final eight months in 1929 made only one difference: the Dow fell 89% instead of 86%.

It is imperative to understand that the Dow has fully realized, for all practical purposes, the big potential that lay ahead 21 and 13 years ago, *no matter what happens* on the way to "top tick." There is no way that latecoming bulls will enjoy anything close to the 640% gain that the bull market has provided so far, and every reason to believe that they will pay for whatever sin they commit in buying stocks at this late date. What's more, when the Dow shot up its last 27% in 1929, the advance-decline line went *down*, so the average stock did not participate in the Dow's final climb. Stocks then lost half their value in two months. As then, the reversal from the peak of this bull market is likely to be swift, and the higher it goes, the swifter it will be.

Recognizing the coming top may be possible upon the event, and may even be forecastable. Those exercises have been reserved for *The Elliott Wave Theorist*, where they are pursued with the usual gusto. Perhaps a future edition of this book will contain an appendix that discusses Fibonacci price relationships and even more precise time relationships, just for the record.

Pattern, price and time, then, all argue emphatically that a major peak is forming. It is *not* a "new era." A Golden Age does *not* lie directly ahead. On the contrary, we are ending one.

Chapter 5

EXPECTATIONS FOR
THE GREAT BEAR MARKET

ANALYTICAL PERSPECTIVE

Readers of this book must understand that long term forecasts are exactly that; they will not be fulfilled by a week from Thursday, and the path the market takes to achieve a target may include wide intervening swings. The elements of a forecast under the Wave Principle, in order of predictability, are direction, degree, extent (price target), pattern and duration. Time, then, is the least predictable element. For instance, when in 1982 *The Elliott Wave Theorist* made the case for the Dow Jones Industrial Average to (1) go *up* (direction), (2) go up an amount proportionate to the 1932-1937 and 1942-1966 rises (degree), (3) reach 3500-4000, with specific targets at 3885 and 3686 (extent), and (4) trace out *five waves* (pattern), all of those forecasts were considered virtually certain. However, the *duration* eluded our analysis entirely, as the 1978 expectation that the bull market would end in 1983 or 1987 and the 1983 forecast that it would end in 1987 or 1990 proved well off the mark. Still, these three time forecasts were not entirely without merit, as those years did contain the three most important highs of the past thirteen years.

In the same way, some elements of the current forecast are virtually certain and others are not. Here is my assessment of the probability of each element that will be discussed in this chapter:

(1) **Direction**: The downward direction of the next major move is certain, despite today's majority opinion that prices will continue rising over the long term forever, with corrections of no more than 10%.

(2) **Degree**: The bear market is almost surely to be of Grand Supercycle degree, and will definitely be of at least Supercycle degree, which for practical purposes is all we need to know.

(3) **Extent**: A drop to at least Dow 1000 is certain. A drop to below 400 at one or more times during the bear market is nearly certain. A precise price forecast will become available after the pattern has progressed substantially.

(4) **Pattern**: Because the forecast involves a correction, not an impulse wave, rules for determining the specific pattern provide far less certainty than they did in 1974 and 1982 to the extent that a *single* likely path cannot even be suggested. Because of the guideline of alternation, though, the style of pattern ("sideways" as opposed to "sharp") *is* virtually certain.

(5) **Duration**: The time that the pattern may take is, as always, uncertain. Nevertheless, two estimating approaches are in agreement at three different times, strongly suggesting a particular overall timing that fits a highly qualified pattern profile. Channeling provides a high confidence estimate of a *maximum* duration.

The enormity of the task of forecasting properly any *one* of the above variables is appreciated by market veterans, while the odds of getting most of them right are so low that any such instance of success is usually considered luck. It is hoped that skeptics will first read *Elliott Wave Principle* and judge for themselves how the authors did in forecasting the great bull market and whether it was luck.

DIRECTION

The next major stock market move will be down.

DEGREE OF THE BEAR MARKET

Because the Supercycle degree advance from 1932 is a fifth wave, it is ending not just its own pattern, but the Grand Supercycle from 1784 as well. Thus, there is virtual certainty that the ensuing correction will be of at least Grand Supercycle degree.

One question to answer is, could the bear market be even *larger* than Grand Supercycle? *Elliott Wave Principle* expressed concern over this question in 1978, stating, "As we read Elliott, the current bull market in stocks is the fifth wave from 1932 of the fifth wave from 1784 of *possibly* the fifth wave from the Dark Ages." At the time, we had no way of determining whether that possibility was a probability. We did know that if the advance from 1784 were itself discovered to be a fifth wave, then the ensuing bear market would then have to correct an advancing wave of at least Millennium degree, which would make it proportionately larger.

In order to become confident about the degree of the bear market, it was crucial to determine the Grand Supercycle's position in the larger development of the Elliott Wave dynamic through history. As discussed in Chapter 2, the critical data allowing us to conduct an investigation into the expected degree of the bear market are the prices for British stocks in the 1700s, which show that the 1720-1784 bear market and the bull market since that time are of the same degree: Grand Supercycle. The question is, are these structures waves Two and Three or waves Four and Five of a larger impulse? Answering that crucial question involves a good deal of supposition because a continuous record of stock price data before the year 1695 is not available. However, prior suppositions of this type have so far all proved correct, as detailed in Chapter 2.

One observation is critical to the analysis: The Grand Supercycle correction that took place from 1720 to 1784 is a *zigzag*. Its pattern, labeled (A)-(B)-(C), is unmistakable in the plots of both ac-

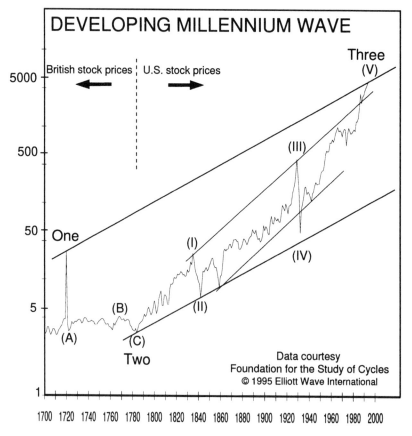

Figure 5-1

tual prices, shown in Figure 2-2, and inflation-adjusted prices, shown in Figure 3-3. A zigzag is far more typical of *second* waves than fourth waves. There are exceptions to this common characteristic, such as the 1929-1932 zigzag wave (IV). However, even in that case, the correction was a *triangle* in inflation-adjusted data (see Figure 3-3), which is a classic fourth wave pattern.

The appearance of a zigzag in the fourth wave position is so rare in the stock market that I do not hesitate to conclude that the 1700s bear market was wave Two of a larger advance that began centuries ago. The advance from 1784, then, is wave Three, as shown in Figure 5-1. The next event at this scale must be wave Four, which means that *the degree of the imminent correction is limited to Grand Supercycle.* As strong as that conclusion may be from a single piece of evidence, there is more to support it.

Confirmation From the Inflation-Adjusted Dow

Another key to the limited degree of the coming bear market is that the corrective pattern from 1966 in the inflation-adjusted DJIA began with *three* waves down, and the corrective pattern contains a new high, as shown in Figure 3-3. This is terribly good news, because had the bear market begun with five waves down, there would be no telling what degree was unfolding, as a "five" could be part of a pattern of any size. A three-wave beginning, on the other hand, indicates a developing flat or triangle, which is always either an entire correction or a component one degree smaller than the entire correction. There is no example of a bear market of any degree that began with a flat or triangle two degrees smaller. Because this flat or triangle must constitute the entire correction *or* Supercycle wave (W) of a Grand Supercycle, we know that a Grand Supercycle corrective pattern will *not* turn out to be part of an even larger structure.

While a Grand Supercycle bear market is quite big enough to worry about, it is nevertheless heartening to know that that is *all* we and our progeny will have to worry about. Although much of the world may return to conditions not unlike those of the 1930s and 1940s, it will not be returning to the conditions of the Dark Ages. This conclusion is hardly trivial; it pertains to civilization itself. While a Grand Supercycle bear market portends major war, which will be devastating to be sure, we can now retire any fears of an all-out global nuclear holocaust that devastates the planet and sets civilization back a thousand years, which would have been the implication of a Millennium degree bear market. Such fears will probably be intense and widespread before this Grand Supercycle bear market is over, and not without reason, as it will engender severe global tensions and armed conflict. Nevertheless, while there will be areas of horrible devastation, the entire world will not end up "On the Beach." Whatever occurs, and whatever fears permeate the globe, we will *know* this to be so, and that, comparatively speaking, is quite a comfort.

Happily also for analytical purposes, we have a firm basis now for forecasting the *extent, pattern* and *duration* of the coming bear.

EXTENT OF THE BEAR MARKET

Whether forecasting at the Subminuette or Grand Supercycle degree, the most reliable support area for a correction is the area of the preceding fourth wave of one lesser degree. This is particularly true when the correction *itself* is a fourth wave, as this one will be. If you examine Figure 2-5 closely, you will see, for instance, that the low for wave II occurred in the price territory of wave ④ of I. Similarly, the low for wave IV occurred in the price territory of wave ④ of III.

Using this approach, Chapter 8 of *Elliott Wave Principle* telegraphed our general expectations with respect to targeting the bear market that would ultimately *follow* wave (V):

> If our scenario proves correct, a new Grand Supercycle will get underway once the current Supercycle (V) has terminated. Eventually, the Grand Supercycle bear should carry to its expected target within the range of the previous Supercycle fourth wave, between **41** and **381** on the Dow. The best efforts of the leaders of the financial community [will] not stem the panic once the tides of emotion [take] control. Situations of this nature that have happened over the last two hundred years usually have been followed by three or four years of chaotic conditions in the economy and the markets.

This long-standing forecast is no longer something for a future time. Rather, it is the expected range for the low of the bear market we now face. If the current bear market is of Grand Supercycle degree, prices *will* fall to this area.

Potential Support Levels

Specific downside targets for the Supercycle degree lows within the bear market will be reliably provided only by assessing the relationships among the smaller waves, and that opportunity is years away. At the onset of a new corrective trend, the only reference points available for determining potential support levels are those provided by the preceding wave structure. There is some record of success with this approach, but it has been of less specific value than calculating typical price length relationships within patterns. For example, in early 1966, Charles Collins and Hamilton Bolton gave a preliminary estimate, based upon wave form only, that the bear market that had just begun would last several years and ultimately bottom near Dow 525. That was an excellent first estimate, but it was not until the 1966 low was established that A.J. Frost was able to say, based on typical wave length relationships, that a final low was likely at 572, a level that was met to the dollar on December 9, 1974. (For the full story, see *The Complete Elliott Wave Writings of A. Hamilton Bolton* (New Classics Library, 1994) and *The Complete Elliott Wave Writings of A.J. Frost* (New Classics Library, due 1996).)

Though we are restricted to using previous structure to identify some possible stopping points for the Grand Supercycle bear market, it is of some value that these support levels will retain whatever applicability they have no matter where the Dow peaks. As illustrated in Figure 5-2, the four most strongly indicated support levels from previous wave structure are as follows:

295, which provided support and resistance in 1928, 1930 and 1953;

195, which provided support and resistance in 1929, 1937 and the late 1940s;

161, which provided support in 1949 at the end of the inflation-adjusted wave IV; and

95, which provided support in 1942 at the low of wave II.

Due to the upward slope of the Millennium degree support line shown in Figure 5-1, the 95 level will be eliminated from consideration if it is not met within a decade. I rule out **41** (the 1932 low) as an acceptable target because it is below the *current* level of the support line. Given ideal upside targets and these support levels, the Dow should fall at least 91.5%, but no more than 98.3% from its high. These percentages will be adjustable to a narrower range once the high is registered.

While such talk appears outrageous, the only precedent available for the first drop in a Grand Supercycle degree bear market is the collapse in British stock prices from 1720 to 1722. Of the 130

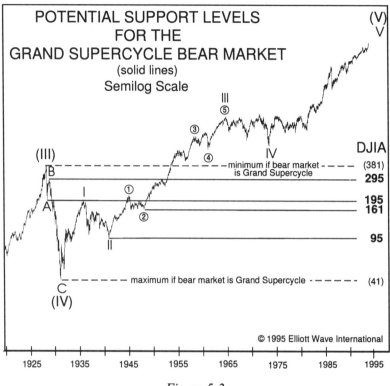

Figure 5-2

issues that were traded at the high, 118 went to zero in the aftermath of the great South Sea Bubble, while the remaining dozen dropped 80% from extreme peak to trough. The average stock, then, lost 98% of its peak value in the debacle, which is at the high end of our projected range. (The figures in Chapters 2 and 5 show a 91% drop in the annual averages of daily readings for 1720 and 1722, not the intra-year extremes.)

Again, while the levels identified here are excellent *candidates* for the low, they are *not yet targets* and should be considered properly in that light. The internal wave structure of the bear market is the only thing that will allow the application of specific targeting techniques, and that opportunity lies several years hence.

For the same reason, we will have to wait for a fair portion of the bear market to unfold before determining *interim* support levels. Until then, I would observe that the **1000** level stands out from the previous wave structure as solid structural support that was built from 1966 to 1982. In 1978, before that 16-year "ceiling" had been penetrated on the upside, *Elliott Wave Principle* observed, "The first phase of the bear market should bring the market down from its peak to about the 1000 level again." Our idea was that that level might mark an intra-correction low, such as wave (A) of an expanding flat or triangle. If the market slices right through the 1000 level initially, it could later mark the end of wave (C) or (E) of a contracting pattern, just as the higher low of wave C in 1942 in the inflation-adjusted plot (see Figure 3-1) ended at structural support that was built from 1915 to 1924.

A market drop to the range discussed in this section is considered an impossibility by virtually everyone. One reason is that people typically conceive of such a decline in arithmetic terms. For a perspective on this mental view, take a look at the Dow on arithmetic scale, as shown in Figure 5-3. Another reason is that most people form opinions using only recent history as a benchmark, and of course recent history displays no such event because the market has been

Figure 5-3

in a bull trend of Cycle degree for years, Supercycle degree for decades, and Grand Supercycle degree for over two centuries, which is exactly why we should be concerned that a drop of this magnitude is possible.

PATTERN OF THE BEAR MARKET

Since the bear market will be wave Four, it will alternate in form with wave Two to satisfy the guideline of alternation. Because wave Two (see Figure 5-1) was from the "sharp" family of corrective patterns, being a *zigzag*, wave Four will be from the "sideways" family and trace out a *flat, triangle* or *double three.*

Most sideways patterns contain at least one rally carrying prices above the peak of the preceding impulse wave. As an example of such an occurrence, Figure 5-2 shows that although the Dow hit a new high in 1973, it was part of the corrective pattern that began in 1966 and ended in 1974. As another example, Figure 3-3 shows wave (B) reaching a new high in the ongoing flat or triangle from 1966. Therefore, we should expect a similar new all-time high, by a small margin, within Grand Supercycle wave Four.

It is extremely fortuitous that the data available is sufficient for us to discern the parallel trend channel for the Millennium wave, as demonstrated in Chapter 2 and shown again in Figure 5-1. This channel allows for substantial confidence and precision in some of our projections.

If Figure 5-1 shows the proper channel for the Millennium degree advance, it should define the lower boundary for wave Four (and ultimately the upper boundary for wave Five, which will end two or three centuries from now). We also know that most fourth waves produce or precede a brief break of the support line, called a "throw-under," such as in 1932 at the low of wave (IV) (shown in Figures 2-1 and 5-1) and in 1982 after the low of wave IV (see Figure 2-5). With this much information, we can reliably discern the approximate *size* of the expected sideways pattern.

Given that the form of wave Four should be a flat, triangle or double three, that it may contain an all-time high, that the downside target range is 95-381, that the bulk of the correction should take place within the channel, and that a break of the lower channel line is probable near the end of the correction, I propose four compatible scenarios. As each one is described below, you may wish to examine the real-life examples referenced in parentheses.

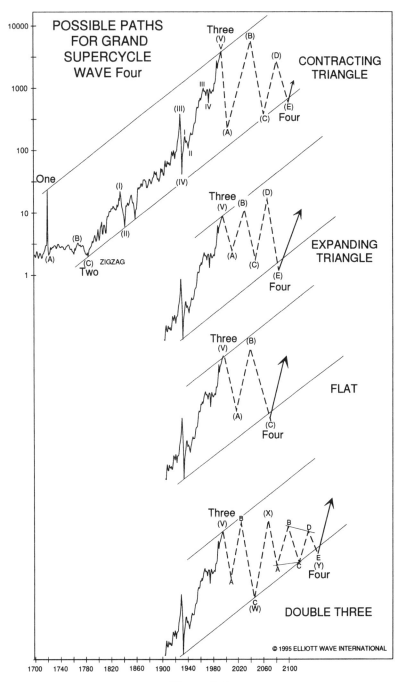

Figure 5-4

The dashed lines in Figure 5-4 first show a *contracting triangle* (reflecting the form of wave (IV) in Figure 3-1). A contracting or ascending (i.e., one with a horizontal top) triangle would fulfill the greatest number of Elliott Wave guidelines. In such a pattern, the Dow would stage its deepest drop early, which is the best way to achieve the downside target zone and have prices remain within the Millennium degree channel. Because of the long duration of Supercycle wave (V), the lower parallel line of the Millennium wave is on a path that will make the target zone otherwise unattainable several decades hence. A substantial decline for wave (A) of the triangle would nicely fit the outlook for wave (C) down that is due in the inflation-adjusted Dow.

The second diagram shows an *expanding triangle* (reflecting the form of wave IV in Figure 2-5). The third diagram shows an *expanded flat* (reflecting the form of wave ④ of III in Figure 2-5). The fourth shows a *double three* (with a triangle in the position of the second three, reflecting the form of the 1966-1982 pattern, as shown in Figure 2-7).

As explained earlier, when a market has several levels of structural support, sometimes corrections oblige by producing reversals in subwaves at more than one of those levels. All of the patterns postulated in Figure 5-4 allow the market to meet more than one of the support levels discussed under **Extent**, at the lows of waves (A) and (C), and/or (E).

Despite the fair probability that the downside target will be met early in the pattern, there is no way to be certain of it. When dealing with Intermediate and Primary trends, the lowest point is ultimately achieved within weeks or months, so there is little practical difference in whether the price low occurs early or late in the pattern. However, the scale of the upcoming bear market will be many times larger. If the Dow is still well above its ultimate downside target a decade from now, do not assume that it will not be met. One could have made a similar erroneous assumption in 1968 or 1973 about a correction of Cycle degree.

Even though the look of the pattern will be "sideways," the size of the Grand Supercycle correction has extremely important practical implications. The price swings are likely to be so dramatic as to provide phenomenal investment returns to a successful long term market timer, while battering the so-called and recently rediscovered long term investor and his successors out of the game.

The Outlook for the Inflation-Adjusted Dow

For thirteen years, the forecast for the inflation-adjusted Dow, discussed in Chapter 3, has been relentlessly consistent. The success of the upward projection for wave (B) suggests that we should also pay attention to the projection for wave (C) made years ago. The January 1982 report, which laid out the whole scenario up to today, even addressed the question of targeting the low for the upcoming decline:

> After an intervening speculative boom, how low might we expect stock prices ultimately to fall? One of the rules of the Wave Principle is that corrections, particularly when they are themselves fourth waves, tend to terminate *within the span of the previous fourth wave of lesser degree, generally near the low end of the pattern*. Thus, normal wave behavior would indicate an ultimate bottom in values equal to those at the 1932, 1942 or [1948-]1949 lows.

Because wave (A) already attained the general target area by falling to 7.68 in 1982 (see Figure 5-5), the entire Grand Supercycle corrective pattern has several options for the path its remaining waves may take. By every scenario, however, the inflation-adjusted Dow must return to the span of wave (IV). Because the 1982 low is not quite as low as the ideal target levels listed above, the bear market could begin with an *expanding triangle* or a *flat*, as postulated in Chapter 3. These two patterns are illustrated in the top and bottom drawings in Figure 5-5. In each case, the next decline would fall moderately below the 1982 low, bringing it closer to one of the lows of the wave (IV) triangle, which are 3.85, 5.45 and 6.03. The entire correction may also be developing as a contracting triangle, as shown in the middle illustration in Figure 5-5. These depictions at least provide some perspective on the downside potential for inflation-adjusted stock prices from today's lofty level of 34.68.

Reconciling the Actual and Inflation-Adjusted Dow Patterns

The first major low in the bear market in the actual Dow will ideally be of Supercycle degree, completing wave (A), as shown in Figure 5-4. As labeled in Figure 5-5, the next low in the inflation-adjusted Dow will also be of Supercycle degree, completing wave (C) of a triangle or wave (W) of a double three. Thus, the two mea-

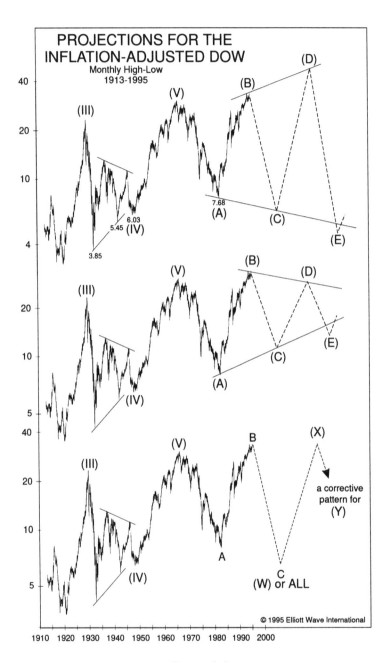

Figure 5-5

sures at that point will be ending a wave of the *same* highest degree for the first time since 1929. From there, both measures will enjoy a Supercycle degree advance that will be labeled wave (B) in the actual Dow and wave (D) or (X) in the inflation-adjusted measure. (The technical difference among the three labels will pertain only to the final resolution of the inflation-adjusted pattern many decades from today.)

A Milder Scenario

There is only one way to extract from the Wave Principle the possibility that the upcoming bear market will be of smaller than Grand Supercycle degree. It involves the idea that the last 63 years of rise are not a complete fifth wave, *but only the first wave of a developing Supercycle extension.* This interpretation is possible because almost every impulse contains an extension, and the Grand Supercycle to date lacks a clearly extended wave.

The triangle wave (IV) and the completed wave (V) shown in Figure 3-3 for the inflation-adjusted Dow disallow a fifth wave extension and at first appear to make such a scenario impossible. However, the *entire advance* in that measure might have been an extension, leaving waves (II) through (V) yet to occur. Figure 5-6 shows how this less negative outcome would unfold in these two Dow indexes. Under this scenario, the low of wave II in the actual Dow and wave (II) in the inflation-adjusted Dow would lead immediately to many decades of advance more spectacular than those of 1932-1995.

Notice that under all scenarios outlined so far, the decline that is currently imminent must be at least of Supercycle degree, which is substantial enough to justify arranging one's affairs in anticipation of a severe price collapse. By either scenario, the imminent decline will almost assuredly be a *sharp* correction, because in the preferred scenario it will be an "A" wave, and in the milder case it will be a second wave, each of which is typically a zigzag. At the same time, the inflation-adjusted Dow would require a relentless five waves down for wave C to complete its flat pattern from 1966 (see Figure 5-6).

This wave interpretation and the forecasted pattern shown in Figure 5-6 will increase in probability if over the next decade the Dow falls *below 1060, but not below 572,* which by this labeling is the zone of support provided by the previous fourth wave of one lesser degree. If a zigzag ends in that range (the 1982 low of Dow

777 would provide a focal point of support), then we will have to let
the technical and fundamental health of the ensuing advance tell
us whether it is a "B" wave or a third wave. Fortunately, the difference is as night and day. As *Elliott Wave Principle* explains, "B"
waves are technically weak, while third waves are powerhouses of
breadth. Since we may be afforded an opportunity to buy stocks for
what will be anticipated as the wave (B) advance anyway, a decision to continue holding them should hardly induce trauma. On the
other hand, if 572 is broken, we can discard this idea.

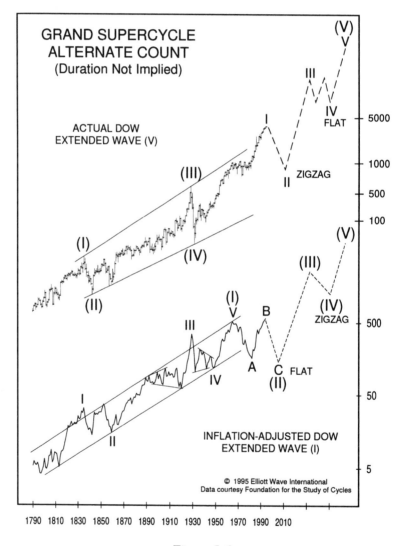

Figure 5-6

The Low Validity of Other Interpretations

In my opinion, all other long term wave counts are erroneous. Although most of the Elliott Wave analysis that crosses my desk from subscribers and others is quite competent and even insightful, there has been a proliferation of unsound analysis in recent years. "Elliott Wave" articles calling for a continued advance to "Dow 10,000" and even "Dow 100,000" have been published. However, such targets are merely a reflection of the market psychology typical of major tops. *Elliott Wave Principle* made the basic point seventeen years ago, when the Dow was in the 800-900 range:

> With the DJIA in a persistent downtrend until just recently, pervasive pessimism has worked to produce several distorted "Elliott" interpretations that call for a calamitous decline to emerge from what is only a Primary second wave correction. Targets below 200 DJIA have been forecast for the near future by taking Elliott's principles and twisting them into pretzels. [Note: the same phenomenon recurred in 1984.] To such analyses, we can only quote Charles Collins from the 1958 Elliott Wave Supplement to the *Bank Credit Analyst*: "Whenever the market gets into a bear phase, we find correspondents who think that 'Elliott' can be interpreted to justify much lower prices. While 'Elliott' can be interpreted with considerable latitude, it still cannot be twisted entirely out of context."

When the market is in a bull phase and nearing a peak, as it is now, the same phenomenon occurs and the same observation applies, but in the opposite direction. The best interpretation of the data says that the Dow will not continue to 10,000 without first falling to one-tenth that level or lower.

The Comparative Uncertainty in Forecasting the Path of a Corrective Pattern

The scenarios displayed in Figure 5-4 are the most likely candidates for wave Four. Indeed, I would say that they are the *only* candidates were it not for the experience of 1987. In that year, an expanded flat correction was stretched so dramatically in terms of price and contracted so dramatically in terms of time that there is no remotely comparable event in the stock price record.

Figure 5-7 shows what the Primary wave ④ correction of 1987 would look like at Grand Supercycle degree. Given an exact replica of wave ④ in 1987, this pattern would last 40 years (about ⅔ of the

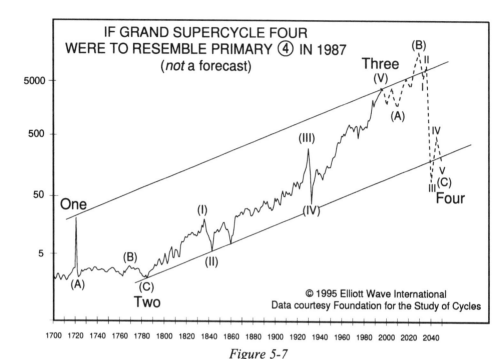

Figure 5-7

time of wave Two). It would trace out a drop to 1700, a move to a slight new all-time high, a drop back to 1700, a move to 16,000, then after a few years of topping, a crash in less than three months to below Dow 100 (one might assume it to be a panic associated with a nuclear attack), and it would all qualify as an expanded flat! What's worse, it would start with three waves down at Cycle degree, not a neat and easily analyzed "five" such as will be shown in Figures 5-8 and 5-9.

Figure 5-7 is not a forecast. Indeed, the chances of such a recurrence are nearly nil. The point this illustration makes is a larger one, that the exact path of the bear market could be extremely difficult to manage in real time, despite all we know about what it must accomplish before it is over. Corrections in progress are far more difficult to forecast than impulse waves, so it could be dangerous to rely upon any preconceived scenario. Alert analysis will be required throughout.

The Crash Of 1987 and the *Next* Crash

Elliott Wave Principle forecasted that "stock prices should not develop a bear market downswing similar to 1969-70 or 1973-74 for several years to come, most likely not until the early or middle eighties, at least." The first decline approximating those magnitudes occurred in 1987, a full nine years later.

The crash of 1987 occurred almost as if it had desired to accommodate the description given near the end of Chapter 8 of *Elliott Wave Principle*. More important, though, is that it occurred despite virtually universal disbelief that anything like October 1929 could ever happen again. History may eventually forget the litany of arguments for why a crash was impossible. "We have no 10% margin like the 1920s." "We have no pool operators as we had in the 1920s." "Government won't let it happen." "Institutions control the market; professional money managers will never panic." "Futures and options allow hedging, which will dampen extremes." "There are too many safeguards."

The mere fact that crashes occur demonstrates that the governor of stock price behavior is mass psychological change, not the latest news. There was no proportionately important news event just prior to the 1987 crash, despite several imaginative but transparently weak analyses to the contrary made months after the event in an attempt to justify the theory that markets move because of news. Other attempts were made to "explain" that the crash was due to the *mechanics* of market operation, specifically, computerized futures-based arbitrage, ironically called "portfolio insurance." This idea can be dismissed with two observations. First, the panic was global and occurred in markets that had no futures contracts.

Experts agree they can't agree on cause of crash

WASHINGTON — Despite four months of intensive study on the Oct. 19 stock market crash by some of the best minds in the nation, no one really knows what caused the plunge, let alone what needs to be done to prevent another one, a blue ribbon panel of experts agreed Wednesday.

Second, declines in those markets without futures trading were *worse*. More important, though, is that such "explanations" fail to reveal why massive futures contract selling initially occurred or why a discount to the cash market, which triggered the computer programs to sell, would have persisted for so long a time. These factors, simply, are governed by the *market*, and it is the market that crashed. Finally, lest we forget, the programs were designed by human beings to act when *they* would have acted. If computers "panicked," it is because their designers would have.

Viewed in the proper perspective, the October 1987 crash was *perfectly normal market behavior*. Such crashes occur all the time, though usually at much smaller degrees. When the Dow opens down 1% in the first few hours of a trading day, relative to the previous week's advance, it is a crash. Within the context of a Grand Supercycle, the 1987 crash, despite the fact that the October 19th meltdown was the single biggest down day (in arithmetic terms) in Wall Street history, was a minor event. The next decline will prove that assertion, as *the crash that Elliott Wave Principle was talking about hasn't even occurred yet*. The worst weeks of the Grand Supercycle bear will exceed the destruction of October 1987.

Today, eight years afterward, that crash is forgotten. It is once again accepted wisdom that "it can't happen again." The vast majority of analysts have written off October 1987 as "an anomaly," "an aberration." Portfolio insurance is no longer a factor, we are told, and besides, the Federal Reserve Board gained experience in 1987 and is in full control this time. As an antidote to this prevailing attitude, keep in mind *Elliott Wave Principle*'s description of the last Supercycle bear market:

> In 1929, as bids were withdrawn, "air pockets" developed in the market structure, and prices tumbled precipitously. The best efforts of the leaders of the financial community could not stem the panic once the tides of emotion took control. We have not seen a 1929 situation in fifty years and, while it is to be hoped that it never recurs, history suggests otherwise.

That paragraph described the first subwave (wave A) of a bear market of only Supercycle degree. We now face a Grand Supercycle bear market. *The Elliott Wave Theorist* prepared for the current potential back in October 1988:

If you really want to see a crash of historic proportion in stock prices, root for the count that allows wave V to be still in force. On the bigger picture, this is the more bearish interpretation. It eliminates the case that a sideways correction began in 1987, and makes a crash (perhaps as much as 2000 points) probable from whatever high is registered. With valuations squeezed back to historic extremes at such a peak, another crash would not be an unreasonable concern.

If you cannot imagine a crash of even greater percentage, just take a look at Figure 5-1 and realize that relative to the two centuries of uptrend that preceded it, the 1987 decline is almost invisible. Today we face a correction not merely larger, but *three degrees larger* than the one that included the 1987 crash.

A bear market need not *begin* with a crash. Price collapses are assured only in the third wave of a "C" wave, which was exactly the position of the market in October 1987 at Primary degree. Nevertheless, many "A" waves are crashes. Two examples are the declines of 1929 and 1937, which are discussed below.

How the Pattern Will Start

Regardless of which specific long term pattern ultimately unfolds at Grand Supercycle degree, there is no question that the first (or only, under the milder scenario) Supercycle degree decline will be of the *zigzag* family. It will be composed of *three* waves, to be labeled A-B-C or W-X-Y. Every initial decline through Primary degree (the "first" waves), and probably through Cycle degree (wave A), will be composed of *five* waves in order to be compatible with the larger trend. The declines of 1929 and 1937-1938 were "A" waves within Supercycle and Cycle degree bear markets respectively. Figures 5-8 and 5-9 show pictures of what these first declining waves looked like. Expect the first major decline of the coming bear market to reflect the form of these waves.

PRELIMINARY TIME FORECASTING

Time Forecasting for the First Major Low

Regardless of the total duration of past major corrections, in most cases, as previously stated, the deepest selloffs have occurred sooner in the pattern rather than later. In Grand Supercycle wave Two, the initial price low of 1722 was reached 2 years after the peak

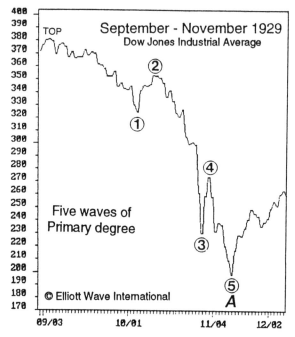

Figure 5-8

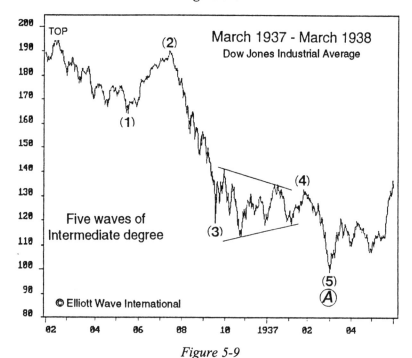

Figure 5-9

of 1720. In Supercycle wave (II), the price low of 1842 was met **7** years after the top of 1835, while the low of 1857 was reached **5** years after the wave B peak of 1852. In Supercycle wave (IV), the price low of 1932 was reached **3** years after the price peak of 1929, while the low of 1942 was reached **5** years after the wave B peak of 1937.

Given the tendency of the market in those prior instances to decline for a relatively short period of time and to decline for a Fibonacci number of years, we can reasonably expect the first major bottom of Grand Supercycle Four (and possibly its price low) to be registered between **2** and **8** years from the top. Since 1995 is the probable year for a top, and since 8 years is the longest probable time for the initial decline in the bear market, then the year 2003 is indicated as the *last likely year for a bottom*, exactly as suggested by the most reliable fixed-time cycles (see Appendix B).

From a presumed 1995 peak, Fibonacci numbers point to the following years as possibly providing turning points within the bear market:

1995 + 3 years = **1998**;
1995 + 5 years = **2000**;
1995 + 8 years = **2003**.

Needless to say, while the time *lengths* of 3, 5 and 8 years will remain valid estimating distances from whatever year the final high is recorded, these specifically projected dates are dependent upon 1995 being the year of the top. If it proves otherwise, these distances will have to be adjusted forward accordingly.

The inflation-adjusted Dow also indicates an important turning point around that time, as shown by the following Fibonacci time spans, illustrated in Figure 5-10:

— The end of wave (II) in 1859 + **144** years = **2003**.
— The end of wave (IV) in 1948 + **55** years = **2003**.
— The end of wave (V) in 1966 + **34** years = **2000**.
— The end of wave (A) in 1982 + **21** years = **2003**.

These lists of dates unequivocally support the years **1998, 2000** and particularly **2003** as probable years for the first major bottom. Strengthening these dates yet further, 2003 corresponds to a major cycle low, 1998 corresponds to smaller cycle low (see Appendix B), and 2000 is a Fibonacci 13 years after the crash year of 1987. It is possible that like our earlier projections for tops in 1983, 1987 and 1990, all three of these years will mark lows.

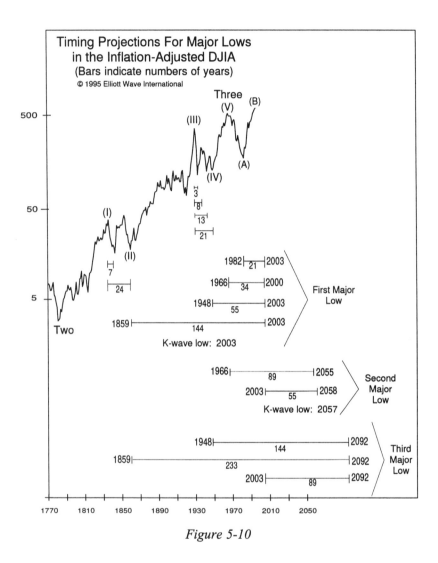

Figure 5-10

The year 2003 may be further strengthened as a target year for a major low by an analogy to the 1921-1932 experience. Wave V of (III) from 1921 to 1929 lasted **8** years, and wave V of (V) from 1974 to (presumably) 1995 will have lasted **21** years, or **2.618** times as long. The 1929-1932 bear market lasted **.382** times as long as the preceding wave V, or **3** years. (See Appendix A for a discussion of these ratios.) The bear market beginning in 1995 might also last **.382** times as long as the preceding wave V and **2.618** times as long

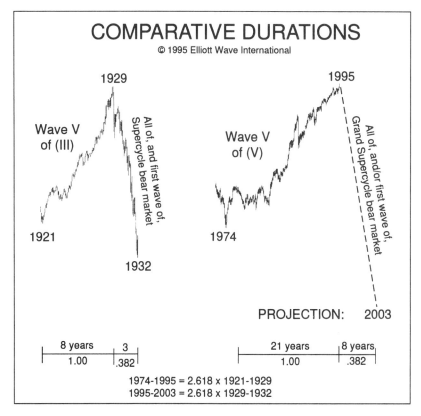

Figure 5-11

as 1929-1932, or **8** years. From 1995, this duration would project a low in **2003**. Figure 5-11 is notated to show that a low at that time could mark the end of the entire Grand Supercycle bear market or only wave (A). The 1932 low was both the end of a Supercycle bear market (in dollar terms) and the end of Cycle wave A (in inflation-adjusted terms).

To conclude, a major low is still expected to fall within our long standing target time of 1998-2003 first suggested a dozen years ago in *The Elliott Wave Theorist* (see Appendix to *Elliott Wave Principle*). The most strongly indicated specific year is **2003**. This analysis should not be construed to mean that a longer decline is impossible. This is a "best guess" and should be treated accordingly.

Time Forecasting for the Next Major High

Three of the last four Kondratieff cycles (see Appendix B) saw inflation-adjusted stock market peaks 23 years (1722 to 1745), 33 years (1896 to 1929) and 20 years (1948 to 1968) after their lows. These durations are each close to a Fibonacci 34 and 21 years, deviating by up to two years. Wave (B), then, might last 19-23 years or 32-36 years. The former time is the more strongly indicated because the "21" year period governed two out of the three instances, one of which took place in the last Grand Supercycle bear market. Thus, if wave (A) bottoms in 2003, the next high has a chance of occurring in **2024 ± 2 years** (i.e., 2022-2026), and a lesser chance of occurring in **2037 ± 2 years** (i.e., 2035-2039). *This is not yet a forecast*, simply an advance indication of a possibility. Only if the market declines as expected and then rises into one of these times will it become a forecast.

Time Forecasting for the Second Major Low

If wave (A) ends early in the century, when will wave (C) bottom? *The Elliott Wave Theorist* offered its first estimate back in December 1986:

> Once wave B is over in constant dollars, all the bear market structure will need for completion is wave C. Of course, that may only be the first A-B-C in a *double* three, and the bear market could continue with a net sideways series of ups and downs carrying as far out as the year **2057**.

The year cited above was based upon the projected ending date for the low of the next Kondratieff stock market cycle (see Appendix B), which is ideally due 54 years after the upcoming low is ideally due, in 2003.

As it happens, the Fibonacci time aspects of prior bear markets in the inflation-adjusted Dow support this projection. In both Supercycle corrections of the past two centuries, turning points came not in adjacent Fibonacci numbers of years, but at *alternate* Fibonacci numbers of years, i.e., skipping one Fibonacci number. From the 1835 peak of wave (I), **8** years marked the 1842 low for wave A (off by 1), and **21** years marked the 1857 low of wave C (off by 1), skipping the 13-year duration. From the 1929 peak of wave (III), **3** years marked the 1932 low for wave (IV), **8** years marked the high for wave B of (IV), **13** years marked the low of wave C of (IV), and **21** years (off by 1) marked the end of wave (IV), skipping the 5-year duration. If the Grand Supercycle reflects the same dynamic, then its first low might occur near 2000, **34** years after it started, while its final low might occur near 2055, **89** years after it started, skipping the 55-year duration, as shown in Figure 5-10. Past Fibonacci durations have sometimes been off by 1 year when the lengths are in the range of 8 to 21; the one length of 89 years was off by 2 years, expanding the range to 2053-2057. Add the observation that a Fibonacci **55** years after the projected low of 2003 is 2058, and we obtain a time window for a major low in the inflation-adjusted Dow in **2053-2058**. That time could mark the end of the Grand Supercycle corrective pattern if it is a flat. However, there is a fair probability that the final low in the actual Dow will occur a few decades later, as described below.

Time Forecasting for the End of the Bear Market Pattern

The last recorded Grand Supercycle bear market took place in the 1700s and lasted 64 years as measured by actual prices (it was 60-61 years in inflation-adjusted prices). While some limits do apply, there is no way to determine exactly how long the coming Grand Supercycle correction will last. It could be swift or prolonged. The wave (III) advance, for instance, which lasted 87 years, from 1842 to 1929, was corrected in just 3 short years, or 3.4% of the total time of the advance. On the other hand, the advance for wave III of (V), which lasted 24 years from 1942 to 1966, was corrected in 8 years, or 33% of the time. (By the interpretation shown in Figure 2-7, it took 16 years, totaling 50% of the time.) In each case, it should be noted, the downside price targets were *always* achieved, whether sooner or later. Since the Grand Supercycle uptrend has lasted 211 years, the corresponding corrective pattern will be commensurate in form and price extent, *regardless of duration*.

Despite this caveat, there are two main guides to a high probability conclusion in the current instance. Grand Supercycle wave Four is expected to be a *sideways* correction *and* remain inside the larger parallel trend channel (excepting perhaps the final low, for a brief period). Sideways corrections typically last longer than sharp corrections. In fact, they often last 1.618 times as long. As one prominent example, wave II, a sharp correction from 1937 to 1942, lasted 5 years, and wave IV, a sideways correction from 1966 to 1974, lasted 8 years, a Fibonacci relationship. There is an excellent probability, then, that wave Four will last between a Fibonacci ⁵/₃ and ³/₂ of the duration of wave Two.

As explained in Chapter 2, we are unfortunately hampered by the uncertainty of the data for the late 1700s. British stock prices show a low in 1784, completing a 64-year bear market. If wave Two ended in 1779 or 1788 (or in 1781 when adjusted for inflation) in the United States rather than in 1784 as in Britain, then the duration of wave Two could be as short at 59 years and as long as 68 years. Without putting too fine a point on it, we can conclude that wave Four will last about 1.618 times as long as wave Two, or about a century. This is also an excellent estimate for the *maximum* duration, since a century is about half of the time of the Grand Supercycle *advance*, and of the examples listed above, a 50% duration is the longest. It is also a *reasonable* relationship in this case, as the 50% duration was achieved by a sideways correction. A sideways correction of this duration would also meet the lower parallel line quite satisfactorily. The bear market, then, should end no later than the **2090s, plus or minus a decade**.

Supporting this time zone for a change in trend is the fact that a Fibonacci **144** years from the end of the Supercycle wave (IV) bear market in inflation-adjusted terms in 1948 is **2092**. A Fibonacci **233** years from the inflation-adjusted low of wave (II) in 1859 is **2092**. A Fibonacci **89** years after the low due in 2003 is also **2092**. (Once the date of the low due in the next decade is available, we can adjust this date if necessary.) All these durations are illustrated in Figure 5-10. The Decennial Pattern (see Appendix B) argues for a low in the first four years of each decade, with the *second* year the most strongly indicated, so 2092 date is strengthened by that cycle. Since durations of 89 years and higher have been off by as much as two years, and because the Decennial Pattern leaves open about the same leeway, we have a strongly indicated time for the end of the Grand Supercycle bear market of **2092 ± 2 years**. Perhaps the earliest year would be 2084, 89 years after 1995, and the latest year would be 2111, the projected time for the Kondratieff cycle bottom due after the one mid-century. Both of those dates will be subject to change upon verification of the year of the high and the time of the next two Kondratieff cycle bottoms.

AN IDEAL SCENARIO

I should have enough sense by now to refrain from outlining overly specific scenarios. Over the years, had I stuck to revealing only the aspects of my forecasts that were certain under the Wave Principle and omitted all conjectural aspects, even critics would have been hard pressed to find fault with any of it. In 1974, Frost and I might simply have said, "A great bull market for Cycle wave V is due, and will carry beyond 2700. We'll let you know when it's over." In 1982, after the wave was partially developed, I could have added, "Now we know that wave V will carry beyond 3600." Today, the only certainty is that a great bear market of Supercycle or Grand Super- cycle degree is due to begin this year and carry the Dow to below 1000. That's quite enough specificity for a scenario that no one ex- pects.

Nevertheless, I cannot resist trying to solve every aspect of a puzzle in my field. That challenge is what makes the profession engaging and fun. With the caveat, then, that the following is an ideal scenario far down the continuum of probability, I will proceed to put the puzzle together from the pieces we have discovered so far in this chapter.

Ideally, the Dow Jones Industrial Average should top out in 1995, then fall into a low in 2003 that marks the end of Supercycle wave (A). Wave (B) is then likely to carry the market upward for two or three decades, probably, though not necessarily, to a new high. Wave (C) will then unfold, probably ending in 2053-2058 amidst world turmoil. Either wave (A) or (C), or both, will bring the Dow down into the 90-390 range. The bear market could end there, com- pleting a flat, but only if wave (C) has carried the market below the low of wave (A). More likely is that subsequent waves in a triangle or double three will carry the pattern into the end of the century, ideally in 2090-2094 and no later than 2112.

A *triangle* that fits into the Millennium degree wave channel would satisfy with exceptional precision all pattern requirements, price requirements and time forecasting considerations discussed in this chapter. Figure 5-12 shows this ideal pattern as it would fit into the Millennium wave channel.

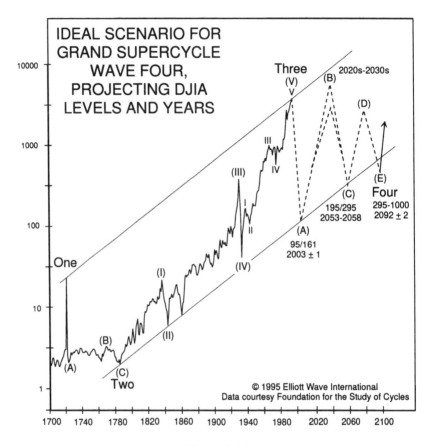

Figure 5-12

PERSPECTIVE

That the beginning of a historic decline in stock prices is near is the single most crucial fact facing every investor and portfolio manager today. Anyone still invested and not selling into this market rise is ignoring the most crucial message from the stock market pattern since 1929. As then, the stock market is stretched far out on a limb. You can rest assured that when the first wave of stock market losses hits, it will once again catch the financial establishment completely off guard.

The coming bear market need not catch you off guard, and indeed can be used to your great advantage, as discussed in Chapter 13. Once you have prepared for the downside, you can spend your time and energy focusing on how you will take advantage of the upturn due thereafter, which is not, after all, that far away in the future. When contemplating the implications of wave structures of the size discussed in this chapter, it is well to keep in mind these words from *Elliott Wave Principle*:

> If the existence of the planet Earth is conceived to have lasted so far one year, life forms emerged from the oceans five weeks ago, while manlike creatures have walked the Earth for only the last six hours of the year, less than $1/100$ of the total period during which life forms have existed. To put these time periods in perspective, we should note that on this basis, Rome dominated the Western world for a total of five seconds. Viewed from this perspective, a Millennium wave isn't really of such large degree after all.

Introduction to Technical Analysis Section

Has the bull market that began in 1974 had the ancillary characteristics of a *fifth wave*? As *Elliott Wave Principle* explains, "the average fifth wave is almost always less impressive than the third." The key to knowing whether a bull market advance is truly a fifth wave is to compare its quality in *action* ("technicals") and *foundation* ("fundamentals") to that within the supposed third wave. If an improvement is clearly evident, it is probably not a fifth. If the wave is "less impressive" both technically and fundamentally, then a fifth it is. How does wave V from 1974 compare to wave III from 1942 to 1966? The differences between waves V and III have been clear throughout. Chapters 6 and 9, covering momentum and fundamentals, explore these differences.

Chapter 6

MOMENTUM CONSIDERATIONS

"Momentum" is the word market analysts use to denote the speed and breadth of progress or regress in a market. Speed is measured by rates of price change, while breadth is determined by the percentage of markets subsumed by the larger one that are participating in the overall trend. A market's momentum status is extremely valuable information because momentum in markets is not random, but patterned.

The real value of momentum studies is in their confirmation or challenge of an Elliott Wave analysis. Momentum studies on their own are substantially unreliable because without the Wave Principle, an analyst has no way of knowing the degree of the top or bottom expected. He therefore has difficulty in assessing what momentum characteristics should be considered "normal" under the circumstances.

OVERBOUGHT/OVERSOLD

Markets respect loose limits of trend persistence that are commonly labeled "overbought" and "oversold" levels. This concept has proved useful at both major and minor market junctures. An example of a major trend juncture that was supported by an oversold condition was the second half of 1982. In December of that year, *The Elliott Wave Theorist* showed the chart reproduced here as Figure 6-1 and presented this commentary:

> Is such a super bull market really likely from here? There are plenty of reasons to answer "yes," but here's one that is strictly technical. This chart shows a 20-year forward-weighted rate of change plotted with the Dow Industrial Average. As you can see, the extreme "overbought" level reached in 1929 was fully corrected by the crash into 1932. Similarly, the overbought level reached in 1966 *has now been entirely corrected by the long sideways trend that finally ended in 1982.*

Elliott Wave analysis was crucial to this conclusion, because it was certain that the 1966-1982 corrective process was a wave of

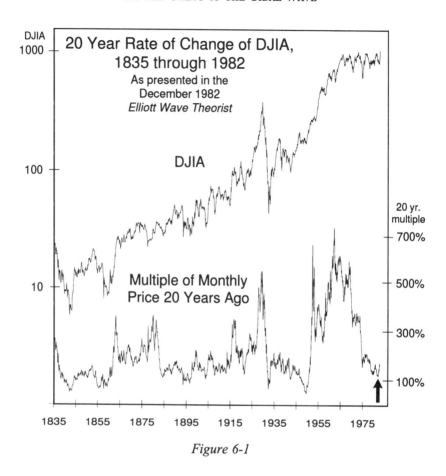

Figure 6-1

Cycle degree and therefore would not produce an even deeper oversold condition like those of 1933 and 1949.

As you can see in Figure 6-2, the updated 20-year rate of change
for the DJIA now shows an *overbought* condition commensurate with
those of 1929 and 1962. Those dates respectively preceded (1) an
89% drop in the DJIA and (2) twenty years of zero net gain in the
DJIA during a mostly inflationary period, which included a decline
of 75% in real terms beginning four years after the peak overbought
condition was registered. The current overbought condition is likely
to mark no less an important market juncture. For reasons discussed
under **Divergence,** the fact that the overbought condition in 1995
is *less* than that of 1962 supports the conclusion from the Wave
Principle that the trend change is of even *larger* degree than either
1929 or 1966.

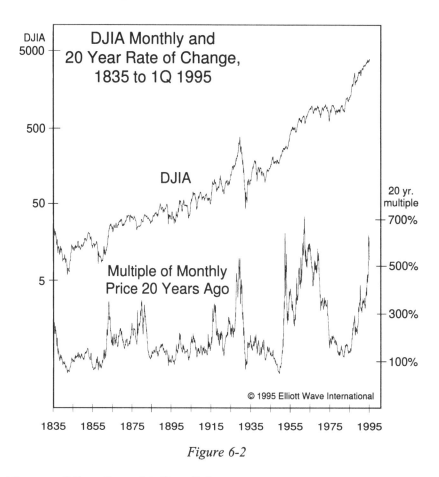

Figure 6-2

Types of Overbought Conditions

An overbought condition by itself is no proof of a top. The stock market most often reaches its peak short term rate of change and breadth in the third wave, i.e., the volatile center of an impulse, and sometimes reaches it in the first wave. The difference between a peak-of-market overbought condition on the one hand and an early or mid-trend overbought condition on the other is subtle, but crucial to a correct interpretation of the indicators. Rates of change that measure the appropriate durations will always show one or more *lower peaks* by the time a top in market prices arrives. When the stock market is overbought in mid-trend, all or most rates of change concurrently register *new highs*. With a knowledge of the difference, *The Elliott Wave Theorist* correctly identified the bullish implication of the powerful overbought condition achieved by the S&P Composite index in 1983, as measured by its annual rate of change. That indicator is created by computing the percentage difference between the S&P Composite's average daily closing price for each month and that of twelve months prior.

In August 1983, the bull market was one year old and had continued higher despite its relentless near term overbought condition. The persistence of the trend produced the most extreme overbought condition in the 1-year rate of change since 1943. *The Elliott Wave Theorist* concluded, "August 1982 marked the start of something more than what has come to be regarded as the norm, a two-year bull market followed by a two-year bear. The highest overbought condition in forty years signals that our Elliott Wave forecast for the launching of wave V is right on target." (See the full analysis in Appendix A of *Elliott Wave Principle*.) Figure 6-3 is labeled exactly as shown then through "Kickoff for Cycle Wave V" and is then updated to today.

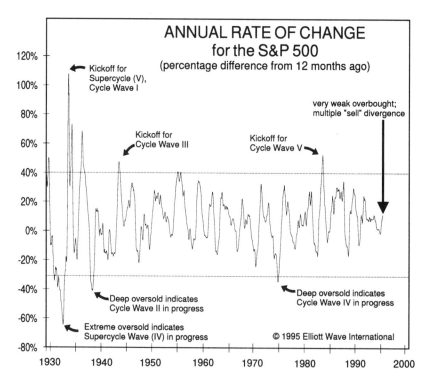

Figure 6-3

After the wave ② correction of 1984 had run its course, *The Elliott Wave Theorist* returned to that momentum study in January 1985 and reaffirmed its implication: "Any time an oscillator retreats to *moderately* oversold territory after an *extreme* overbought condition has been reached in a normal cyclical manner, the market is almost always on the verge of another significant advance." Advance it did, nonstop for over three years.

DIVERGENCE

As described briefly above, what distinguishes the overbought condition at a top from that at the start or middle of a trend is a *slowing* in the rate of advance and a thinning in breadth. Such occurrences are called "divergences" because they produce a divergence of direction between rate-of-change and breadth indicators and the market's price averages. The stock market *always* slows down and becomes thinner before reversing from an uptrend to a downtrend. Kickoffs and mid-trend accelerations typically show no such divergences, while top formations display them in countless ways.

On a long term basis, the momentum condition of today's stock market has been anticipated for over a dozen years. Here is the description from the December 1982 *Elliott Wave Theorist* concerning what to look for at the top:

> [It is] my expectation that wave V will register a lesser overbought condition than did wave III in 1966. A few years from now, a lower peak in the rate of change *against higher highs in the market* is expected to give a typical "sell" signal of the type so often used in shorter term divergence analysis.

The 20-year rate of change in Figure 6-2 shows exactly that situation in place today: a mammoth divergence between today's overbought condition and that of 1962. As long as the market does not accelerate dramatically enough to bring that rate of change to a new high, this indicator is and will remain compatible with the case that the stock market is creating a top of at least Supercycle degree, because that is the degree of the slowing of upside momentum.

Let's examine the 10-year rate of change in the DJIA to see if the bull market has been slowing at Cycle degree. First study each of the extreme overbought conditions in this measure over the past 150 years shown in Figure 6-4. There have been four extreme overbought conditions in this period, the fourth being that of the

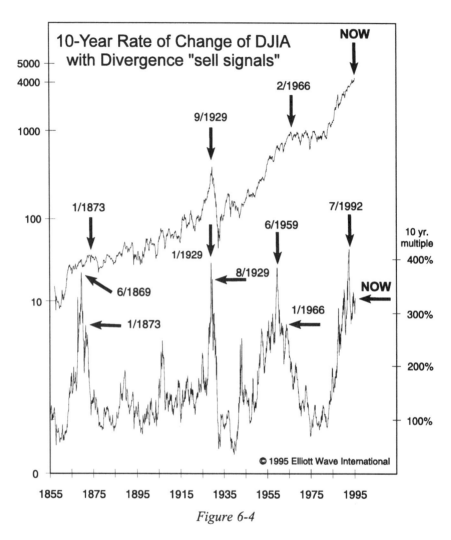

Figure 6-4

early 1990s. Notice first that the extreme reading of July 1992 was the highest of all and therefore the highest in U.S. history, edging out that of 1929. One legacy of raging inflation was a distortion of this indicator in the latest cycle, as nothing of the kind shows up on the inflation-adjusted chart. Yet even with that inflation, the 20-year, 3-year (see Figure 6-5) and 1-year (see Figure 6-3) rates of change are below previous highs, so we do not have to fear that the market is at a high acceleration midpoint. On the contrary, the three-year divergence that is now in place on the 10-year rate of change (along with the others) is emphatically announcing an aged topping process. As you can see in Figure 6-4, in every instance that the 10-year rate of change reached an extreme overbought condition, the market did not peak until the indicator had first retreated to a lower level, reflecting a slowing of the upside rate of change. Each vertical arrow in Figure 6-4 marks a peak overbought condition, while each sideways arrow marks the level of the indicator when the market made its final high. Durations between the high in the indicator and the high in the market have ranged from seven months in 1929 to nearly seven years in 1959-1966. Now observe that wave V's upside rate of change on a 10-year basis peaked in July 1992, nearly *three years ago*. The indicator has since fallen and bounced back up to a lower level. *The divergence at Cycle degree in place today is commensurate with those of the most important tops of the past 150 years.*

Let's investigate this latest slowing more closely. Observe in Figure 6-5 the striking divergence of the 3-year rate of change on the DJIA against the new highs it has been making since 1987. A 5-year rate of change (not shown) shows the same thing. Primary wave

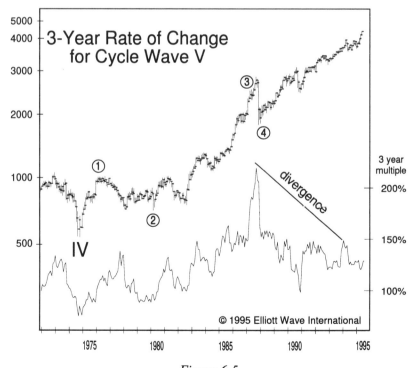

Figure 6-5

⑤ has clearly been much slower than wave ③, the classic precursor to a downside reversal. We can now add to the divergence at Cycle degree a divergence at Primary degree. Is there a divergence at Intermediate degree as well?

Figure 6-3 updates the 12-month rate of change that *The Elliott Wave Theorist* used in 1983 to confirm the start of wave V. Examine its behavior of the past eight years, and you will see that this indicator has been giving one of the clearest and longest lasting "sell signals" in its history. Not only has the latest all-time high in the S&P Composite index failed to generate new extremes in upside momentum, it has accompanied a massive *quadruple divergence*. The advance into the 1987 and 1990 peaks had already displayed a slowing in upside momentum relative to the 1982-1983 rise. The peak "overbought" readings in 1983, 1987, 1989 and 1991 were **+52.5%, +34.3%, +29.8%**, and **+24.4%** respectively. As we enter the second quarter of 1995, the Dow is potentially creating yet another divergence as the rate of change has reached only **+13.8%**, making the latest one-year rise the slowest of the entire bull market. These last two readings are divergences at Intermediate degree. The progression of lower peaks, coupled with the fact that the oversold conditions of 1988 and 1990 were deeper than that of 1984, presents a clear picture of a market that is finding it increasingly easy to decline and increasingly difficult to advance. These lower peaks create a momentum profile not unlike the one that accompanied the market into the 1966 top. It is therefore the most urgent long term sell signal since the peak of Cycle wave III.

There is also a divergence at Supercycle degree, although it does not show up on the chart of the actual Dow because of the powerful inflation that has persisted since the 1940s. Turn back to Figure 3-3 and recall that since 1948, the inflation-adjusted Dow has performed in a strikingly weak manner compared to its gains in Supercycle wave (III). Although there is no rate of change plotted on that chart, you can see at a glance that the rise into 1929 would generate an extreme overbought condition, while the appropriate rate of change would be diverging dramatically against the moderate new highs of 1966 and now. The current status of long term momentum, then, with divergences at fully four degrees of trend, is precisely what one would expect if the Elliott Wave analysis presented in this book is correct.

Non-Confirmation

A "non-confirmation" is a special type of divergence. When a long standing prior trend fails to continue in one or more subsectors of the larger market, the subsector at a new high is said to be "unconfirmed" by those that are not. Non-confirmations do not guarantee an approaching trend change, as they sometimes appear for periods of time in the middle of a trend. Their value is that they *always* accompany stock market tops and usually accompany bottoms. Any case for a stock market top must include non-confirmation, then, while a trend that is confirmed across the board is not at a top. At the 1968 top, the Value Line, S&P, NYSE and Transportation indexes registered new highs, but the DJIA, after rallying all the way back to within a few points of its 1966 high, never confirmed, nor did the Utilities. The stock market then fell for 18 months to below its late 1966 lows. At the 1974 bottom, the Value Line, S&P, NYSE and DJIA registered new lows for the decade, but the Transports, holding above their 1970 low, did not confirm. At the final month of the bottom, the DJIA made a new low, but no other index did. From this double non-confirmation, a new bull market was born.

Today's non-confirmations reflect a significant top in the making. With the DJIA at a new high today, the Utility average and the advance-decline line are below their highs of 1993-1994. While the a-d non-confirmation may be overcome, the lagging Utility index is consistent with analysis indicating an approaching major top.

Wave V has been a worldwide affair. While minor non-confirmations would be expected on such a scale at almost all times, the Japanese Nikkei index is in a serious state of long term non-confirmation. The Nikkei was the world's star performer through 1989, outpacing all other countries' stock indexes. After rising 1143.4% from 1974 to December 31, 1989, the Nikkei turned down. While the DJIA and other countries' stock indexes have continually made new highs over the past five-plus years, the Nikkei has declined over 60%. Following fifteen years of joint uptrend, this dramatic non-confirmation, shown in Figure 6-6, is bearish for the entire global bull market. Figure 6-7 shows the result of a brief 8-month non-confirmation between the world's two biggest stock markets in 1929.

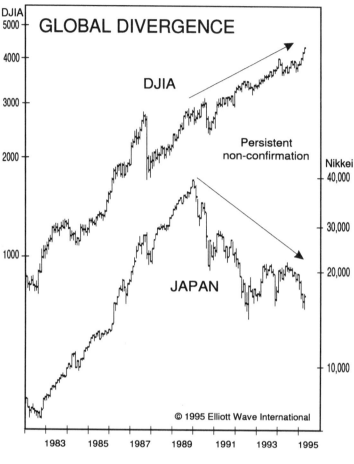

Figure 6-6

Breadth

The advance-decline line is the number of stocks advancing minus the number of stocks declining on a daily basis continually added to a running total. Thus, the a-d line is a reflection of the breadth of participation of the smallest subsectors in the stock market, the individual stocks that compose it.

The a-d line is not a reflection of market value, because it does not take into account whether a stock goes up or down a lot or a little; it reflects only direction. The value of the indicator is nevertheless substantial because *it acts differently at different times in a market cycle.* For whatever psychological reason, investors' buying and selling impulses cause a greater percentage of stocks to go up

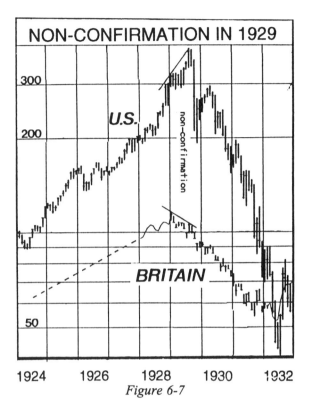

Figure 6-7

daily in third waves than in fifth waves. Even if the rising stocks' price changes are greater in a fifth, fewer stocks rise on the average day. As *The Elliott Wave Theorist* pointed out in a special section in the April 1983 issue (see Appendix A of *Elliott Wave Principle*), "There is no question that in fifth waves, a lagging advance-decline line (the cumulative net daily advances minus declines) *is a normal occurrence.*" As the chart then illustrated, a weak a-d line has been a dominant characteristic of fifth waves. Prior fifth waves of comparable or similar degree occurred in 1921-1929 and 1962-1966, during which periods the a-d line was flat or only moderately upsloping after the initial "kickoff" year. *The Elliott Wave Theorist* placed its expectation for wave V in this perspective:

A relatively poorly performing a-d line from 1982 to (I expect) 1987 will be a "sell signal" for the entire Supercycle from 1932. The lesson for now is, don't use that underperformance as a reason to sell too early and miss out on what promises to be one of the most profitable uplegs in the history of the stock market.

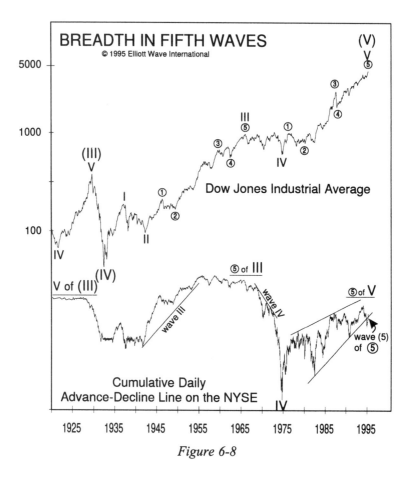

Figure 6-8

Had the advance from 1974 produced a relative *expansion* in the number of stocks advancing vs. declining, the entire analysis that the bull market was a fifth wave would have been negated. However, as you can see by Figure 6-8, wave V performed in the required lackluster way compared to wave III. During wave III, the number of stocks advancing so outstripped the number declining that the advance-decline line soared. During wave V, selectivity has been such that in 21 long years, the a-d line has retraced only half of the losses it incurred during the 8-year sideways correction of wave IV from 1966 to 1974, which in price terms was a mild correction. The anemic retracement by wave V is even worse than the chart makes it appear; over the years, more stocks are traded, so the daily net differences should normally be expanding over time to create wider and wider swings on the chart. If this chart were constructed as a/d, not a-d, it would more properly convey the extent of the relative weakness of wave V. This chart further overstates the breadth performance of the past dozen years because during that time, hundreds of bond funds, equity funds, preferred stocks, foreign stocks and foreign funds have been listed on the NYSE. The breadth performance of all U.S. common stocks of individual manufacturing and service corporations (i.e., traditional common stocks) has been even worse. Breadth has been dismal in the over-the-counter market since 1983. For *twelve years*, the NASDAQ index has risen while on the average day more stocks closed lower than higher. This indicator reveals that daily buying in the index (and by extension in traditional common stocks) over that time has been selective, quite in contrast to the wholesale accumulation of 1974-1983. The trend of breadth among traditional common stocks is clear even in the deteriorating advance-decline figures for the impeccably blue chip S&P 500 index. While the cumulative advance- decline line fell for only the last eight *months* of the great 1921-1929 bull market, in this bull market it has fallen for the past *six years*. The difference is due to the fact that 1929 marked a top of Supercycle degree, while this one will mark a top of Grand Supercycle degree, which is sporting a longer period of breadth deterioration. In conclusion, what *Elliott Wave Principle* forecasted to be Cycle wave V of Supercycle Wave (V) fits the typical character of a fifth wave like a glove.

Within wave V, wave ⑤'s breadth has been the narrowest among the three Primary degree rises, generating the weakest upward slope, confirming that it is indeed wave ⑤. What's more, within wave ⑤, wave (5)'s breadth reveals a dramatic non-confirmation in that the advance-decline line is failing to accompany the DJIA above the high registered in January 1994. Both of these phenomena are noted in Figure 6-8. Similarly, there are fewer stocks on the NYSE at one-year highs now than in January 1994, when there were in turn fewer than in early 1992. Despite headlines about how "the market" is making new highs, then, there have been more stocks down than up on the average day, and fewer stocks making new all-time highs, for quite a long time.

Unfortunately, there are no breadth statistics for Supercycle wave (I) from 1784 to 1835 or wave (III) from 1842 to 1929. However, wave (III) took place during a period of essentially zero taxes and no government regulation. There is no doubt that such an environment would produce a greater breadth of successful business enterprise than the period from 1932 to today, which has encompassed wave (V). I am willing to state unequivocally that had we breadth statistics for the 19th century, the 20th century would show a bearish divergence at Supercycle degree.

Because in a-d terms, wave (5) is below wave (3), wave V is below wave III, and wave (V) is almost certainly below wave (III), the current situation is a non-confirmation at Intermediate degree on top of a non-confirmation at Cycle degree on top of a non-confirmation at Supercycle degree. This behavior is *extremely* divergent and supports the case that today the stock market is in the "fifth of the fifth" wave from Supercycle degree at least down to Intermediate degree. Such breadth behavior is a classic precursor of a downturn in the blue chip stock averages at any single degree, much less three together.

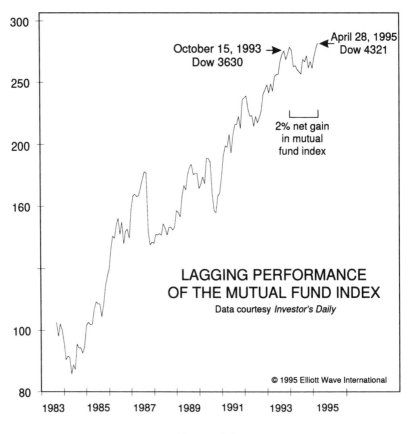

Figure 6-9

The Hidden Forces of Divergence

As a result of divergence and non-confirmation, the transition phase from a bull market to bear is a period in which profiting on the long side still looks easy, but isn't. This condition has certainly been in force recently. From October 15, 1993 to today, the Dow Jones Industrial Average has risen nearly 700 points, or just under 20%. At the same time, the NYSE Composite index, a broader reflection of the market, has risen only 6.5%, the average stock fund is up *less than 2%*, and the advance-decline line has lost ground. Take a look at Figure 6-9 and see how mutual fund owners have done since October 1993 while the headlines keep announcing new highs. The Dow is telegraphing the *feeling* that making money is easy, but the average market participant has experienced almost no net gain for a full year and a half, thereby underperforming Treasury bills by 6%. While the conventional opinion today is that this condition means that stocks have had an "internal" bear market and are therefore on their way in "a brand new bull market," it is classic behavior in a transition phase, and this one is living on borrowed time.

Quiz: How many stocks among the 30 Dow Industrials do you think pushed that index to its headline-making record in the first quarter of 1995? Three-fourths? Two-thirds? Half? The truth is that only six Dow stocks made all-time highs in the first quarter of 1995. All the others topped long ago. This is the kind of thinness characteristic of the final months of a rise into a *major* top such as those of 1929, 1937 and 1973. In other words, "the market" is not at new highs; only a few stocks are. In fact, seven Dow stocks are below their 1987 highs!

Divergence in Seat Prices

A seat on the New York Stock Exchange recently sold for $900,000, $200,000 *less* than the $1.1m. peak price registered in 1987. The last time that seat sales were below a previous high despite a new high in the averages was January 1973, at the top of a corrective wave rally within a larger bear market (see Figure 6-10). Exchange seat prices are sensitive to market momentum. Professional traders can feel the difference when a market's breadth and upside rate of change weaken, and therefore bid less for seats. A persistent rise in wave (5) may still force some newcomer to grab a seat at a new all-time high price, such as occurred at the 1929 top.

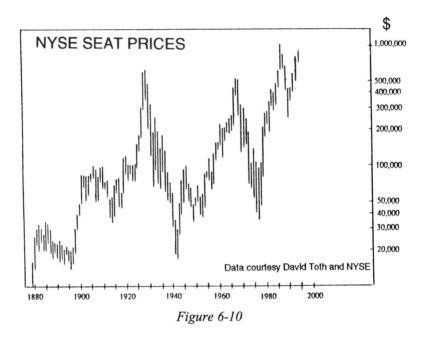

Figure 6-10

However, any new record is in no way likely to reflect the extent of the stock market's gain since the 1987 high, thus maintaining at least a subtle divergence.

VOLATILITY AND COMPLACENT BUYING

1992 and 1993 set consecutive all-time records for narrowness of range in the S&P Composite. More important, the period from 1991 through today has set an all-time record for the longest time without a 10% correction. Four years is twice as long as the previous record stretch. The market was not content with setting a new record in 1993, so it has maintained the performance for four years (and may be going for a fifth).

Cycles expert Peter Eliades of Santa Rosa, California adds that the five longest periods of the century without a 12% correction were those that preceded the highs in 1937, 1946, 1966 and 1987, and *now*. These previous instances marked tops of Primary, Cycle and Supercycle degree. The current period has not only set at least a one-century record, but is over a year longer than the previous record and isn't over yet.

Market analyst James Stack of Whitefish, Montana has conducted a similar study from 1928, producing a table of annual percentage price ranges, listed in order of volatility. I am reprinting

S&P Annual Ranges from 1928, in order of size					
Year	%Average	Year	%Average	Year	%Average
1993	9.3	1967	19.3	1991	29
1994	9.4	1981	20.2	1955	29.2
1992	11.2	1950	20.4	1970	29.7
1959	12.5	1978	20.7	1962	30.5
1965	12.7	1948	20.8	1946	30.7
1964	13.4	1968	21.1	1975	30.9
1944	13.9	1949	21.4	1958	31.1
1952	14.1	1983	22.1	1982	33.1
1951	14.2	1986	22.1	1934	34.3
1984	14.2	1990	22.1	1940	34.7
1956	14.3	1957	23	1980	35.4
1960	14.4	1961	23.1	1928	35.8
1979	14.6	1943	24.9	1954	36.8
1971	15	1966	24.9	1987	40.3
1988	15.6	1985	25.7	1974	46.4
1972	15.8	1941	25.9	1938	47.5
1953	16	1939	26.1	1935	50.2
1947	16.6	1973	26.4	1930	56.9
1977	16.9	1989	26.6	1929	57.5
1976	17	1942	26.7	1937	59
1969	17.4	1936	27.6	1932	71.6
1963	17.9	1945	28.9	1933	75.2
				1931	80.7

this table because it shows not only that 1992, 1993 and 1994 have been the least volatile years during this time, but that 1931, 1932 and 1933 were the *most* volatile years. In other words, the three years surrounding the last Supercycle *bottom* were the most volatile, and the *past* three years have been the least volatile. (Since volatility subsided after the first quarter of 1991, this span is actually now four years in duration.) Is it simply coincidence that the Wave Principle identifies these years as completing a Supercycle bottom and leading to a Supercycle top?

The entire span of the past four years, then, is setting an all-time record (perhaps for any stock market ever) for its dearth of price-related psychological upset near an all-time high. What explains this phenomenon?

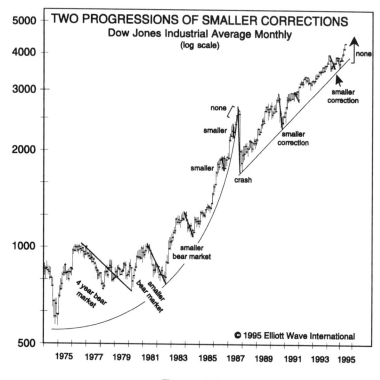

Figure 6-11

The lack of volatility in today's market is both an *effect* of the bulls' complacency and a *cause* of further complacency. The market's calm is widely presumed to be "normal," when in fact, *it is so abnormal that it is unprecedented.* Such long periods of uncorrected advance do not suggest that "a 10% correction is due." They reveal deep investor complacency and therefore market tops, which is why they have preceded major downside reversals. The next ten years will witness volatility equal to or greater than that during 1931 to 1933 and shake investors out of their carefree dream world for many decades.

The current state of investor complacency has been attained through a long process of decreasing fear and smaller setbacks. This progression always leads to a top. For example, as the bull market from 1974 progressed over its first thirteen years, each corrective phase that occurred was *milder* than the preceding one. As Figure 6-11 reveals, this phenomenon continued until August 1987, when there were no corrections in the monthly figures. The aftermath of

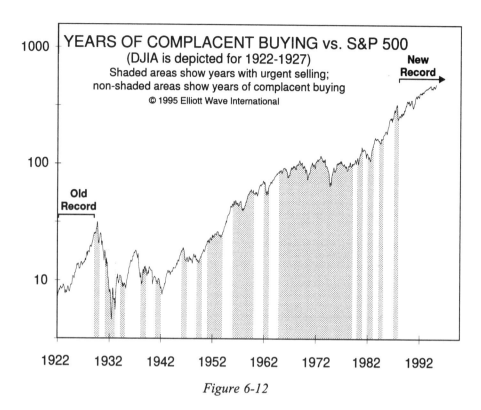

Figure 6-12

this parabolic curve was the crash of 1987, which took the DJIA down 36.1%. The 1990 decline took the Dow down 21.2%. In 1994, there was a correction of 9.7%. The latest rise has been so persistent that since March 7, there has been no close-to-close correction bigger than of 1%! If the Dow continues in this manner past May 15, it will set a record for its entire century-plus long history. The phenomenon of 1974-1987, then, is repeating. Whether it ends now or after a pullback and final rally, the resolution should be a bear market.

Another aspect of this phenomenon is revealed by a subtle indicator called "urgent selling." In 1978, the late stock market historian and analyst James Alphier developed a study of periods of persistently declining prices for the S&P Composite stock index. Specifically, he noted periods of fifteen or more trading days among which at least 80% were down days in the market. Urgent selling is normally quite common and has occurred one or more times in 51.6% of the years within this century. Moreover, he found that the few extended periods that *lacked* urgent selling preceded the biggest bear markets. As revealed in Figure 6-12, the previous record duration lacking a single instance of urgent selling was November 1, 1922 to October 28, 1929, a period of seven years. It preceded and accompanied the start of the biggest bear market in the history of the country. As of today, *that record has been broken.* As Peter Eliades points out in an update of Alphier's study, the S&P Composite index has exhibited not a single instance of urgent selling since October 1987, which was seven years and six months ago. We may dub the lack of any urgent selling over a period of more than two years "complacent buying." While nearly every investor, professional and public alike, behaves and speaks as if a persistently rising market is perfectly normal and will maintain for the indefinite future, it is in fact both (1) monstrously abnormal in the context of all market behavior, yet (2) perfectly normal for a market that is capping a multi-decade advance.

Another incredible thing about the current period of complacent buying is that it began from a level of *fair to high market valuation* (see Chapter 7). The corresponding period in the 1920s began from *low* valuation. The new record of complacent buying and the consistently higher valuation reflect the Elliott Wave case that a Grand Supercycle, a trend one degree larger than the one that ended in 1929, is cresting. Like 1929-1932, the next event should be a period of urgent selling that does not stop until it has set all-time records.

Some people argue that markets are unpredictable because people learn and therefore act differently at different times. The truth is that markets are largely predictable *because* people learn. As discussed in Chapter 1, their learning is weighted toward recent experience. Progressions of smaller corrections, for instance, are due to learning. Initially bearish investors "learn" over time that market setbacks are buying opportunities, so upon each new occurrence, the general fear is less, so the response time for committing new funds is less. The same is true of periods of less and less urgent selling. Investors keep "learning" that markets always come back after falling, so they buy during and after every pullback so quickly and persistently that no urgent selling occurs. This trend continues until there are no more corrections, investors having learned that there will not be one deep enough or long enough to buy at lower prices. At that point, the last dollar is soon committed, and the market is ripe for a crash.

OUTLOOK

Figure 6-3 shows that the annual rate of change for the S&P Composite index in November 1929 reached minus 35% (indicating a net decline of 35%, using the monthly average of daily figures, in twelve months). This was an extreme figure that signaled the onset of Supercycle wave (IV). The maximum downside rate of change on a one-year basis was achieved in July 1932 at minus 64%. Supercycle wave (II) produced a nearly identical oversold condition in 1857 with a twelve month decline of 52%. The developing Grand Supercycle bear market will at some point generate a one-year net decline greater than these. In fact, it should set two- or three-century records for the depth of oversold condition on every indicator discussed in this chapter.

Historically extreme readings on all momentum indicators, including short term ones, will be a natural part of the process of broad and intense selling that must take place if prices are to go substantially lower. Do not assume prematurely that these conditions indicate a market low. For example, the depth of the oversold reading in the ten day average of the Arms index (a measure of momentum utilizing breadth and volume) in September 1987, just a few weeks off the all-time high, was the deepest in three years, yet it was *not* a "buy signal," as was popularly assumed. In fact, it was one of the earliest hints that the tide had changed, as the measly 9% correction of the time was accompanied by great selling pressure. Two weeks *after* the rally into October 2, the oversold level achieved by this index was not only huge, it was historic. During bull markets of Primary degree, most mild oversold readings indicate Intermediate degree bottoms. In the bear market, most mild overbought readings will indicate Intermediate degree tops. During the bull market, the best strategy has been to look for oversold conditions and short term downside divergences to buy. During the bear market, the best strategy will be to look for overbought conditions and short term upside divergences to sell short. Any bottoms that will lead to tradable rallies will be marked by oversold conditions that are both deep *and* divergent, and not all of those will be trustworthy.

Chapter 7

INVESTOR PSYCHOLOGY: VALUATION

When pessimism about the future course of a market is widespread, the market is nearer a bottom than a top. When optimism about the future course of a market is widespread, the market is nearer a top than a bottom. This fact appears perverse to novice investors who read the news for guidance, but in fact is true by definition. A market top is the point at which the most money has been committed, and a market bottom is the point at which the least money has been committed. People commit money when they are optimistic and withdraw it when they are pessimistic.

There are several gauges of optimism and pessimism that are useful in confirming an analysis based upon the Wave Principle. As with momentum analysis (see Chapter 6), measures of investor sentiment are insufficient for an accurate market analysis because they do not address the question: How bullish is enough or how bearish is enough to indicate an approaching trend change in the current environment? Some tops and bottoms are of Intermediate degree, and some are of Grand Supercycle degree. The only way to anticipate the extremity of market mood is with an approach that can address that crucial factor. Once that approach is available, psychological measures can be invaluable in *confirming or negating* a market opinion. If the sentiment picture fits, fine; if it does not, then the analyst must reconsider. As an example of an application of this approach, read this quotation from our 1978 book, *Elliott Wave Principle*:

> One of our objections to the "killer wave" occurring now or in 1979, as most cycle theorists suggest, is that the psychological state of the average investor does not seem poised for a shock of disappointment. Most important stock market collapses have come out of optimistic, high-valuation periods. Such conditions definitely do not prevail at this time, as eight years of a raging bear market have taught today's investor to be cautious, conservative and cynical. Defensiveness is not in evidence at tops.

Are today's investors still "cautious, conservative, cynical and defensive," or has the market since that time reached a "high-valuation period"? We will examine that question in this chapter from the point of view of valuation indicators and in the next chapter from general manifestations of investor psychology.

VALUATION

Monetary value is what people will pay for something. It is objectively definable only with regard for the existence of people and their attitudes. This fact particularly pertains to investment prices, which are governed almost entirely by the mental states of those bidding and asking in an auction market. The stock market bestows greatly divergent values upon various real things at different times, the most important of these being (1) dividends, (2) the value of corporate assets, and (3) the yield on high grade bonds. When it comes down to valuing stock certificates apart from their appreciation potential, these are the only values that matter. An investor trades his money for a quarterly payment called a *dividend* plus the guarantee that if the company had to, it could *liquidate* and divide up the result among shareholders, and he takes this action in lieu of lending his money out at *interest* to a solid, healthy debtor. In past markets, stocks have yielded as little as 3% in dividends and as much as 16%. They have been valued as high as 4.2 times corporate book value (which is the dollar value of assets on the firm's balance sheet) and as little as .57 times. They have yielded as much as 4 times as much as bonds and as little as 0.4 as much. The difference is due to one thing: people's opinion about the *capital gain potential* from stocks, i.e., the extent to which they are bullish or bearish. Therefore, the extremity of such valuations is a direct measure of investors' optimism or pessimism.

Earnings: the Least Reliable Basis for Valuation

Many analysts include stock prices vs. earnings among their valuation models, but earnings are not real to the investor. This fact disqualifies earnings as a good benchmark of value. Even those who do not accept this argument must admit that earnings themselves cycle so severely that the ratio can fluctuate substantially regardless of stock price movement. For proof of this observation, study Figure 7-1, which shows aggregate earnings for the S&P 500 companies over the past forty years annotated with comments regarding the bull and bear markets of the period. Strictly from this juxtaposition, one might be far more likely to postulate that there is

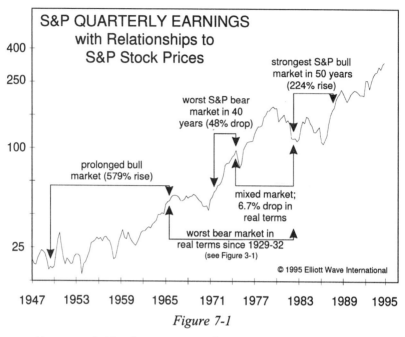

Figure 7-1

a negative correlation between stock prices and earnings than that there is a positive one. This independence, along with the extreme movement in the measure, makes it a tenuous one for valuation purposes. Whatever the price/earnings ratio, one can never be sure whether its level is a function of the latest trend in earnings or the latest trend in stocks. The only reason the P/E ratio has any correlation to the market at all is that the numerator, P, *is* the market. The values for E gyrate so independently as to be almost arbitrary. A P/price-of-peanuts ratio would probably provide no less a stock market indicator. As a result, the P/E ratio has been as much a basis for rationalization (a process that will be discussed in the next chapter) as for analysis.

Perspective

From 1979 (the first year of publication) through 1984, *The Elliott Wave Theorist* argued continually that despite (in fact, because of) all worries, stock prices were cheap. More important, the Elliott Wave outlook prompted a forecast regarding the psychological indicators themselves: that the widespread worries of the day would turn into a record-breaking orgy of optimism. In early 1983, *The Elliott Wave Theorist* predicted that "The long term sentiment gauges will give off major trend sell signals two or three years before the final top, and the market will just keep on going." "Remember," said the October 1983 issue, "that the Elliott Wave position calls for a speculative environment of historic proportion by the end of this bull market." Even after the market had *doubled*, the case remained that considerable long term upside potential remained based on valuation. Read this commentary from the first quarter of 1987 and see how it pertains to today:

> Many investors have already missed hundreds of points of this bull market because they concluded that prices were "too high" with respect to past readings on multiples such as stock prices to corporate earnings or dividends. Late last year, many commentators began using the measure of book value to argue that stock prices were expensive. The current market is priced at 2.2 times the book value of corporations, an area that has coincided with major market tops over the past 50 years. However, what these studies always neglect to mention is that the stock market reached 2.3x book value in 1925, 2.6x in 1927, 3.6x in 1928, and a peak of *4.2 times book value* in 1929, reflecting the euphoria that accompanies the peak of a fifth wave of Supercycle degree. Since, as EWT has argued for years, the 1980s market's closest analogy is that of the 1920s, this observation is of more than passing importance. A similar multiple today, assuming no change at all in book value itself, would project a DJIA at **4150**, which certainly places my long standing target of 3600-3700 in the realm of the reasonable.

Today the market has indeed achieved an overvaluation commensurate with a Supercycle peak, and in fact a Grand Supercycle peak. In doing so, it is telegraphing historic risk. Let's examine the position of each key measure.

Price/Dividend Ratio, or Yield

The most important stock market valuation indicator is dividend yield. Stocks are owned for one reason, to make money. There are two ways to make money, via *dividends* and via *capital appreciation*. The price an investor is willing to pay for dividends is a direct statement regarding his valuation of the speculative component of stocks. When dividends are high, an investor is saying, "I'm getting a good return. I don't expect much capital gain, but if the stock goes up, it will be 'gravy' on the side." This is a conservative

stance. When yield is low, an investor is saying, "I know I am re-
ceiving insignificant dividends, but that's O.K., because this stock
will definitely go up, so I will make money that way." This is an
entirely speculative stance. When investors in the aggregate are
willing to own stocks almost solely for their capital gain potential, it
is a sign of extreme optimism, and therefore of a market top.

August 1987 saw a historically high valuation of dividends,
beating out even that of 1929. The result was a 1000-point crash.
Figure 7-2 shows that the 8½ year climb since then has created a
state of overvaluation *greater* than that of 1987. This bull market,
then, has set two all-time records of optimism, a fitting tribute to a
Grand Supercycle top. The extent of the records is shocking. At press
time, the dividend yield on the Dow Jones Industrial Average is an
all-time low 2.55%. A year ago, the dividend yield on the Dow Jones
Transportation Average reached the lowest of any stock index in

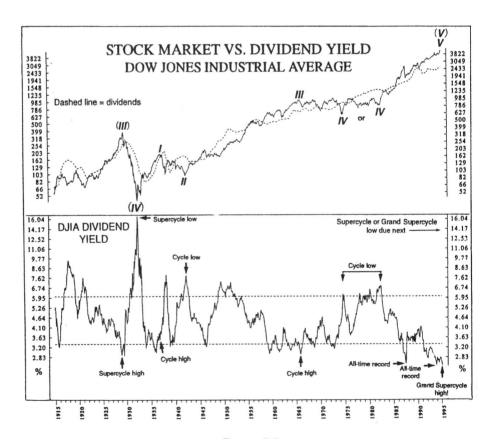

Figure 7-2

U.S. history: 1.05%. As the current wave (5) progresses to its destination, the average of these figures will fall even lower. Consider
the fact that the commission charges on a purchase and sale of stock
(a "round trip") at an average brokerage firm are *at least* 2.5 to 3%,
sometimes much more. Investors today, then, are buying stock that
for the first one to three years has *no yield*. In other words, they are
willing to trade a one- or two-year *negative return* for the promise of
a capital gain and in preference to a riskless yield provided by Treasury bills of 5.7%! These facts eliminate dividend return as a current
reason for owning stocks. They show that people who own stocks
are relying solely on a conviction that the market is headed substantially higher. They show that people view stocks as being less
risky than Treasury bills. Indeed, article after article refers to the
"risk of missing gains" as being more important than the risk of
loss. This is an optimism so extreme that is has not been seen in the
West for nearly three centuries, when the South Sea Bubble and
Mississippi Scheme were running wild in England and France.

Notice in Figure 7-2 that levels of overvaluation and undervaluation have been reached in proportion to the degree of the wave
that is terminating. Cycle degree extremes are less than Supercycle
degree extremes. The fact that the current extreme is greater than
those of 1929, 1937 and 1966, which were Cycle and Supercycle degree tops, confirms our thesis that the approaching top is of Grand
Supercycle degree.

The case of the Dow Jones Transportation Average is of particular interest. The index has suffered several years of "negative
earnings" (i.e., losses), so the record high valuation is apparently
based upon the less than awe-inspiring projection that the companies in the DJTA will actually earn a profit. If investors were buying
a vision, it would have to be one of an unprecedented industry turnaround and twenty years of record growth. Even after such events,
though, these stocks would be only *fairly* valued, so what would
push them up yet further to give current owners a gain? In truth,
there is no vision at all, because none can be justified. Accompanying today's market optimism, then, is simply plenty of denial.

Needless to say, if the economic outlook presented in Chapter
10 comes to pass, thousands of companies (yes, including many in
the Fortune 500 and even the DJIA) will be cutting or eliminating
dividends. Widespread dividend reductions will serve to retard the
progress of the aggregate dividend yield to more palatable levels
even as stock prices are persistently falling.

Individual Stock Yields

Geraldine Weiss of *Investment Quality Trends* has developed an indicator of the percentage of undervalued stocks based upon dividend valuation. The indicator is prepared by comparing the yield from each of the 350 stocks the service has been monitoring since 1966 to its historic range in order to categorize it as "high" or "low."

When the number of undervalued stocks rises above 70% of the total, the market has typically been at or near a bottom. When it falls below 20%, the market has typically been at or near a top. As you can see in Figure 7-3, the percentage has actually been persistently in single digits since 1991, four long years. In March 1993, it touched 6%, the lowest figure in the history of the indicator. Not only is this measure reflecting a top of historic proportion

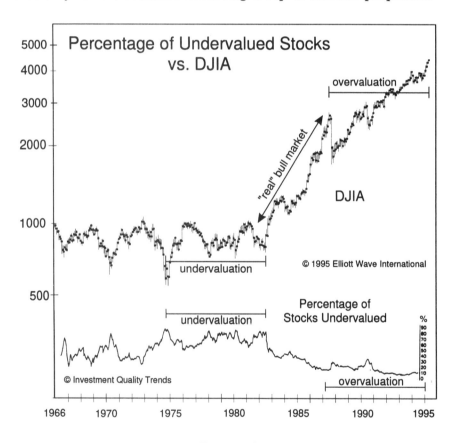

Figure 7-3

because of the level that it has reached, but also because of the long time that it has been there. At this point, the 8-year period of overvaluation from 1987 to 1995 balances the 8-year period of undervaluation in 1974-1982.

Corporate Value

Owners of corporate shares do own something outright: the assets of the company. How the stock market values those assets is a measure of investor caution or exuberance. Two widely used measures of a corporation's net assets are the replacement cost of those assets (which compared to the stock's value is called the "Q ratio") and book value. While the concepts differ, their depiction on a chart is nearly identical. Since there is more historical data on book value, that measure better suits our purposes.

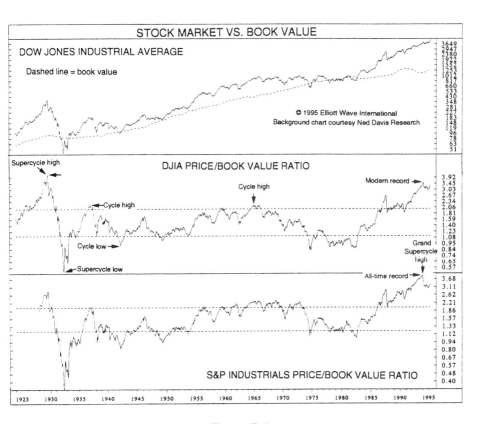

Figure 7-4

As you can see in Figure 7-4, stocks are extremely overvalued in terms of corporate book value. Up from a low of .82 in 1974, the price-to-book value ratio for the DJIA is now 3.81. Only the month-end reading for August 1929 was higher, at 4.23 times. If the Dow rises another 30%, this indicator could actually spike to a new all-time high, though it isn't necessary. The S&P Industrials, a larger group than the Dow Industrials, have already surpassed their 1929 peak of valuation based upon book value, as shown at the bottom of Figure 7-4.

Bond/Stock Yield Ratio

Finally, how do investors in this environment value stocks against their chief competitor, presumably safe U.S. government bonds? Figure 7-5 shows the market's historical valuation of the yield from stock dividends vs. the yield from bond coupons. The higher the ratio, the more investors value the capital gain potential of stocks; the lower the ratio, the more they value the safety of bonds. Our data back to 1870 show that for at least 70 years, the normal

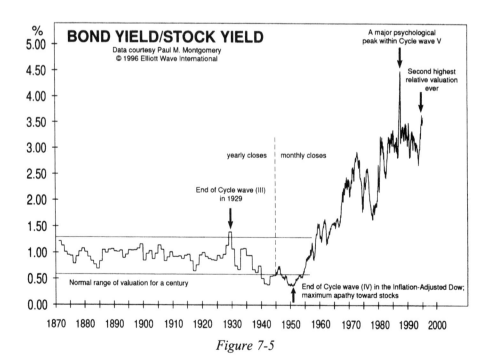

Figure 7-5

range for the ratio was .6 to 1.3, a moderate zone of fluctuation around equality that reflected minor adjustments in people's evaluation of the two sources of income. During that period, the all-time high annual average valuation was 1.4, which was registered in 1929 at the top of Supercycle wave (III).

The period from 1940 through 1954 saw stocks valued at below their historical norm. Low tick on a monthly basis was reached in December 1950, near the end of Supercycle wave (IV) in the inflation-adjusted Dow. At that time, a dollar of stock yield "sold" for $^{36}/_{100}$ of the price of a dollar of bond yield. Stocks were cheap because investors were afraid. They felt they could depend far more upon a small bond coupon than a high return from stocks despite the high dividend because they so feared a capital loss from a falling stock market.

At that point began an upward march in stock valuation that has dwarfed all other rises undoubtedly since the year 1720. At the October 1987 peak, a dollar of stock yield sold for an amazing 4.38 times the price of a dollar of bond yield, an increase of over 11.8 times and the highest relative stock market valuation in U.S. history. This record level of relative value reflected a powerful belief in both the safety of stocks and a continuation of the bull market, which would be necessary to make up for the difference in yield.

Today, the bond/stock yield ratio is at 3.56, its highest level since October 1987 and nearly ten times its 1949 low of .37. This high multiple reveals that stock market psychology is still historically bullish in favoring corporate shares over high grade legal obligations. This situation is particularly alarming when one notes that bond market psychology *on its own* remains bullish to an extreme as well, as described in Chapter 12.

The Consensus Opinion About These Indicators

Among the several litanies contributing to the mantra for today's Wall Street bulls, including, "stocks always go up long term," and "secondary stocks are going to explode before the bull market ends," the most cavalier is, "despite the statistics, stocks are still undervalued." It's true: Conventional analysts today simply *dismiss* the long standing warnings from all these indicators of record investor optimism. Their reasons fall into two camps, either that (1) it is a new era, so the indicators no longer matter, or (2) the indicators are flawed.

One general complaint against using book value as a measure of a company's worth is that accounting actually requires companies to set up a *reserve* for retired workers' benefits, as if that is an invalid charge against book value. This liability is quite real, however, and in a bad economy will be crippling. Today's money managers are not considering prospects for anything but growth. It is also argued quite strenuously that the historically low dividend payout is actually bullish because its means that "companies are plowing more money back into the company" instead of paying it to shareholders. Under the February 7, 1995 *Wall Street Journal* headline, "Flaws in Market Gauges Make Stocks Seem Expensive," an article reports on explanations by analysts and money managers as to why not just one indicator of value, but *all* of them, are misleading. In April, at press time, appeared a companion piece, "Debunking Low Dividends."

Denial is alive and well on Wall Street. Go back and read those articles in eight years. *The Elliott Wave Theorist* addressed the impulse to explain away indicators a decade ago, when no one wanted to believe their *bullish* message:

> We have often heard lately that these sentiment indicators "used to work, but now they can't be trusted." This is a symptom of bearishness, pure and simple, just as its opposite at the top is a symptom of bullishness. It is a common occurrence at turns.

Today we are witnessing the same impulse, but with an opposite purpose: to explain away a bearish message. Such exercises are absolutely necessary for the avoidance of cognitive dissonance between reason on the one hand and a decision already made based upon socially shared emotional forces on the other. Thirteen years ago the bears were rationalizing, and now the bulls must do so to avoid having to admit that the stocks they own or recommend are historically overpriced. The arguments that they present are themselves a reflection of the overall lack of worry and contraindicate the very fact that their proponents are trying to claim. A shocking number of analysts go as far as to say, "stocks are *under*valued," a statement justified with reference to the price/earnings ratio. Besides the essential irrelevance of P/E, the high earnings making the headlines are mostly accruing to the companies with multinational dealings as a result of the weak dollar. When the dollar turns up (see Chapter 11), these high earnings will disappear.

The preceding presentation suffices as an analysis of today's market psychology, which dramatically reflects the making of a Grand Supercycle top. However, it is a clinical analysis, and market psychology derives from *feelings*. The next chapter is devoted to communicating an understanding of not only what forces are behind these indicators, but how investors have progressed to the emotional state that produced today's readings.

Chapter 8

MANIFESTATIONS OF INVESTOR PSYCHOLOGY

A MASS PSYCHOLOGICAL JOURNEY

Bull markets climb a "Wall of Worry." When the wall has been climbed, there is no more worry, just optimism. One way or another, the culminating market psychology always snares just about everyone, public or professional. How it happens is subtle and insidious. Although most market players profess to understand how psychology progresses in a market, in the vast majority of cases, they ultimately fail to act upon what they claim to know. You will be no exception unless you experience and document the progression of market mood from bear to bull and back again *and commit it to your emotional memory*. Otherwise, your professed knowledge will be useless as a weapon against the powerful forces of social psychology that work their ways upon even the most individualistic person. Only a true understanding of the nature of people's behavior as it relates to markets will allow you to reason through emotionally charged situations and deal with them properly.

I would like first to take you on a journey through time back to the bear market bottom and lead you through a classic progression of market psychology. I want you to learn what a bottom *feels* like and what the changes along the way feel like, so that when you consider the case argued in Chapter 7 that today's market sentiment reflects a major top, you will not respond, like everyone else, "Yeah, *but*...." If you can have what you know in your head permeate your bones, you will never again let a powerful public mood persuade you to follow the crowd.

Psychology At The Bottom

Turn your mind back to the late 1970s and early 1980s, when U.S. investors were in a panic over uncontrollable inflation, labor unrest, slipping world power, consumer shortages, expensive energy, stifling regulation, all-time high interest rates, and nearly two decades of dishonest or incompetent politicians. Stocks were subject to what observers called "massacres" in 1978, 1979 and 1980.

The overwhelming consensus was to concentrate investment in gold stocks, Swiss francs or short term Treasury bills. The social mood then was quite the opposite of what it is today. In fact, in December 1978, Roper showed that for the first time in the history of its poll dating back to 1959, Americans rated the future as less promising than the present. The President's popularity was the lowest in modern political history, even lower than President Nixon's two months before he resigned. In each of 1978, 1979, 1980 and 1981, the percentage of advisory services bearish climbed to the 60% level, a record string of bearish readings. In 1980, even the big guns in the major brokerage houses, typically bastions of bullishness as a matter of self-interest, were staunch and vocal bears. By 1982, ads in *Barron's* reached the point that offers of booklets entitled "Widows & Orphans Guide to Short Selling" would have fit right in. On June 10 of that year, a broker jumped from a window, committing suicide.

That state of sentiment was not without reason. Headlines in mid-1979 included, "Chaos in the Gas Lines," "Record Jump in Money Supply," "Inflation 'Uncontrollable'," "Recession Looms," "Nationalize Big Oil?," "Odd-Even Plan: Disaster," "Price of Wheat Soars," "Farmers: Food 'Rotting in Fields,'" and "Severe Food Shortage Due Next Week." U.S. Senator Patrick Moynihan was widely quoted as saying, "This is the most serious economic crisis since the depression." In October 1979, *The Wall Street Journal* ran a series of articles entitled "The Depression Remembered," a reflection of the widespread fear (and something that would never appear at a top). *The New York Times*, *U.S. News*, and other publications recounted the 1929 crash, which was also paid tribute in a "special" by the *Wall Street Week* television program. A May 7, 1981 *Wall Street Journal* article entitled "Surge in Interest Rates Puts Squeeze On Already Ailing Economic Sectors" included these excerpts: "I think the economy is starting to crack," says an economic consultant. "The savings and loans are bleeding to death." Auto sales "are in the sub-basement; how can Chrysler make it under these circumstances?" "Housing is dead; sales are nonexistent." On June 2, 1981, West German Chancellor Helmut Schmidt warned publicly that high U.S. interest rates would precipitate world depression. On the same day, rumors circulated on Wall Street that the low level of free reserves in banks had reached a crisis and that if the Federal Government did not step in within one hour and save the banks, the entire U.S. banking system would collapse. Countless articles and interviews reflected the same fears over the ensuing year and a half. As late as January 1983, the immensely popular *60 Minutes* television program featured a round-table of ex-U.S. Treasury Secretaries who forcefully argued that continued budget deficits would collapse the economy and that President Reagan would do nothing to stop it.

During this 1979-1981 period, with the Dow fluctuating in the 740-1000 range, *The Elliott Wave Theorist* continually communicated the meaning of the widespread worry: "Contrary opinion would seem to support the Elliott thesis that a bull wave of great power may be developing...This is the stuff real bull markets are made of.... The majority opinion can be summed up in one sentence: 'A bull market here is impossible...' This overall period of excess bearishness [has] Cycle degree implications." In other words, the intense bearishness was long term bullish.

After a respite in 1983 associated with the market's blast-off and an upturn in the economy, the dark sentiment returned in 1984 and lasted right through 1985. "The bottoms of second waves," said *The Elliott Wave Theorist* at the time, "are points when bearishness is not only rampant, it is positively fashionable." In June 1984, *The Wall Street Journal* ran a five-page special section quoting countless experts forecasting continued soaring interest rates. This unprecedented commentary was published three weeks *after* the low in bonds and within points of that year's low in the Dow. Proof of the assertion that bearishness was fashionable was the market psychology of 1985, a year that saw the Dow make new all-time highs for several months before undergoing a mild "wave two" pullback into the fall. In that year, a seat on the American Stock Exchange sold for *one-third* of its value of 1983. Brokerage houses, said the WSJ's front page that August, have "dismal" bottom lines, with one racking up "the biggest single-year loss in Wall Street history." The general public remained so disinterested and uninvolved in stocks that a brokerage firm in June 1985, within one day of another all-time high in the market, filed for Chapter 11 bankruptcy protection. Market letter ads in late 1985 were no longer being coy, but announcing, "Market Top Has Been Seen," "Bear Market," "Sell Short," and "On the Brink of Great Depression II." Newspaper headlines continued to reflect the general psychology: "Bears Take Floor at Investment Conference," "Big Run Almost Over, Brokerage Warns," "Aging Bull Looks Ready to Stumble—Analysts Hear Growl of a Hungry Bear," and "What is There to be Bullish About?" One state governor made headlines when he said he "Fears National Disaster Looms Ahead." Even after the last pullback low ended in September 1985, the barrage of scary articles continued. October's contributions included "Market Still Looks Dangerous Here" (10/7),

"An Appraisal: Institution Managers Don't Have the Cash to Buy Stocks" (10/7), "Diverging Indexes Spur Grim Stock Price Forecasts" (10/14), "Analysts Take Cautious View" (10/18), and "Gurus Predict Best Bull Market Gains Over" (10/25). On October 7, *Forbes* ran a commentary headed, "It's Too Late to Avert a 1929-Style Crash." The only question addressed by the article was how to prepare for it. The U.S. Government even ran a Savings Bonds advertisement in *People* magazine entitled, "Outsmarting the Bear," complete with a menacing ursine visage. The writers, in denial of the new highs, took for granted that the bear was "loose on Wall Street, and he's mean." The most amazing phenomenon of late 1985 was the continued preponderance of bearish analysts at brokerage houses. Brokers sell stocks for a living. To have the official position of any brokerage house bearish is surprising to say the least, but to have the majority of major brokerages bearish, as reported in *Barron's* that November, is one rare occurrence. "How can anyone be bullish," said an investor in one of the articles, "when you can just *look around you* and see how awful things are?"!

That last sentence and the ensuing market behavior convey more about market analysis than a university degree in economics. "Looking around you," *outside the market*, is the kiss of death to successful investing. Today, for instance, that same investor would say, "How can anyone be bearish when you can just *look around you* and see how terrific things are?" (Chapter 9 will cover this point in greater detail.)

All of the events chronicled above were reported in *The Elliott Wave Theorist* as they occurred because they so powerfully impacted and reflected a depressed market psychology. The accompanying market sentiment from 1983 through 1985 was a sign of further market gains to come, and EWT said so. Here are some excerpts from issues published during that period:

> There is a contingent of analysts who are equating today's environment with that of 1929, and I see almost no justification for such an analogy.
> If this is a major top, it is like no other major top in history. Structural explanations such as the relative popularity of mutual funds are not convincing. The fact is that *the stock market has yet to capture the public's imagination.* It is almost certain that that day will come before the market makes a major top. There is still a long way to go before the public reaches a truly euphoric state.

The euphoria expected by the top of wave ⑤ of V should be great, and the setbacks in sentiment along the way should continue to fail to hit the low readings technicians came to expect at the bear market lows of the past twenty years.

The bottom line is that the professionals, despite claims to the contrary, are really not roaringly bullish on stocks. Many of the advisors rated "bullish" are so rated only because they still have stocks on their recommended list, while the accompanying rhetoric over the past six months has usually read something like, "but we're very cautious...take profits quickly...looking for a major top...it's late in the cycle...," etc. Even small town local banks and brokerage houses are putting out bearish reports, and these are businesses that make their best money in bull markets! True story: during a cross-town trip in New York City last month, the *taxi driver* was telling me how many puts he owned! (And that was en route to an interview with a bearish host.)

This is the stage of market development where people *should* be grasping for reasons to justify their bearish feelings. And feeling, or mood, is what this attitude really entails. As one market letter pointed out, the market is making new all-time highs, "but it doesn't *feel* strong." Two recent articles recognized this phenomenon: "Where Are All The Public Investors?" in the *Financial Weekly*, and the WSJ's "Stocks Are Up, Rates Are Down; So Why Aren't Investors Happy?" The simple answer is, because they only get "happy" at tops!

The hard numbers of the indicators show that members of the public are acting on their feelings and what they read and hear; they have sold short heavily and bought puts at an all-time record rate. When the public *buys* stocks late in a bull market, they often enjoy paper profits for awhile, but they are never allowed to keep them. Similarly, when the public *sells short* heavily, they may be profitable for a while, but they are inevitably forced to cover into a powerfully rising market.

History shows that the odd-lot [i.e., small] investor typically sells heavily not only at a major low, but also several months into a new bull market advance. He becomes convinced by the bear market that the trend is down, so feels that the big rally that is in reality the beginning of a sustained bull trend is merely a chance to unload in what is surely an ongoing bear market. The odd-lotter is currently bailing out of the stock market at more than a 3.5:1 sales-to-purchases ratio, the highest rate of selling to date in this decade! This is exactly how the odd-lotter should feel in the early months of a Primary third wave up. [Similarly,] margin accounts have been liquidating stock at a rate that exceeds all readings since the September 1981 low at Dow 800. I have kept those figures for almost ten years, and they have been highly reliable. *The prevailing psychology is an expression of the cumulative experience of the past 16 years.* It is typical that such sentiment occurs just prior to the onset of a third wave up.

After watching market behavior closely for fourteen years, I feel that these developments are, if anything, a *requirement* in the market's preparation for takeoff. Whatever the cause of the bearish sentiment, it doesn't matter. That fact is that it is there, and for that reason, most of the selling which is to be done has already occurred. Whether the market drops below the August 19 [1985] low is irrelevant. Such action (along with, perhaps, some "surprise" bad news) will only serve to keep the sentiment figures at levels compatible with a major bear market low.

According to the current polls of investment advisors, there is more skepticism with regard to the market now, at 1550, than there was in the summer of 1983 at 1250! The simple answer to that mystery is that in 1983, the market was at a Primary wave top. 1550, then, is not a Primary wave top.

Some who called for a big bear market in September are trying to justify missing the rally by claiming that the average portfolio has not kept pace with the Dow. Do not be misled by this claim. *The Wall Street Journal* reported on December 19 that the latest poll of 2000 money managers finds that while most of them underperformed the S&P 500 index in 1985, it was only because of their inordinately high cash reserves. In the aggregate, their stock holdings for 1985 outperformed the S&P 500 index for the first time in three years! In other words, this data confirms our position on two fronts: (1) This *is* a great bull market in stocks, and (2) the majority lost out only because they were bearish and underinvested.

It is difficult for the casual observer to conceive that market professionals would get powerfully and increasingly negative in the face of rising prices, or to understand that such an event is a virtual guarantee of further advance, but that is the way psychology is positioned at a "wave two" low. How gloomy was stock market psychology in September 1985, the month of the very last pause before the bull market accelerated? On September 17 of that year, the Market Vane polling service of Pasadena telephoned, as they did every Tuesday, to add my opinions on the major markets to their

"Bullish Consensus" figures. The next morning, as the Dow touched its low, they announced the second lowest bullish consensus on stocks since they had been keeping the figures. The low in August 1982 had provided a single week at 19% "bulls," while the September 17, 1985 figure was just *23%*. Market Vane called again that afternoon with some interesting news. In their tally of the opinions of all the major advisors, from brokerage houses to money managers to market letter writers, *The Elliott Wave Theorist*, they said, was the *only respondent* who answered "bullish and long" on the stock market. One reason that the figure was even as high as 23% was because Market Vane rated those "neutral" or "on the sidelines" as partly bullish and partly bearish. Notice also that if EWT had been just an interested observer and not a double weighted (letter and hotline) participant, the Bullish Consensus figure would have been *even lower*, probably matching that at the 1982 bottom. EWT was very alone, and truly in accord with contrary opinion.

By the end of 1985, despite the skeptical and bearish professional psychology, the stock market had nevertheless captured people's *attention*. *The Wall Street Journal* for the first time ever became the largest circulation daily newspaper in the world. In years past, the fastest growing magazine circulations were for titles such as *Life*, *Time*, *Newsweek* and *People*. By year-end 1985, the fastest growing of all major magazines in the previous twelve months was *Money*. Its circulation by then had climbed to over 1 million, it pulled in $25m. of ad revenue yearly, and its newsstand sales alone in the first half of 1985 were more than those for *Time*, *Fortune*, *Forbes* and *Newsweek combined*. (Needless to say, its circulation today is far higher.) A headline in the 10/8/85 *USA Today* noted that "Youth Rocks to the Beat of Wall Street." The article documented the surprising increase in teens' interest in the stock market, and concluded by saying that for some, "even the Big Board is old hat...[they're now] eyeing the Chicago Board Options Exchange."

Preparing for a Psychological Change At the Point of Recognition

There is a point along the way in every bull market when investors suddenly seem to get the message. It always happens in the "third wave of the third wave," the centerpoint of the entire structure. As that point approached, *The Elliott Wave Theorist* prepared readers for a big change and counseled them not to be spooked by it:

From the black sentiment conditions of December, *we should now expect a rapid shift toward bullish sentiment*. Primary wave ③ in the Dow will be the phase during which most investors *change their minds* on the long term trend from cautious to bullish in a flash of recognition.   — February 4, 1985

The psychological setup for the acceleration phase of Primary wave ③ is as close to perfect as it can get.   — September 30, 1985

The acceleration phase began right then, and in January 1986, the stock market passed the "point of recognition." The abruptness of the public's change from apparently total disinterest to full-bore participation when the Dow crossed 2000 was as if someone had flipped a switch on the collective mind. The entire psychology of the market changed dramatically, and in a flash. Brokerage houses rushed out "Dow 3000" bullish reports. Market letter writers dropped to a paltry 13% bears. *USA Today* headlined, "Small Investors Dive Into the Market." A single article in March 1986 contained all the following quotes: "This is the easiest market in the world to call" (September, October, November, December, January and February, on the other hand, were tough!); "There is nothing negative on the horizon"; "For any kind of [economic] number that comes out, investors will come up with a favorable interpretation"; "Look out for 70- to 100-point days — we're going to get 'em"; "Everyone's talking about 1800, but the next step is really [to] 2000." On March 17, *Business Week* magazine, which had announced "The Death of Equities" on its cover in August 1979 with the Dow in the 800s, put a bull on its cover, subheadlining "The Stock Market Rally is Far From Over."

Was this change an immediate "sell signal?" As *The Elliott Wave Theorist* reiterated, "This is a change in psychology typical of the 'point of recognition.' Emerging enthusiasm, however, is *not* an immediate sell signal. The resulting publicity is drawing in more public participants, which adds more fuel to the trend."

The summer of 1986 displayed numerous indications of an emerging enchantment with the stock market. Newspaper clippings from June, July and August told the story. "Money," said a media expert in *The Wall Street Journal*, "is becoming the new sex," a source of "endless fascination." "A new crop of celebrities will be picked from business," said another. Even the new board games reflected the focus on finance. "Last year it was murder; this year it's money," said a New York merchandise buyer in the August 28, 1986 WSJ. New game titles that summer included "Condomoneyum," "Go For It," "Your Money," and "The Bottom Line." Then the media joined in. "Television is suddenly bullish on business news," said a July 30, 1986 article entitled "Lineup of TV Business Shows Expands." "Local Stations are Giving Business the News...And the Viewers Like It," read another headline. Financial News Network (now CNBC) became standard viewing not only in trading rooms, but in New York bars. After decades of nearly total ignorance of business, television began flooding the market with business and market news. Why? Because Cycle wave V of Supercycle (V) had passed the point of recognition, and the public demanded it. In December 1986, *USA Today* proclaimed, "A New Breed is Bullish On the Market," noting that 57% of the new stock investors since mid-1983 were women. Whatever their age or sex, a new breed is a new breed, and it takes a new breed to recreate the follies of the past.

Though the bullish fever was beginning to take hold, it had a long way to go even at that juncture. On November 7, at the end of the late 1986 consolidation, which included two record down days in terms of Dow points, *The Elliott Wave Theorist* concluded as follows:

> *Long term* sentiment measures are still in an extremely bullish position. These indicators argue powerfully in favor of the Elliott Wave conclusion that the Dow will *double yet again* before the bull market is over.

In fact, the Dow has more than doubled from that point, though by a circuitous route. The bull market roared into August 1987 and then crashed. The crash prompted analogies to 1929 in the press, and even *The Elliott Wave Theorist* (which had finally sold its stocks near the 1987 high) conceded erroneously that the bull market had probably ended (see discussion later in this chapter). The market recovered slowly, but finally reached new highs in 1989 at the start of wave ⑤, and then sold off into late 1990. The entire time marked a pause in the swelling bullish psychology. The market pullback into January 1991 was the final point of restraint in stock market bullishness on the part of both the public and professionals. Skepticism was dispelled once and for all when wave ⑤ accelerated following the start of the Gulf War. The public threw caution to the winds after the Dow crossed 3200 and has spent the last four years becoming invested to an extent never before attained in the history of the country. From the dark mood of 1979-1982, the investment world has reached its psychological destination. Let's examine the myriad manifestations of this mood, as well as its unequivocal implications.

MANIFESTATIONS OF A PSYCHOLOGICAL EXTREME IN TODAY'S MARKET

Investor sentiment today reflects the rarefied atmosphere of the crest of a major psychological trend. The market has made a long journey to get to this state. The "super bull market" thesis put forward years ago by *Elliott Wave Principle* and *The Elliott Wave Theorist* was met with terrific skepticism from the start, as the idea of Dow *1200*, much less Dow 3700, was considered extreme. Yet the Wave Principle told us exactly how bullish people would ultimately be, as shown by this description from the Special Report entitled "A Rising Tide," from April 6, 1983 (see Appendix to *Elliott Wave Principle* for a complete reprint):

> Finally, what might we conclude about the psychological aspects of wave V? The 1920s bull market was a fifth wave of a *third* Supercycle wave, while Cycle wave V is the fifth wave of a *fifth* Supercycle wave. Thus, as the last hurrah, it should be characterized at its end by an almost unbelievable institutional mania for stocks and a public mania for stock index futures, stock options, and options on futures. In my opinion, the long term sentiment gauges will give off major trend sell signals two or three years before the final top, and the market will just keep on going. In order for the Dow to reach the heights expected by the year 1987 or 1990, *and* in order to set up the U.S. stock market to experience the greatest crash in its history, which, according to the Wave Principle, is due to follow wave V, investor mass psychology should reach manic proportions, with elements of 1929, 1968 and 1973 all operating together and, at the end, to an even greater extreme.

This vision was expanded in July and August 1983:

> As for the long term, even if you can prove that some sectors of Wall Street are very optimistic, you may have to wait until *half the population* is euphoric about stocks before the *final* top occurs. Remember, this is just the setup phase. The average guy probably won't be joining the party until the Dow clears 2000. The market's atmosphere by then will undoubtedly become out-and-out euphoric.

Then you can start watching the public's activity as if it were one huge sentiment indicator. When the stock market makes the news reports every single day (as gold did starting about two months before the top, remember?), when your neighbors find out you're "in the business" and start telling you about *their* latest speculations, when stories of stock market riches hit the pages of the general newspapers, when the bestseller list includes "How to Make Millions in Stocks," when Walden's and Dalton start stocking *Elliott Wave Principle*, when almost no one is willing to discuss financial calamity or nuclear war, when miniskirts return and men dress with flash and flair, and when your friends stay home from work to monitor the Quotron machine (since it's more lucrative than working), then you know we'll be close. At the peak of the fifth wave, the spectacle could rival Tulip Mania and the South Sea Bubble.

The Elliott Wave Theorist added in December 1985, "What's important now is that we remain on guard to recognize the polar opposite emotions of good feelings, confidence and complacency at the top of Cycle wave V. When the majority is bullish and happy, we'll be close to the end." It has been a long road to reach that point, but reach it we have.

Public Optimism in the Past Four Years

In 1991, NASDAQ volume exceeded NYSE volume for the first time ever. That year, the ten largest brokerage firms raised their recommended average investment in stocks to 65% (and only 5% cash), the highest percentage since the figures began being compiled in January 1987. Bullish sentiment became so extreme in 1992 that to attract and keep investors, the best known short selling firm switched to stock buying strategies. Stock market advice began to appear so easy to provide ("buy and hold for the long term") that two of the country's largest mutual fund companies went into the business of giving clients advice on asset allocation. In 1993, the public began pouring its savings into stock, bond and money market mutual funds at the rate of one billion dollars a day. Merrill Lynch's customer assets rose to half a trillion dollars and are still rising. New stocks introduced to the market began rocketing up fifty percent or more on their first trades, fueling the fervor among issuers to create more "product." On September 20, 1993, the S&P futures contract began trading almost around the clock (today it is open all but 9-9:30 a.m. and 4:15-4:45 p.m. EST) weekdays for the first time ever, on the Globex exchange. $1.5 trillion worth of *new* stocks and bonds were issued worldwide in 1993, an all-time record that was 36% above 1992's all-time record. Fidelity Investments' sector funds reached a level of only 7% cash, a record low that is still in place. The first Russian stock issue of modern times had taken place as wave ⑤ was emerging, in 1988, starting a trend even in the world's bastions of anticapitalism. By March 1994, the stock mania had permeated the world so extensively that citizens of the People's Republic of China were lining up by the thousands at banks in Beijing to buy shares in four of the city's Communist government-owned enterprises. In four short years from 1991 to today, the number of brokerage firm offices has *doubled* in the United States, from 29,000 to 58,000.

According to a poll from June 1994, *ninety-one percent* of the wealthiest 1% of the U.S. population regard a stock market crash as unlikely. Brokers relate stories of clients who are deciding to start investment clubs, or who suddenly put all their retirement money into stock mutual funds after previously owning only government bonds. On financial television, the ratio of bulls to bears being interviewed is about 100 to 1. "Never," comments an *Elliott Wave Theorist* subscriber, "have I seen the Schwab office so crowded." "*Barron's*," reports another subscriber, "is selling out at my local convenience store every Saturday in a few hours." In a reflection of the widespread public acceptance of the idea of investing (as opposed to saving), banks now offer customers the option of buying and selling mutual funds at their automatic teller machines. In the past four years, the success of *Money* magazine has spawned three competitors: *Worth, Smart Money*, and now *Mutual Funds*, which is devoted entirely to that one subject. You could not have given these magazines away in 1975 or 1985, but 1995 is a different story. "Investors," says a *Wall Street Journal* headline at press time, "See Stocks Rising For Rest of '95." When asked about 1996, 1997 or 2004, they have answered in the same way.

Figures 8-1 through 8-11 show the extent of the public's conversion in mid-1991, when investors dove headlong into the stock mania that had been building for over sixteen years. The charts depict mutual fund assets, the number and growth of mutual funds, common stock offerings, the value of initial public offerings (IPOs) of stock, household liquidity and stock ownership, purchases of growth stock funds and "aggressive" (i.e., even riskier) growth stock funds, and customers' margin debt with brokers. Every single one of these measures is at an all-time extreme. While 1993 set a record to date of $130 billion worth of mutual fund purchases in a single year, 1994 set a record of $124 billion worth of mutual fund purchases *in a down year*, when the average fund lost 1.7%, implying that bullish psychology is still swelling. Preliminary reports reveal a high level of buying in 1995 so far as well, so the mania has continued to this day. As a result of all this buying, and because pension funds that invest in stocks cover so many people today, 37.1 % of the U.S. households now have investments in the stock market, the highest figure ever recorded by economist Albert Sindlinger, who has been compiling these statistics since 1955. A record was also set in September 1987, when 33.4% of the population was in the market (just before the crash). In the past three years, households have put money into stocks at a high *rate* as well. Never in fifty years of data has households' net money flow into the stock market consistently represented nearly 5% of disposable income, as it has from middle of 1991 to now. As a result, household liquid assets (cash, CDs, commercial paper and U.S. savings bonds) are at an all-time low percentage of total assets, having exceeded the previous low readings of the late 1960s when Cycle wave III was topping out. As people have bid up the prices of stocks and bonds, total available liquidity in the economy as a percentage of the market value of paper invest-

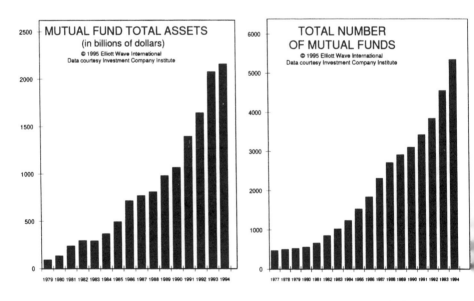

Figure 8-1   Figure 8-2

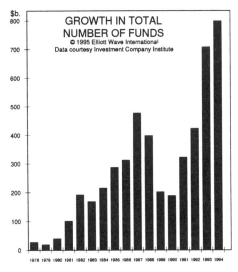

Figure 8-3

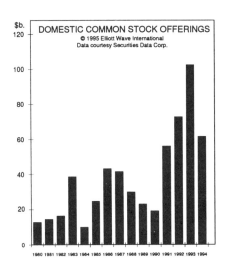

Figure 8-4

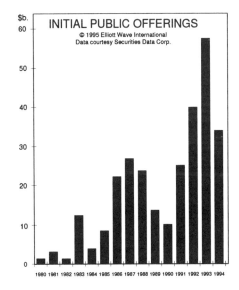

Figure 8-5

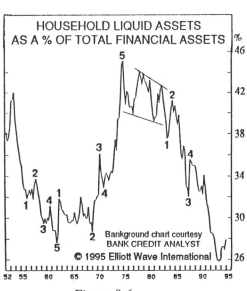

Figure 8-6

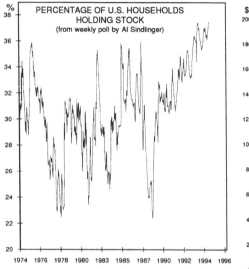

Figure 8-7

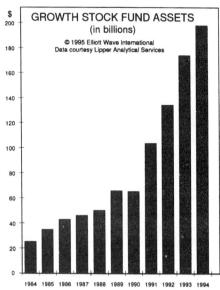

Figure 8-8

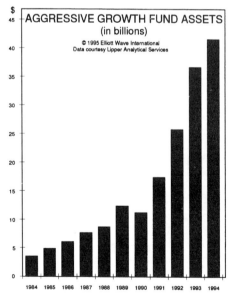

Figure 8-9

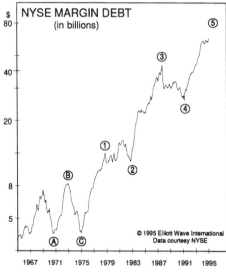

Figure 8-10

For an excellent profile of today's naive stock market investor, read "The New Investors" in the August 30, 1993 *Barron's*. Here is an excerpt: "...Neither she nor her friends worry about a possible market correction. 'That's the first I've heard of the idea,' she says a little coldly. 'Everyone here feels that Fidelity is perfectly safe.' She doesn't ask for more information."

Speculative environments come along at most only once in a generation, as a horde of new, inexperienced players is then available to descend upon the stock market scene. Members of the general public are always latecomers to the market's party, and because of the powerful emotional forces involved in manias, tend to check their skepticism and rationality at the door. This has certainly been the case in the past four years. Because bankers, brokers and high-profile fund managers in recent years have been telling people that investing in stock market mutual funds is (over the "long term") better than *saving*, they have simply taken the promise literally. As a result, average investors profiled in *The New York Times* explain that they have extended their mortgages as far out as possible so that they can put the monthly payment difference into a stock mutual fund, under the assumption that a perpetual 12% return will pay for future college costs. Television programs interview young parents who are moving their kids' savings account money into stock market mutual funds so they will learn about the market. (And learn they will.) Magazine articles instruct parents how to teach *kids* to buy stock in *socially acceptable* companies, as if profits are child's play and as if one may simply choose, based upon personal whim, what type of vehicle he wishes to produce his annual investment gain. The generation of the profits themselves is simply taken for granted, and the choice is presented as if it is little more than choosing among 31 ice cream flavors. "Would you like to receive your steady capital gain from Coca-Cola stock or Philip Morris stock? Don't like the idea of smoking? Well, then, just pick Coke!" Those who have made money owning stocks from 1991 to today are the same types who made money in 1967-1968 and 1971-1972. They may look smart for awhile by being ignorant of the historic market negatives, but they will pay for it later, big time.

The level of sophistication among today's investors is at an all-time low, but it is still not low enough to satisfy the sellers of financial services. The Fidelity mutual fund group now advertises with infomercials on late night TV, sandwiched in between the ads for fishing lures and sunglasses. The NASDAQ over-the-counter exchange has been advertising on *Monday Night Football*, a prime time television slot. Apparently they are trying to ferret out that last guy, the one with the beer and the chips, who does not yet have all of his spare change invested in the stock market. The NASDAQ, furthermore, in 1994 began advertising that it is "the stock market for the next hundred years." That would have been a useful vision in 1974 or 1984. It took twenty years of advance, though, for the exchange to become bold enough to invent that slogan, and it is hypnotizing to those easily swayed.

Today, the public, *because* of its naiveté, has adopted the same chutzpah as the professionals. Television commentators, newspaper columnists and university professors, who are nonprofessional members of the public, have been presenting themselves as market advisors. After all, it is so easy to say "buy and hold," why shouldn't they? One of our subscribing money managers who recently adopted a bearish stance on the market heard from a client who called to say, "A short position is so foolish that my 12-year-old kid could trade better." That may be a true statement, but *when* it is a true statement, the market's long-established trend is near a reversal. I label this attitude with the oxymoron "aggressive complacency," which I feel describes the arrogance and even vehemence with which some people express their disdain for caution.

I saw two Joseph Granville "shows" in the late 1970s and early 1980s. Granville enjoyed explaining that when buyers no longer politely ask, "Please sell me your stock," but instead grab your collar and scream, "Gimme that bag!," don't argue with them, "just give it to 'em!" These "bagholders" are not only dumb, he was saying, they are coarse and demanding, too, so they get what they deserve. Today, the public is screaming "Gimme that bag!" to every imaginable seller of questionable paper, including junk bonds, new issues, low priced stock funds, and repackaged mortgage and consumer debt, stuff that would never cross my mind as a serious investment or even a sound speculation (except for a few professionals who know the game). The sellers, gentlemen all, have politely complied.

The idea, though, that the public is entirely to blame for its attitude does not wash. These are not people who choose to go to a casino because they foolishly believe in luck. The bear market may give them what they deserve for not having taught themselves something about investing before attempting it, perhaps, but in another sense, they have justifiably relied upon people they have been told are experts, the media's pick-stocks-and-forget-market-trends financial heroes, who have told them that the stock market is perfectly safe, that anyone *not* invested in stocks is a fool. Those people are more to blame for the public's attitude than the public itself.

Regardless of who is responsible, the public will be in a fury when the house of cards falls. To amateurs, an uptrend is *normal* and a downtrend is an outrage, so they will not tolerate losses calmly. Evidence of the coming rage has been hinted in two articles recently. *USA Today*, on June 16, 1994, headlined, "Mutual Fund Losses Anger Novice Investors." The Investors Arbitration Service, which usually handles 200 calls a week from irate investors, saw calls shoot up to 1,600 at the April 1994 low following an insignificant 9% pullback in the market *from an all-time high*. Investors are quoted as saying, "I've lost five, ten percent of my principal. What are my rights?" To paraphrase Granville, the *market* doesn't care about your rights! Once you are in the market, you have but one right: *to sell.* The Wall Street Journal further reports that with the virtually unnoticeable losses in stock and bond funds of 1.7% and 3.7% respectively for 1994, "many investors are furious." One letter to a mutual fund family demanded that it not just fire its managers, but "take them outside and shoot 'em." When a single-digit pullback from a record high *angers* someone, that someone is a complete novice who has no concept of where his money is. Now that the market has reached this far down the pyramid of market sophistication, it has few depths left to plumb.

In 1994, *USA Today* reported some investors' perturbation that they had lost a percent or two of their money, but took the step of assuring readers that there were only four reasonable courses of action: (1) Do nothing, (2) keep buying, (3) diversify into more funds, including foreign funds, and (4) adjust your asset allocation. Out of four options, not one was "get out of stocks." The professionals and media commentators who have been catering to the public's whims, thus assuring that they will continue to have no idea what they are doing, will soon have to endure a far uglier mood. How angry will these people be when their assets are down 40%? Or 80%? Because the naiveté of today's investor is at an all-time high, the wrath that the public will feel at the bottom of the bear market will also reach an all-time high. When the public becomes enraged at its losses in coming years, it should remember where to direct its anger.

Professional Optimism

The public has felt safe in throwing billions of dollars of its discretionary investment capital and pension fund money at stock fund managers under the assumption that professionals know what they are doing and will handle the money correctly. The managers have simply put all that money into stocks, because in the narrow field of stock picking, they may know what they are doing, but in the market analysis field, they do not.

In the aggregate, professionals' experience is exactly that of the stock market. Fund managers (like economists; see Chapter 10) are people too, and in the aggregate, they become optimistic at market tops and pessimistic at bottoms. When the over-the-edge bullish psychology took hold of the public in 1991, it also took hold of professionals. One manifestation has been the flood of bullish books since that time, including *Beating the Street*, *Riding the Bull*, *The Warren Buffet Way*, *Of Permanent Value*, *The Common Sense Guide to Picking Stocks and Beating the New York Experts*, *Making Your Living From the Stock Market*, and a host of others.

Long time technicians remember the famous *Barron's* headline of January 1973, "Not a Bear Among Them," which summed up institutional investors' opinion at the onset of the biggest stock market drop in 36 years. Today, that situation is repeated. Fifty-eight economists surveyed by *The Wall Street Journal* last June agree: The best investments are stocks and bonds. This opinion is supported by the widely accepted observation, as expressed by Federal Reserve Chairman Alan Greenspan, that the country "is experiencing the ideal combination of rising activity, falling unemployment, and falling inflation." Money managers are so certain of these factors and their meaning that they have been calling the current juncture "cheerful tidings" and "nirvana" for stocks. This attitude shows up in the indicators.

One indicator of professional sentiment is the percentage of cash equivalents (such as short term money market paper) held by pension funds, mutual funds and insurance companies. Fund managers, whose job is often to remain more or less fully invested, nevertheless adjust their cash positions to higher levels if they feel that the market will fall and provide bargains. Because their decisions are based on an assessment of extramarket conditions, just like most other people's, their cash holdings are invariably highest at bottoms (just when funds should be fully invested in stocks) and lowest at tops (just when they should be out of the market). The reading of

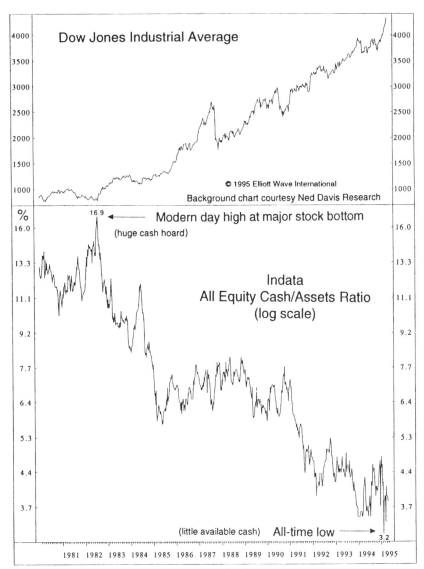

Figure 8-12

approximately 17% cash in 1982 was extremely bullish. It was 7% in early 1987, when *The Elliott Wave Theorist* remarked, "When the peak of this bull market really does arrive, stock market mutual funds will be nearly fully invested. Until then, no major top is indicated." According to Indata Corp., which has been collecting data for an all-equity institutional cash/assets ratio since 1979, institutional cash levels were down to 3.2% on February 10, 1995, the lowest

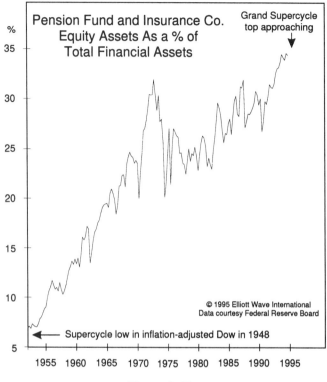

Figure 8-13

level ever, as shown in Figure 8-12. They are now "nearly fully in-vested," as forecast, which should mean that a "major top is indicated."

Institutions invest in both stocks and bonds, so it is useful to check the relative percentage of assets devoted to stock ownership as well. At the January 1973 top, pension funds and insurance companies had a record 31.95% of their assets in stocks. At the 1987 top, they had a nearly equivalent 31.90% of their assets in stocks. In 1994, they reached a new record high 34.38% of their assets in stocks, as you can see in Figure 8-13. That amount has almost certainly been exceeded here in the first half of 1995. The 1973 and 1987 market peaks led to drops of 46% and 36%. What will an all-time high percentage precede? *Corporate* pension funds have an amazing 57% of their assets in stocks, which is double their bond percentage. The drop in the bond market last year forced a new opinion that "stocks are now safer than bonds." If you liked bonds at 125, shouldn't you love them at 105, a comparative bargain? Not if fear and linear extrapolation are more in the driver's seat than reason. In a reflection of the fact that the mania is worldwide, British pension fund managers, who were deeply affected by the decline in gilts (UK bonds) in the 1970s, have an amazing 76% of their funds in equities. In Australia, investors have even snapped up shares in a brothel.

Today's money managers are not only more bullish than their high-flying predecessors of 22 and 27 years ago, but far more swashbuckling. Managers of closed-end mutual funds (which can accept no new money after their formation and closure) have invented a way to bring in more money with a concept called "rights offerings," which allow existing shareholders to purchase new shares on the basis of shares already owned. A record 22 such offerings took place in 1993, and the trend has continued. According to an article, the reason fund managers want more money (besides to earn higher fees) is that they can't "pass up" all the new stuff they want to buy. Institutions are also becoming increasingly involved in derivatives (i.e., securities that are created from other securities to increase leverage). Eastman Kodak's pension fund made the first major commitment to futures trading in 1987, when it allocated $50m. for the purpose. From that humble beginning, pension funds now have $1.5 billion allocated to futures trading, much of it in the hands of commodity trading advisers. Thus, even the most historically conservative sector of investors has become willing to speculate in leveraged instruments. Institutions have also purchased countless complex illiquid securities. For instance, they have very recently become heavily involved in "restricted securities," i.e., stock offerings that cannot be sold to individuals because they are not registered with the SEC. The irony is that in many cases the public indeed owns them, it just does so through the institutional intermediary. Mutual fund managers bought a whopping $80b. worth of restricted issues in 1991-1993 after the SEC relaxed its rules on their sale. Guess the last time that restricted securities were popular. That's right, in 1968, right at the top of a heated market preceding a 75% collapse in the average stock over the next six years.

Why are money managers taking such a cavalier attitude toward the risk their funds represent? One answer is inexperience. Lipper Analytical Services reports that only 9.8% of the 2657 stock market mutual funds in existence today (which is more funds than there are stocks on the NYSE) existed during the 1973-1974 bear market. Only 36 funds were both around for that bear market and have the same manager. Most fund managers, then, have never grappled with a bear market, nor have their investors. Only *seven* of today's funds have a manager who during 1973-1974 lost a lesser percentage of his portfolio than the Dow did, i.e., outperformed the market. There are, of course, *no* fund managers around today who *made money* in the 1973-1974 bear market, which means there are none that ever made money in *any* bear market. For them to prepare their portfolios to profit from one would be as foreign an idea as preparing to be abducted by aliens.

Perhaps the most dangerous manifestation of the complacency of recent years is the 1993 decision by several major banks and brokerage firms, including Banker's Trust, Merrill Lynch and Paine Webber, to guarantee *no loss of principal* to stock investors. Investors who buy certain securities are promised that they will receive on a specified date all of their principal regardless of market action, plus all of (or in some cases more than) the gain that they would have made in a particular stock index if it went up! Clearly the issuers believe in (1) a continued bull market, (2) their ability to derive enough income from dividends and leveraged trading to be able to pay the obligation *and* make a profit, and (3) inflation, since they want to return the invested principal years in the future. Four things that will kill this apparent golden goose are a bear market in stocks, a drop in dividend payout, unmanageable market volatility, and deflation, all of which are virtually certain to occur over the next decade. Most such investments sold today come due in the years 1998 to 2002, right in the time span that *The Elliott Wave Theorist* has forecast for the first major bear market low. The probability of default on these securities is very high.

Even the activity of *would-be* professionals reflects the ongoing mania. The annual exam for becoming a Chartered Financial Analyst is given midyear. A year ago, there were 16,000 chartered financial analysts in the U.S. How many people do you think registered to take the CFA exam in mid-1994? Answer: 22,000, 38% more people than were in the entire industry! Remember in 1986-1989, when Everyone & Spouse were getting their real estate brokerage licenses? That was the end of a 40-year rise in property prices. At that time, employment in the real estate industry was at its all-time high. Today, employment on Wall Street is at a new all-time high of nearly ½ of 1% of total U.S. employment, which is double the .22% of 1974-1979. Today, then, we are witnessing the same psychological phenomenon in every respect, only the name of the investment-related profession is different. The end will be the same.

Corporate Optimism

One way that companies express optimism is by taking over other companies. The dollar amount of mergers and acquisitions reached the highest level ever last year, $339.4 billion, surpassing 1988's record volume of $335.8 billion, as you can see in Figure 8-14. The pace has picked up further in 1995 so far, suggesting another record year in the making. In the past fifteen years, the number of mergers and acquisitions has come from about 1,000 per year to 7,469 in 1994, also a record. The merger mania of 1994-1995 has dwarfed the M&A frenzy of 1969, which according to the *Bank Credit Analyst* saw only a bit more than 6,000 announced deals that had a far smaller total market value. Such activity is indicative not of minor bull market tops, but of ones that precede prolonged and devastating bear markets. Making the current situation even more

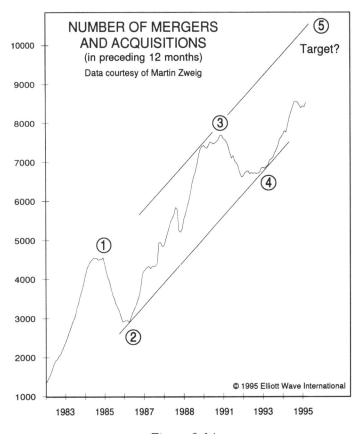

Figure 8-14

impressive from a psychological standpoint is that unlike the late 1980s period, merger activity in the 1990s has been financed more commonly with *stock* than with debt. Buyers like it, because unlike the junk bond financing of the 1980s, stock financing allows the buyer to owe nothing after the transaction; the stock is payment in full. The fact that the sellers are happy with the deal is quite a comment on the attractiveness of stocks to virtually everyone. If there is a cherry on this sundae, it is the newest craze on Wall Street: "blow-out bids," whereby a company buys another by offering so much for it that no sane company will make a competing offer. Recent such bids have represented nearly 30 times expected 1995 earnings and 50%-70% more than the market valued the stock just days before.

How can we recognize the end of the frenzy? As you can see in Figure 8-14, the expansion in M&A activity has followed an excellent Elliott Wave that is now in wave ⑤, which appears to have a bit more to go. It is crucial to mention that the peak of activity relating to the 1942-1968 bull market occurred in the year *after* the top, when bullish fever and hopes for a resumption of the old trend ran high, earnings were excellent, and the economy was peaking. Thus, the peak in M&A activity this time might occur a year or two after the stock market top, at or below the upper channel line in Figure 8-14.

Companies sometimes decide to "take over" their *own* companies. In 1994, corporations bought their own stocks so aggressively that it was a record buy-back year. Companies buy their own stock when prospects for future business appear attractive. In a bull market, they are often smart enough to do so when their stock pulls back in price. However, on the larger trend, company officers are part of the market's psychological fabric just like everyone else, and they tend to become bold when the company outlook appears strongest, which is usually near a top. As evidence for this observation, previous big buy-back years were 1987 and 1989, at or near market tops.

Further evidence of how deeply corporations have become permeated with bullish stock market psychology comes from the fact that the biggest trend today in directors' compensation is payment in the form of stock and stock options. Some major companies pay directors *nothing* but stock options. After all, they're better than cash!

Finance has become so lucrative and running a business so difficult that Kansas City Southern Industries tried to sell its flagship railroad unit so that the company can focus on mutual fund asset management. The announcement caused the stock to rally 11% in one day on four times normal volume. Why? Because everyone knew that they had made a smart decision. Question: If industry disappears, what will stock market mutual fund portfolios contain?

Government Optimism

Government has become optimistic as well. In 1934, two years after the Supercycle low, laws were passed to restrict the activities of investment providers. Today, the SEC is more inclined to *reduce* restrictions. It is considering one proposal allowing insurance companies to offer investment packages, and another allowing mutual fund companies to sell funds by mail and through newspaper ads without first furnishing the formal offering document known as a prospectus.

In recent weeks, a U.S. Congressman has proposed that the Social Security trust fund be allowed to invest in *equities*, not just Treasury bonds as it has in the past. "Listen, guys. It could save the program!"

Optimism is not limited to the federal level. Several states in the U.S. are discussing establishing stock funds for investing their own money. Why? Because stock investing will so assuredly bring in steady profits that they will not have to raise taxes! It took over two hundred years of stock price rise in a Grand Supercycle to entice state governments into such undertakings. There is little question that this plan will lead to huge losses in the bear market, and as a result, *higher* taxes than would have existed otherwise.

Buy-and-Hold is a Stance, Not a Philosophy

The Elliott Wave Theorist took a "buy and hold for the long term" stance back in the late 1970s and early 1980s, when the idea was out of favor. At that time, fundamentals reflected what appeared to be the worst of all possible worlds, therefore being the best of all possible worlds *for stocks*. The upside potential in the market then was truly great. From 1979 to 1983, during the resolution of a sixteen year trading range, *The Elliott Wave Theorist* hammered home this point at a time when few would listen:

We are exiting a period when well-timed trading was the only key to profits in the blue chips. We are entering a period when "buy and hold" is again a sensible approach. And how many money managers would dare utter that phrase after the pummeling of the last thirteen years?   — August 3, 1979

This bull market should be the first "buy-and-hold" market since the 1960s. The experience of the last sixteen years has turned us all into traders, and it is a habit that will have to be abandoned.
                                                                              — October 6, 1982

Legions of brilliant short term traders who have been weaned on the jerky markets of the past few years are not psychologically prepared for the first real bull market in 20 years. By the time the public gets into this game, the speculation will be wild. If you're a professional, it will be the easiest money you have ever made. If you're not, try to think like one. It may sound easy now, but it will be tough not losing your perspective when this market is boiling into its final peak.   — November 8, 1982

Large institutions will probably do best by *avoiding a market timing strategy and concentrating on stock selection*, remaining heavily invested until a full five waves of Primary degree can be counted.   — April 6, 1983

Would it have been possible to *anticipate* investors' switch to a *full embrace of this approach* at the ultimate top of the market? In fact, that is exactly what *The Elliott Wave Theorist* did. The June 1985 issue prepared readers for the eventual extension of time horizon by the majority of investors:

The professionals' focus on the near term, as Robert Farrell of Merrill Lynch has pointed out, is becoming increasingly obsessive and myopic. On Friday, a major national newspaper quoted an optimistic broker as saying, "you might soon see the start of a 10-15 point rally." What kind of perspective is that?! More and more often, both the media's and industry's focus is not the next two years, but the next two hours (or more accurately, the *last* two hours). As pointed out in a classic little book from 1917 called *One-Way Pockets*, the public is always *trading* oriented in the early stages of a bull market, *and "investment" oriented at the top*. As yet, the "buy and hold" strategy is still a minority view. It hasn't been easy for any of us, holding 100% long for a full year now against the shouts of "sell now, you fool" emanating continually from all directions. But hang in there; what's easy rarely pays off.

Has the forecast that investors would become "investment oriented at the top" (as opposed to trading oriented) come to pass? What a difference there is today, one decade later! The single most popular buzz phrase today, bar none, is "buy and hold for the long term." Today it is impossible to go through a single day and not read or hear someone pontificating on the wisdom of buying stocks "for the long term." That the long term trend will remain up is doubted by virtually no one. The stock market will probably never experience a big bear market, we are told. If it does, it will just go back up; the aftermath of the 1987 crash, and even the 1973-1974 bear market, proved that. So, then, why should you ever sell? Why should you even hedge against the occasional decline? Why should you ever be anything but fully invested on the long side? Says one typical fund manager solemnly, "Investment success over time is more a function of time in the market rather than timing of the market." Just this week, at press time, financial newspapers have published these articles: "Buy and Hold Strategies," "Long Market Slides Aren't Always So Bad," and my personal favorite, "Where's the Reward in Hedging Against Risk?" Such sentiments are the epitome of linear trend projection and were nowhere to be found in 1974 or 1979-1982.

When the public is deathly afraid of stocks, such as in 1974, 1980, 1982, 1984 and 1988, the market is safe. On the other hand, "focus on the long term and hold your stocks" is what people said in 1929, 1946, 1968 and 1973, major tops all. At this juncture, the validity of such comments is nil, and their value is negative (the error of this stance is further explored in Chapter 13). Yet the professionals are now (after 21 years of bull market) so comfortable with the market that they repeat the idea tirelessly, and the public has swallowed it whole. Fidelity Investments, the country's largest mutual fund company, conducted a poll revealing that a mind-numbing 95% of its customers proudly state that they are "in the stock market for the long haul." Said a Vice President of Fidelity, "You clearly have a U.S. investor who has made the switch from short term to long term gratification." Most people interpret this switch as bullish, a market stabilizer. It is precisely the opposite, as no market top-heavy with public involvement fails in the end to punish the average investor for his gullibility. The public has, in its own eyes courageously (where was that courage in 1974?), stepped up to the plate during recent corrections and bought more stock. So far, it has worked. An advertisement from October 1993 depicts an investor faced with three situations: a market that has risen, fallen and stayed flat. His sensible response in each case? "Buy more shares." Well, now they are *in*. Let's see what happens.

Properly applied, the phrase "focus on the long term" is in no way synonymous with "close your eyes and buy." It means what it says: adopt a long term orientation. To do it properly, you must have a method of anticipating long term trends. As my readers know, I am a passionate advocate of a long term orientation. Focusing on the long term is exactly what should have persuaded you to become fully invested in the early 1980s. *Focusing on the long term is exactly what should persuade you to get completely out of the market today.* It should further persuade you to *remain* out of stocks for several years regardless of intermediate term rallies, arguments that stocks are undervalued, forecasts of imminent boom or recovery, and above all, exhortations for you to "focus on the long term and buy, buy, buy."

Academic Optimism

When academia catches up with a social trend, it is over. One example is the mid-1980s conclusion that secondary stocks always outperform blue chips. In the past three years, professors have released several studies concluding that with respect to stocks in the United States, market timing has been inferior to "buying and holding." In essence, these studies tell investors what they *should* have done years ago: buy U.S. stocks and hold them. Well, thanks, but we can all make market calls retrospectively.

Concluding in retrospect that having bought at the bottom of some market and held through a long rise would have made money is simply a tautology; it is true by definition. Selecting the U.S. stock market from all others, as these studies do, proves the point and negates any possible validity of the generalized conclusion. We have not yet seen a study that focuses on the silver market from the same time, which fell 93%. We have not seen a study concluding that investors should buy and hold another blue chip market, U.S. Treasury bonds, which have lost 50% of their value over the past half century. Solemn academic studies purporting to justify buying in a particular market always come out at tops. Similar ones were issued in the mid-1980s concluding that rare coins and real estate should only be bought and held. Doubtless if we were to visit the Tokyo library, we would find a similar study on the Nikkei dated 1989.

In one representative new book, *Stocks For the Long Run*, a Wharton professor takes the continuation of the long term uptrend so for granted that he even argues that stocks are less *risky* than bonds or even Treasury bills because of their "historical return." This is simply another statement that in the past fifty years, stocks have outperformed bonds and Treasury bills. Thanks again, but we *know* that; the question is, what will happen over the *next* investment period? Echoes another analyst, "The greatest risk for most investors is that they don't have enough of their capital in stocks, not that they have too much." See how rationalization works to satisfy a psychological imperative? What was seen in 1942 at the 100 level as a *high* risk is seen in 1995 in the 4000s as a *low* risk. Indeed, high risk is now purported to *mean* low risk because the trend will protect you.

In another related study, an economic think tank recently showed, quite accurately, that money managers who have had the least turnover, i.e., who held onto their stocks, have tended to make the most money. A similar study demonstrates that portfolio managers who occasionally hedge their long positions with options and futures have not made as much as the managers who have remained fully exposed to downside risk. The conclusion of both presentations is again that you should have bought stocks long ago and held them unhedged. The implication is that you should *purchase stocks now and never sell or hedge them*. The data used for these studies was from 1982 to 1992, conveniently encompassing almost the entire gain of Cycle wave V. If they had utilized data between 1966 and 1982, it might not have produced the same results or the same implication.

Yet another recent study claims to reveal that even the best market timing advisors are utterly worthless because they did not outperform the bull market in stocks from the bottom until today. The idea that a particular period of gain in a retrospectively chosen

market is some kind of yardstick of judgment on one's investment
ability is transparently invalid. Real people have to make their decisions in current time, not in retrospect, and correctly choosing the
best markets for investment with consistency is an extremely rare
and valuable talent. The only valid benchmark against which to
measure investment advice is against (1) a safe haven, such as a
savings account or Treasury bills, or (2) the performance of people
for whom the advice is designed and who do not take the advice.
Advice that beats either of them is valuable advice. As for the latter
benchmark, in the past fifteen years, the average investor was too
timid to buy stocks until mid-1991. A study by market analyst James
Bianco of Arbor Trading Group, using data from the Investment
Company Institute, reveals that 80% of all the money committed to
stock mutual funds over the last 70 years has been committed in
the last 5½ years. Figure 8-15 shows the commitment to stock funds
at each Dow increment from January 1980 to the present. Of all
mutual fund investors currently in the market, the average pur-

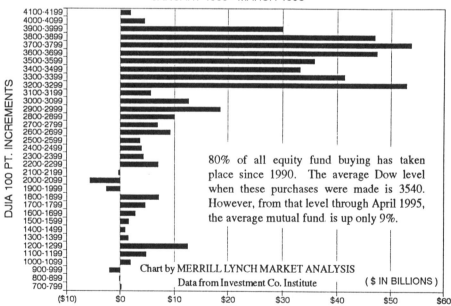

Figure 8-15

chase price is Dow 3540, which was *after* a 378% gain from 1980 and which has yielded a gain to Dow 4300 of just 22%. But, wait. Investors have not owned the Dow, but *mutual funds*, which have lagged the Dow considerably since late 1993, as shown in Figure 6-9. Since Dow 3540, the average mutual fund is up less than 10%! *That* is how much the average investor made in stock market mutual funds in the entirety of Cycle wave V, which has gained well over 600%! Most seasoned market timers certainly beat that gain by a handy margin and helped their followers do it, too. What's more, most of them will keep their profits, while the average investor will give his small gain back, and much more. The bad news for the typical stock market investor is that his average purchase price is rising faster every month, thanks in part to the encouragement provided by the latest slew of studies from universities.

Unfortunately, academic studies do not stop at telling people what they should have done. By linearly extrapolating past trends and *then* publishing their conclusions, these studies, in some cases implicitly but often explicitly, advise people what they should do *now*. The book mentioned above projects past stock market performance indefinitely into the future and proclaims that stocks are the #1 choice for investment *now*. A professor interviewed by *USA Today* states that even investors as old as 65 should have 90% of their money in stocks *now*. After years of stock market gain, the study decrying market timing advises all of us to ignore market analysts and buy and hold U.S. stocks *now*. The grand irony is that the authors of these studies, who were nowhere to be found in 1980 or 1982, have waited throughout the bull market and have finally issued what amounts to "buy signals" to investors, *thereby assuming the role of market advisors*. Without realizing it, these professors are engaging in market timing. It is just terrible market timing. Let the rating services track these buy-and-hold "signals" *from the day they were issued*, and we will see how well they do.

When asked on one occasion what the stock market would do, Bernard Baruch replied, "It will fluctuate." Then, his answer was a smart aleck remark. Today the same sentence is apparently profound wisdom. Academics who tell us today how reasonable, indeed how *imperative*, stock market investment is today will be conducting studies a few years from now revealing how obviously irresponsible it was to own stock at all-time highs in 1995.

The Proliferation of Investment Types

Specialization of stock mutual funds has reached an absurd extreme. There are general funds, blue chip funds, small stock funds, income funds, growth stock funds, aggressive growth stock funds, index funds, futures funds, hedge funds, sector funds, short selling funds, shortable funds, funds for women, funds for Catholics, funds for people against apartheid, funds for the environmentally conscious, and funds for the politically correct. In April 1994, Stein Roe introduced a fund designed to lure young investors with stocks of companies such as McDonald's, Coca-Cola and Toys "R" Us. Just invent it, and it will sell.

Derivatives (securities based on other securities) were essentially nonexistent prior to Cycle wave V. Last year, Merrill Lynch reported that its annual revenue from derivatives for 1993 soared 67% to $761 million, the first time ever that the company's revenue from derivatives exceeded its revenue from stocks. The total value of all monitored futures and options contracts traded in the U.S. alone in 1993 was $217 trillion, which is ten times the total value of all private real estate and publicly held companies in the entire country. During wave V, the marketplace, not satisfied merely with stocks, preferreds, warrants, futures, options, options on futures and options on options, has additionally devised "PIK-Preferred" stocks, "cash index participation" shares, leaps, "unbundled units," including "primes" and "scores," "look-back" options, and a host of other tools of risk assumption and transferal. Indeed, over two-thirds of all currently available *types* of securities have been introduced just since 1981. Within the types, such as index futures, there are subtypes issued continually. A futures contract was even created, for instance, for an index of stocks devised by a financial television network. Over-the-counter strategies specially created for select clients are even more exotic.

The array of investment instruments has most definitely expanded to a complexity and diversity one might expect at a Grand Supercycle top. You may enjoy reading this opinion, written by a lawyer. It reveals how complex the laws merely regarding stock options can become:

> As to whether the regulation is applicable to *option contracts*, the opinions of experts diverge widely. I have not found any decision that might serve as a precedent, though there are many cases at law from which one [should be able to] draw a correct picture. All legal experts hold that the regulation is applicable to both the

seller and the buyer [of the contract]. In practice, however, the judges have often decided differently, always freeing the buyer from the liability while often holding the seller [to the contract]. If the assumption is true that the regulation applies to both seller and purchaser, I can rely on it if, as a trader, I have received call premiums and am forced to deliver the stocks on the day of settlement, or if, as a receiver of a put premium, I have to take shares on the day of settlement. If, on the contrary, the opinion is correct that it applies only to the seller, the regulation will be of no use to me [as a person wanting to seek shelter] when I receive call premiums, for in this case I am in fact a seller; but it will help me if I have received a put premium, as I am then the buyer of stocks. With regard to the put premium, however, there are also great differences of opinion, for, while the scholars assume that no [legally valid] claims can be made because of the regulation, there are contrary decisions by the courts, so that law and legal opinion, the regulation and the reasons for the decisions are contradictory. The theory remains uncertain, and one cannot tell which way the adjudication tends.

However, if the payer of a put premium possesses the stocks on the day of the negotiation of the contract so that he could offer to make delivery to me and to have them transferred to my account [within] two weeks after the offer, it is unlikely that in such a situation, embarrassing though it might be to me, the regulation can be appealed to. According to the opinion of some people, it is sufficient if the payer of the premium possesses the shares on the day when he declares [himself ready to make] the delivery and not already on the day when he entered into the premium contract, in order to make all objections on the grounds of the regulation ineffective.

Got that? There will be a quiz on this legal point on Friday! Do not be of the opinion that such complexity with respect to derivative securities is an innovation, a "first" to be explained away as simply a natural result of modern market sophistication. Three hundred years ago, the Amsterdam, Holland stock exchange had a put and call market every bit as sophisticated as today's. Did you guess? The above description is from a book, *Confusion de Confusiones* by Joseph de la Vega, that was published in 1688. "Joey D" was a trader and lawyer in Amsterdam. When was the last time you traded options on the Amsterdam exchange? When was the last time *any* market traded options as widely and cavalierly as we do today? *It was in the late 1600s/early 1700s, near the last Grand Supercycle peak.* Though it appears unthinkable, I expect that the seemingly permanent options market will ultimately fade from popularity once again, to return centuries hence.

Is Indexing a Magic Answer?

An index fund is one that moves exactly with a market index, such as the S&P 500. While index funds are a good vehicle for market timers, they are not the answer to everyone's dreams. The selectivity of Cycle wave V, as revealed by its lackluster breadth, has prompted many money managers to give up on stock selection to outperform the averages. They have "indexed" their portfolios, i.e., bought stocks in the S&P 500 in order merely to match the performance of "the market." One of today's great ironies is that the newly-popular "indexing" requires being *fully invested*, when in fact the thin breadth, like that of the 1920s, is a long term warning signal that you should become fully *un*invested.

The very popularity of indexing is a statement that investors take the long term uptrend for granted. Countless market professionals have stated incorrectly that the criterion for performance is whether one has "beaten (or matched) the market," a view that can only be comfortably held for a particular market when prices have risen for a long time. This goal may pertain to fund managers who pledge to remain fully invested in order to allow *investors* to decide whether to be in or out of the market via their funds. However, the correct goal of every investor is *making and keeping money*, an entirely different thing.

Buying an index fund was a great idea 13 years ago, 7 years ago and even 4½ years ago, when such funds were not popular. Index funds are popular now because they *were* a good investment, and because they *are* a bad investment, i.e., one that investors desire because of recent past performance. Now that many fund managers are comfortably indexed, they will find themselves indexed to a bear market. By the time the bear market enters its final stages, indexing will be scorned, and market timing will be back, more popular than ever. Then it will be time once again to buy and hold.

Is Diversification a Magic Answer?

As the argument for diversification goes, an investor should not restrict himself to owning domestic stocks and bonds, but he should also buy stocks and bonds of as many other types and from as many other countries as possible. The purpose of this strategy is to spread the risk and thereby ensure *safety*. Nor does the exhortation stop there. The June 24, 1994 *Wall Street Journal* ran a large article on the idea that "venturing into *high-risk* funds...makes your mutual fund portfolio more tranquil and *lowers the risk* by diversification." (Here again, high risk magically means low risk.) Diversification is a tactic always touted at the end of a highly inclusive (in this case global) bull market. Without years of a bull market to provide psychological comfort, what today is an apparently self-evident truth would not be popular. No one was making this case in 1974 or 1980.

The truth is that diversification for its own sake, absent a method of choosing promising speculations, can only assure mediocrity or loss, thereby hurting an investor in the long run. Extricating oneself from investments in Singapore, Taiwan, France, Mexico and Brazil, or from junk bonds and exotic real estate packages upon which no one is bidding, will be a nightmare in a bear market. *The Elliott Wave Theorist*'s position has been that successful investing requires one thing: *anticipating successful investments*, which requires that one must have a method of choosing them. Sometimes that means holding many types of investments, sometimes few. Anyone championing investment diversification for the sake of safety and no other reason has no method of choosing investments, no method of forming a market opinion, and should not be in the money management business.

Enticing novices into markets on the promise of safety through diversification is irresponsible. Those who have not studied markets should not be investing; they should be saving, which means acting to protect principal, not to generate a return when they do not know how. Ironically, yet necessarily given today's conviction about diversification, the deflationary trend that will soon be upon us will devastate nearly all financial assets except cash.

Rationalization

The engine of markets is psychological change. Its turns are marked by psychological extremes, as investors move from depression to euphoria. What *is* euphoria, anyway? Euphoria is a state of mind that makes reality appear better than it is. For instance, today it *feels* to most people as if the Dow has doubled over the past year, while in fact, it is less than 10% above its January 1994 high of 3978 (while the Transports, Utilities and advance-decline line are as yet *below* their corresponding levels). One can only imagine the feeling that will accompany a further 10%-30% rise to the resistance trendlines shown in Chapters 2 and 5. When performance outstrips feeling, as it did when the Dow rose 100% from 1982 through 1985 while worry prevailed, it is early in a bull market. When feeling outstrips performance, it is late. The difference is due entirely to a change in people's *emotional state of mind*. That state of mind can be so powerful that among those who have not learned to recognize it, its command is total. To maintain control, this emotion requires the sacrifice of reason by a process called rationalization. Rationalization is the visa that allows emotionally based ideas to pass through the cerebral cortex unaccosted. Smart people are very good at it, and employ it continually, particularly if they have little market experience. The process must take place primarily at the unconscious level because the instant that the feeling of euphoria (or dread) is recognized by the conscious mind as an emotional impulse and is examined and dealt with, it utterly loses its power. Indeed, the reason that fewer than 1% of traders are consistently profitable is that consciously recognizing and overcoming unconscious forces is such a rare mental feat.

An interview in *USA Today* with a professor who wrote a bullish book on stocks in 1994 uses both the terms "[new] era" and "this time it's different," classic signs of rationalization. As usual with academics and economists, the entire argument is based upon extrapolating a past trend indefinitely into the future. Stocks have outperformed T-bonds in all 20-year periods since 1871 and have recovered quickly from bear markets, so they always will. The fact that this argument has become widely articulated only in the past four years demonstrates that it is psychologically based, although its proponents do not realize that fact. There have been a dozen books on the same theme published within the past three years. Heeding them will not only bring devastating losses, but perhaps worse, it will keep those following such advice from being able to take advantage of the golden opportunity to buy stocks cheap when they hit bottom. While these books today are an invitation to financial destruction and should not be read, a dozen years from now they will be deeply informative of the psychological climate that existed at the top.

As market history unfailingly attests, when the public is broadly in for the long haul, the market is a time bomb. Nevertheless, today, commentators appear continually on financial television explaining calmly that the public's new found devotion to stocks is

in fact *bullish*. Their rationalization is that the public's devotion
will mitigate or preclude any decline, as investors will be right there
to buy. Fund managers are calling their clients "hardened investors" because they have learned to buy no matter what the market
does. They are, in fact, *softened up* investors, but these professionals must rationalize the public's behavior as intelligent because it
coincides with their own, which, ironically, they also must rationalize. For example, a national column dated June 17, 1994 argues
that the low cash among institutions is *bullish*, contrary to the record.

As previously discussed, many money managers have argued
in Orwellian fashion that more risk means less risk. They say that
if an investor diversifies into riskier investments such as aggressive growth funds, junk bonds, foreign securities and derivatives,
he will reduce his risk because he has "spread" it among many markets. Is this sound advice from a neutral party, or rationalization?
Money managers themselves have followed this policy because they
are rewarded based on relative performance. If a manager of a money
market firm, for instance, makes $1/10$ of 1% more than the competi-
tion, he is rewarded; if he does not follow his daring brethren who
are buying derivatives by the truckload, he can be fired for underperformance. He must rationalize the higher risk he takes as
beneficial to clients, which is how it magically becomes "less risk."

A most blatant rationalization is the idea, reported throughout
the media in 1994, that higher interest rates would prove beneficial
for the stock market and the economy. As rates fell for most of twelve
years, we were informed that the trend was bullish. When interest
rates rose persistently in 1994, which in the past was viewed as the
death knell for stocks, it was hailed as a master stroke by the Fed
that will guarantee a soft landing for the economy, an ensuing recovery, and thus further rising stock prices. The fact that, historically, rising rates have preceded stock market tops by about a year
and a half was nowhere in the rhetoric to be found.

See how it works? In a crowd, the balanced consideration that
is a hallmark of reason is abandoned to a selective focus that reflects the dictates of the mass emotional imperative. The bullish
Elliott Wave opinion of the early 1980s required that bearish arguments be generally publicized and heeded, and today's bearish stance
requires the opposite. We have been satisfied on both counts.

Denial is an important market factor in rationalization, particularly at major tops. As one example of its use today, a Harris
poll from July 1994 revealed that 75% of mutual fund investors said

they had "made money or broken even in 1994 so far." However, Morningstar reported that actually, 83.7% of stock and bond funds had *lost* money up to that time. Sometimes in people's minds, fantasy is stronger than reality.

Hooks

The way the market sustains rationalization is through what one pioneering technician calls "hooks." Hooks are conditions at important turning points that command investors' focus and induce them to conclude that a reversal is impossible. Ten years ago, in January 1985, *The Elliott Wave Theorist* foreshadowed the psychological environment that would hook the unwary:

> Cycle wave V is eventually going to lead to a gigantic crash. The market is uninterested in trying to catch a trout, as each 2-3 year advance has done for the past twenty years. It is after a really *big* fish. To catch a big fish, it is employing a big hook. That hook requires lulling most investors into a false sense of security by the time the top is made, and that, in turn, will require the bearish technical indicators, such as "lagging breadth" and the apparent problem of "too many bulls," to appear for several years to be about as worth heeding as Chicken Little. By the top, few people will be interested in listening to the "sky-is-falling" super bears, who, after all, will have been wrong for thirteen straight years. Remember, the market cannot bankrupt 90% of investors unless it first hooks them into thinking the game is easy. To that end, bullish investors, even blindly bullish investors, are going to have to be *right* for a little while longer.

This major top has hooks for all types of investors, from novice to professional. A number of hooks have been implied throughout this chapter. Let's examine a few others.

"Too Many Bears"

Would you believe that despite the statistics shown in Chapter 7, the majority of analysts and money managers contend that "there are too many bears for the market to go down"? Virtually every sentiment indicator, from valuation ratios to the cash levels held by institutions to the record public buying of mutual funds to the new issue mania to the litany of optimism spread throughout the media, reveals a headlong optimism permeating the investment establish-ment. Today all those indicators are derided, while bulls are focused on only one indicator, to the exclusion of all others: the percentages of bulls and bears among newsletter advisory services. These num-bers have been about evenly split in recent years, whereas at many tops, bullish advisors have outnumbered bears by a 2-to-1 or even a 10-to-1 margin. The professionals' focus on this apparent technical positive (along with the denial that the negatives are negative) is symptomatic of the intense search by most investors to find a rea-son to stay bullish so that their brains will agree with their guts, or more accurately, so that conscious minds will remain in agreement with their powerful unconsciously derived emotions.

There are times in history when the percentage of naive inves-tors is so high that occasional warnings from professionals are irrelevant to net market psychology. This is one of those times. The first point to make is that opinions of market letter writers are vir-tually irrelevant, as so few of today's woefully unsophisticated retail investors read independent analysis. Subscription levels are low and coverage of timing opinions from anyone besides economists and money managers on CNBC is 1/100th of what it was on FNN sev-eral years ago. As many newsletter editors will attest, the public simply decided after the crash of 1987 to hand its money over to managers. Money managers do not read timing services; they pick stocks and heed their own allocation gurus, who are mostly uncon-cerned with timing, a bearish fact in its own right. Indeed, it is likely that there are more market observers using the percentage of ser-vices bearish to argue a bullish position than there are followers of the bearish positions that the services have taken! So the *influence* of bearish newsletters today is virtually nil.

Now let's examine *which* among the advisory services tend to-ward a bearish opinion in today's market. Margo Parrish of *Margo's Market Monitor* recently made an interesting observation in regard to the advisors who are bearish:

> Have you noticed the age delineation between the bull camp and the bear camp? The bulls are, on average, young. They don't know what a long drawn-out bear market is like. On the other hand, the bears are generally older and have vivid memories of conservative pension funds falling 50% in price and individual stocks falling 60% to 80% in value.

Steve Halpern of *Dick Davis Digest* adds,

> A quick perusal of the newsletters received in my office at-
> tests to the accuracy of her comments. Most of those newsletters
> that began publishing in the mid-to-late 1980s are bullish, while
> most of those with a decade or more of experience tend to be bear-
> ish. For now, the younger bulls have the upper hand, but before
> discrediting the "old-timers" for turning bearish too early, remem-
> ber that it's only through their long term accuracy that they've
> survived in the newsletter advisory field for so many years.

So it is the more seasoned among the advisors who are bearish.
Are the vast majority of players who now ignore the warnings from
these few voices a uniquely correct crowd? History answers that
question, too. Here is how one market observer rationalized the
bubble of 66 years ago, right at the top:

> Through the years the old adage, "Buy when everybody is
> selling and sell when the public is buying," has well justified itself.
> But what help does it give today? Old definitions of the public no
> longer suffice. The customers' rooms at brokerage houses have
> been crowded for several years. The amateur investor who ignored
> the old adage in 1926 has a larger credit account with his broker
> than the old trader.
> —Charles A. Dice, *New Levels In the Stock Market*, **August 1929**

Mr. Dice's assertion that the wisdom of the "old trader" was
outmoded was delivered weeks from the historic market top in 1929.
Substitute 1992 for 1926 in the above description, and you can see
that his sentiment exists again today among people who say that
the few staunch bears are just old-timers who do not understand
the fact that it is a new era, that "old definitions of the public no
longer suffice."

At the 1929 top, there was a record amount of stock held short,
just as there is today. So today's short position may not be bullish,
as so many contend. In the weeks that followed the 1929 top, national financial publications stated repeatedly that the market was
safe because there were "too many bears." Books about the 1929-
1932 bear market recount numerous quotations to this effect. After
the Dow had fallen 89% and a depression was underway, there were
undoubtedly arguments that there were too many bulls.

1968 was the most heated market since 1929 until today's. During that year, advisory service bears actually *outnumbered* bulls in

60% of the two-week monitoring periods through December, the month of the top. According to figures from *Investors Intelligence*, half of them did capitulate for six weeks at the very end but quickly returned to their prior opinion.

As in 1968, the cause of today's persistent split among advisory bears is that a fair percentage of seasoned analysts can see the flagrant overvaluation and widespread public speculation, and they know their meaning. In markets ruled by a frenzied public, a few seasoned pros are bearish for good reason and are loathe to change their opinion.

Thus, today's bears have counterparts at the tops of this century's two most similar market junctures in terms of public participation: 1929 and 1968. A stubborn contingent of bearish independent advisors and other seasoned investors at certain market tops is not a unique phenomenon, but in fact normal behavior at the biggest tops of all, the ones that sport heated public involvement. Taking into account participation in pension plans and ownership of mutual fund shares, there has never been a higher percentage of the U.S. population invested in stocks. Indeed, the percentage of the *world's* population invested in stocks (not to mention bonds) undoubtedly has never been higher either — not in 1929, not in 1720, not *ever*. Thus, the cavalier assessment that "there are too many bears" is simply a psychological hook.

Knocking Off The Elliott Wave Theorist

Markets must, by definition (see Chapter 7), turn when the majority is looking for a continuation of the existing trend. The Elliott Wave forecast for a 1987 high was widely publicized. In undertaking a Fibonacci 8-year time extension and exceeding my original target, the market has left that problem completely behind. *The Elliott Wave Theorist* neglected to heed its own warning in October 1983 that "turning major-trend bearish too early will be the biggest mistake you can make." I forecasted my error in *The Wall Street Journal* of March 18, 1987, predicting, "I'm probably going to be wrong about something in a big way around the top. Undoubtedly the top will take too long, and I'll probably express caution too early, in which case people will say baloney on this crash stuff."

Sure enough, after exiting near the high in 1987, I concluded after the crash that the bull market was probably over and did not re-enter the market. Even after the market made new highs, the advent of the new horde of green investors, who were buying stocks like catfish in a feeding frenzy, kept me too cautious to recommend buying the market as a whole. To this day, the 1987 high has stood as the best exit point for the average stock. What's more, EWT's mining stock recommendations plus T-bill interest have done *better* than owning the S&P since that time. Still, few are paying attention. Who wants to heed someone who has been too cautious on one of his markets for eight years? As required and anticipated, the market's imperative has supplied investors a reason to discount Prechter's opinion. As a result, few will be anxiously awaiting the message from this book, just as few cared to read the message from *Elliott Wave Principle* in 1978. It is as it must be, and aside from having predicted it, there is nothing I can do about it. "No system or approach will ever be generally embraced unquestioningly for any significant period of time," said *The Elliott Wave Theorist* in 1985. "When the inevitable error occurs, even if those errors average only 20% of the time, people will give up on the approach just in time to miss its next string of successes." I can only add that this situation is another symptom of the market psychology that is in place for a major trend reversal. As EWT added in December 1985, "It is [bullish] for the market that the majority of readers and listeners keep giving up on my long term forecast. It will be [bearish] if they ever embrace it. Which they won't; at the top, they will be arguing for Dow 10,000!" It had to happen, and it has.

In March 1989, I ceased all public commentary on the market. One reason was an assessment of my increased error potential, stated this way: "Elliott analysis [tells] me to cut back. If my [bearish] conclusions are wrong, there will be no point in continuing to comment publicly, since I would be providing erroneous information." Now, six years later, I believe that my own professional wave pattern has turned up again, and it is time to make a public statement in the form of this book. Despite the wording of my admonition at the start of the bull market, turning bearish too early is actually not the biggest mistake you can make. The biggest mistake you can make is to turn bullish near the top. That is why I wrote this book — to keep you from doing exactly that.

Circuit Breakers and Government Guarantees

One hook that has helped lull investors into complacency is the set of so-called "circuit breakers" that the stock exchange has in place. These mechanisms are designed to curb computer-based trading when markets fall past a certain amount on any given day. For instance, the S&P 500 futures close for half an hour if the index falls 12 points in a session, computer trading is banned if the Dow falls 50 points in a day, and all U.S. stock and futures exchanges are closed down for an hour if the Dow falls 250 points. These trading curbs are intended to give traders a period of calm reflection to consider whether the market has gone too far and whether in fact buying is warranted. Unfortunately for the idea of controlling market psychology, the marketplace has effectively neutered these supposed safeguards to a panic. In September 1993, the S&P futures began trading around the clock on the Globex, an automated international order entry matching system operated by Reuters and used by the Chicago Mercantile Exchange. If the market were to crash overnight on the Globex, halting market trading in New York midday would provide no comfort to investors who know that the market averages were down five times that amount the night before. In a single upcoming session, the confidence that these mechanisms have instilled could evaporate.

In 1992, it was announced that securities administrators from the U.S., Japan and the European Community "have agreed jointly to monitor stock futures and cash markets *to prevent a stock price crash.*" The effect of this agreement, despite its profound irrelevance in actual practice, has been to increase yet further the public's sense of complacency about the potential for loss in the stock markets of the world. With all its safeguards and guarantees to investors, the market is preparing to deliver not just a hook, but a right hook.

"Nowhere Else To Go"

Another hook was produced by the fact that investors got used to the high interest rates of the 1970s and early 1980s. Years of double digit debt yields caused many people to consider a double-digit return on investment not only normal, but a necessity. About a year after yields began falling from the 8-9% range in the spring of 1990, investors suddenly concluded that there was "nowhere else to go" but the stock and bond markets. By the fall of 1993, the rush to buy stocks and bonds reached frenzied proportion as the 3-month bill and 2-year note yields fell to under 3% and 4% respectively. Ironically, while the public withdrew its money from banks and money market funds at a record rate to buy investments that had a recent history of capital gain, those investments themselves were producing far less capital gain than they had in 1982-1987. Needless to say, most advisors have been assuring people all along that the gains will continue and so will serve to maximize their "yield." The resulting mindset has individuals locked into their opinions and their positions. When investors are standing stock still (pun intended) mentally, they are in for trouble.

The Elliott Wave Theorist has in recent years recommended that long term investors hold the shortest term Treasury bills rather than bonds. Many newspapers reported investors as saying that they "couldn't live on 3% a year." Well, now that 3% has risen to 6%. And a 3% to 6% gain looks very comfortable compared to the net *loss* generated by stock and bond mutual funds combined over the past 18 months, not to mention the losses that are coming. Moreover, most investors are poised to fare far worse than the blue chip averages. Read the article that follows.

Chicago Tribune, Sunday, September 11, 1994

Pension secret: Add risk to mix
Little payoff from being too cautious

A little more than a year ago, workers at Tellabs Operations Inc. in suburban Lisle invested about half their retirement savings in conservative insurance contracts that guaranteed a modest but steady rate of return.

Not a bad idea, you think. Safe, secure investments should be the hallmark for retirement savings.

Today, however, the employees are investing more than half their savings in stock funds that range from value-oriented to aggressive growth to international. They are putting less than 15 percent of their retirement funds in relatively conservative investments, such as money-market funds or guaranteed insurance contracts.

Tellabs' managers are delighted that their employees, a relatively young crowd with an average age of 34, are taking on far more market risk with their retirement nest eggs.

The company made projections and found that while employees were favoring investments with 3 to 6 percent annual returns, they need to be earning 8 to 10 percent on their retirement funds to stay ahead of inflation in the long term and to furnish a comfortable retirement.

But most important was an education campaign that Tellabs sponsored to launch its additions, which included a mandatory two-hour investment seminar held on company time to explain investing principles to employees and highlight the perils of investing poorly.

Even the supposedly conservative guaranteed contracts mentioned in the article have been so difficult to cover that they recently sent a major issuer, Confederation Life, the fifth largest insurance company in Canada, into government receivership. These *professional* investors thought it would be safe to guarantee interest at X% and put all the money into junk bonds and mortgage debt at X+1% . They did not consider the possibility that junk bonds might collapse in value and mortgage debt might turn illiquid, but that is what happened. The creators of these products had no backup plan for earning enough interest to honor their contacts, as there was none available. *If those pros cannot figure out how to receive enough yield to pay off GICs, how can average investors expect to earn an even higher return, as they are being encouraged to attempt?* The answer is that they cannot. The risk they take today in hopes of achieving a high yield is real, in fact greater than ever. It has been made to seem irrelevant by arguments that extrapolate past gains in speculative markets indefinitely into the future, but it is true nevertheless. These employees will rue the day they ever listened to these experts.

Today's pitifully uninformed investor, who insists he cannot abide anything less than a double-digit return on his investments, has proclaimed, "Give me yield...*and give me death!*" For the promise of a high yield, either by coupons or by capital gain, he has bought stocks, which will fall 90%, he has bought municipal and junk bonds, whose issuers will default, and he has bought second and third world stocks and bonds, the perceived value of which hardly in fact exists. To some degree, as some articles have reported, these are acts of desperation over declining CD yields, weak household finances and fear of future costs of college and retirement. Acts of desperation by the unknowledgeable usually result in far greater catastrophes than they thought they were facing before they acted.

"Fundamentals"

The biggest hook, always, is the so-called "fundamentals," or extramarket conditions, as will be discussed in Chapter 12. One reason why even discussing economics, politics and news is misleading to a proper investment decision is that there is enough of it to justify virtually any conclusion. That being the case, the decision about what news to focus upon typically becomes an emotionally-based one. As *The Elliott Wave Theorist* explained in 1983:

Part of the character of a fifth wave of any degree is the occurrence of psychological denial on a mass scale. In other words, the fundamental problems are obvious and threatening to anyone who coldly analyzes the situation, but the average person chooses to explain them away, ignore them, or even deny their existence. This fifth wave should be no exception, and will be built more on unfounded hopes than on soundly improving fundamentals such as the U.S. experienced in the 1950s and early 1960s. And since this fifth wave, wave V, is a fifth within a larger fifth, wave (V), the phenomenon should be magnified by the time the peak is reached. By that time, we should be hearing that the global debt pyramid is "no longer a problem," that the market and the economy have "learned to live with high interest rates," and that computers have ushered in a "new era of unparalleled prosperity."

As forecast, investors today are focusing only on the positive aspects of the background conditions. They see the good news, such as the reports of record earnings pouring out of Wall Street, the low inflation rate, and an administration that wants Japan to open up its markets further to U.S. goods. They conclude that "steady growth with low inflation in an expanding global market is the best of all possible worlds for stocks." The fact that the economy lags stocks is ignored; the fact that disinflation can precede deflation is ignored; the fact that the administration is careening toward a trade war is ignored. This optimistic focus on only the favorable fundamentals is, despite claims to the contrary, bearish for stocks, since anyone who would make a decision to buy on such a basis has, for the most part, already done so.

The bearish side of the news is no less real, but it is not *welcome.* To any warning such as that contained in this book, the majority says indignantly, "Today is *not* like 1929." Well, they are right. Today's hidden fundamentals are in fact *far worse* than those of 1929. The U.S. has lost its place as the fastest growing economy in the world, the dollar is weak, trade deficits have been relentless, the Federal budget deficit is huge, and the level of debt among citizens, corporations, and the federal, state and local governments is of historic proportion. Taxes are so high that most working families have more money taken from them in taxes than they spend on food, clothing and shelter, while the combined governments of the U.S. spend more money than every foreign country in the world put together excluding Japan. If anything, these figures are conservative, as they exclude the costs of regulation, inflation, countless hidden taxes, and estate taxes. Today, federal, state and local governments, for the first time in the history of the country, employ more people in the United States than all the manufacturing industries of the country *combined*. This is not an insignificant fact, as ultimately, manufacturing supports all wealth. The fact that manufacturing has been hit so hard and government has swollen so much reveals deep structural damage. (This damage is revealed in the inflation-adjusted Dow shown in Figure 3-4 and discussed at the end of Chapter 3.) Although none of these observations are perceived as current events or acknowledged as legitimate fundamentals, they are certainly poised to be important in shaping the *next* phase of current events. By the time those events are manifest, the "fundamentals" hook will be out once again, but next time baited for bears.

"This Time It's Different"

At market turns, the most naive people say, "This time it's different." Long time stock market watchers have often commented, "It's never different." Obviously I sympathize more with the latter view than the former, as long as the degree of the trend and turn are comparable. However, there is in fact a basis for saying "This time it's different" that ultimately pertains to the degree of the turn. Compared to previous bull markets of the past fifty years, this one, because it marks the end of a trend at least two degrees larger than the others during this time, *is* different. The real question, even if you do not know anything about the Wave Principle, is *how do you interpret that fact?* The vast majority of analysts today improperly interpret the difference as bullish. Sentiment indicators have been crying "wolf!" for a while, so the majority of professionals believes that the indicators should therefore be ignored. "Stock prices have been historically high relative to dividends and book value for eight years now, and the market hasn't fallen, so the indicator must be irrelevant." "There has been no bear market for eight years, so the likelihood of one occurring continues to diminish." "The momentum indicators have given several sell signals over the course of the past eight years, and none of them have been right. They obviously don't work." Are these sensible conclusions? Hardly. If it suddenly looks like rain, you take your umbrella, right? If it spends all day getting darker and more threatening, do you conclude therefore that rain is unlikely? Do you throw out your umbrella and dress for sunshine?

Or do you head for a storm shelter? Multiple signals are not evidence of ineffectiveness; they convey a *higher-degree message*. Bearish indicator readings are extending because what is being created is the most negative technical condition in 275 years. It might be said that the indicators were crying "wolf" in 1987, they yelled "grizzly" in 1989, and today they are shouting "Godzilla!" When the market is building a Grand Supercycle top, such conditions are normal. The longer that bearish factors remain in place, the greater is their ultimate import.

"Making Money Is Easy"

The implication of the latest academic studies, the linear extrapolation of past trends, and the exhortations to buy and hold, is that making money through investments is easy. The truth is that making money in markets is normally difficult; in fact, for most people, *it is impossible*. If you do not believe it, ask Merrill Lynch or the IRS. what is the percentage of nonprofessionals who make a net profit in investments over a lifetime. A principal of a futures brokerage firm once confided to me that never in the history of the company had customers in the aggregate ever made a profit over a calendar year; they lost money *every year*. Stock picking and bond investing are no different in that regard except that the time frame for ultimate loss is extended. Like any skill, investing must be *learned* before it can be successfully applied. Making money in the past four years in stocks has been easy *only if you believe that making money in markets is easy*. If, like the "old trader" referenced in an earlier quote, you know how difficult it is, you probably have not been fully invested in stocks as they have continued to rise in high valuation territory without a significant correction.

The fact that so many investors, particularly naive investors, have looked so right for a four-year period is simply a reflection of how terribly wrong they ultimately will be. Whatever the near term outcome, on a long term basis you can rest assured that the bullish public is not right. Nor are the professionals who are rationalizing holding a fully invested position here in 1995, when they were fearful and underinvested in 1975 and 1985. Those who think making money is easy will not sell before the market turns down, and their profits will be wiped out in a matter of weeks. Those who are positioned to catch the trend change will make more money in one year than the longs will have made in five.

"I Have No Choice"

The most insidious hooks are those that ensnare even people who would prefer to be cautious. According to one article, some professionals admit that they are trapped in this outrageously over-valued market because the public is bullish. A manager of $600 million worth of stocks at a major bank was bearish in 1993 but 95% invested, explaining, "I'm negative, but you either invest or lose clients." Many portfolio managers today are fully invested in stocks and bonds simply because if they were not, their clients would leave. This practice is destructive, of course, since in essence *it consists of letting the naive, uninformed public dictate investment policy.* Truly, the inmates are running the asylum. Even doctors who know better have abdicated their responsibility and are following the impulsive dictates of their patients.

The hooks are exquisitely set to catch schools of fish. The only question is when the market will reel in its catch.

IMPLICATIONS

As EWT speculated at the end of 1986, "It is hard to believe that after so many years of bull market, *The Elliott Wave Theorist* is still far more bullish than the majority, *a situation that will even-tually reverse.*" Well, now that situation *is* completely reversed. *The Elliott Wave Theorist* is incalculably more bearish than the major-ity, which is optimistic to an extent unprecedented in U.S. history. Clearly, this is a situation that fulfills the expectation (quoted near the outset of this chapter) that at the top, "Investor mass psychol-ogy should reach manic proportion, with elements of 1929, 1968 and 1973 all operating together and, at the end, to an even greater ex-treme." In terms of dividend valuation, the market is *more* overpriced than in 1929; in terms of public participation, the mutual fund and OTC manias are *bigger* than those of 1968; in terms of REIT, new issue and blue chip overvaluation, today's buying frenzy *overshad-ows* that of 1973. Contrast today's mood with the gloom of 1978-1982 and even 1985, as described at the outset of this chapter. Can you see the difference? Is it clear why *The Elliott Wave Theorist* was bullish then and bearish now as a result?

Extreme optimism has actually been manifest several times in the past eight years, including August-September 1987, August-September 1989, July 1990, mid-1991, January 1994 and now. What is particularly remarkable about the high optimism today is that it

is so powerfully entrenched despite the fact that the actual performance of stocks and bonds since 1987 has been substantially less
impressive than it was from 1982 to 1987, and in the past year and
a half, these markets together have produced no net gain at all. In
other words, the *disparity* between actual performance and expectations is being stretched to the breaking point. The psychology of
the public, which was ripe for an upside surprise thirteen years ago,
is now ripe for disappointment.

Market justice is the payback that the dependent person (discussed in Chapter 1) receives for abandoning his independent
judgment to the emotions of the crowd. In early 1983, *The Elliott
Wave Theorist* explained the implications of a very broad one-day
drop this way: "The incredible 1631 issues showing declines on January 24 proved that the general investing public was indeed panicked
by the avalanche of bad news stories, and rushed to sell all sorts of
old dusty stock certificates. While anything can happen, it just
couldn't be market justice to allow that type of seller back in at
lower prices." Market justice prevailed, as prices immediately soared.
The way the market will soon treat today's confident investors is
the flip side of how it treated the fearful ones in the early stages of
the bull market. Market justice will prevail again, as always, and
today's buyers will not be allowed another chance to sell at high
prices once the trend reverses. Complacency will turn to concern
and then capitulation in a cycle that never ceases; it is only a matter of time.

How will investors view the start of the bear market? As a hint,
polls conducted by brokerage firms reveal that during the 9% drop
in stocks in early 1994, public buyers outnumbered sellers by more
than two to one. As another hint, one of the few remaining short
selling funds in the country gained a whopping 60% in the first half
of 1994, and guess what. More money left the fund than entered!
The average investor, who has no clue about the behavior of markets, is fearless of a major market decline. He has "learned" that
every pullback is a chance to buy. When the first big down day,
week, month or even year hits, it will actually change few people's
opinion. Recall that 80% of all the money committed to stock mutual funds over the last 70 years has been committed in the last 5½
years at an average price of 3540 on the Dow. This statistic not only
speaks to the level of optimism that created it, *it also explains why
people have to stay bullish and hopeful in the face of any contrary*

evidence. The cognitive dissonance of turning bearish so soon after becoming heavily invested will be too great for most people to handle. With that sentiment in place, investors will be exquisitely primed to buy all the way down. When the first decline occurs, assurances will fly that the fall is a "gift," "no big deal," "just another buying opportunity," "healthy," and "a bargain." Newspapers will fill their pages with interviews of both professional and novice investors expressing limitless confidence in the long term uptrend. Professionals will continue to give decisive advice to buy more, and public investors will brag about their maturity in feeling no fear. In delivering the Pavlovian response that the market has worked hard to engender, investors will buy more into weakness, certain that the long term trend is still up. Here is what you should expect to hear at various points in the decline. At 5% down: "That's everybody's estimate!" At 10%: "That's the gift we've been anticipating for four years!" At 15%: "This is the maximum for the long awaited 10-15% correction!" At 20%: "That's the depth of the average bear market!" At 35%: "It's just a repeat of the 1987 crash!" At 45%: "This matches 1973-1974!" And so on, always referring to the fall as "a healthy, overdue correction in the long term bull market." If bull markets climb a Wall of Worry, I would add that bear markets slide down a Slope of Hope.

Believe it or not, all this bullish sentiment is, in a sense, programmed into all the fancy software that Wall Street is using. The programmers don't know it, but it is true. Most programs use data going back ten to fifteen years, and few use data going back more than twenty years. In other words, the computer programs that are trying to think their way through the stock market have been told that Cycle wave V is normal behavior, the way that stocks always act. The software will be completely befuddled when the bear market hits. Against all the "historical" parameters in their data banks, the market will be considered a bargain when it is down 10%, 20%, 30%, and lower, just as if the conclusion were being reached by real people.

Second waves typically recreate the emotions present at the preceding major turn, so psychology in the wave ② rally (such as is occurring in bonds now) should be extremely exuberant, reflecting certainty that the bull market has resumed. Be prepared to resist the relentless drumbeat of hopeful opinion that will accompany most of the first and second waves of the bear market. Their hallmarks will be that (1) "There are too many bears for the market to continue down," and (2) "Stocks are so cheap now that they are bargains." After the peak of wave ②, the buy-and-hold philosophy will begin its long process of melting away, just as the short term trading psychology of ten to fifteen years ago ultimately did. Even during the first half of wave ③, many commentators will justify their bullish opinion on the grounds that the market has fallen so much, so it will be important to maintain *perspective*. Take a good look at the Grand Supercycle in Figure 2-3 and realize that even at 50% down, the bear market will have hardly begun. This process will repeat on a larger scale during the rally for Cycle wave B and through the early stages of wave C down.

For the majority, the "point of recognition" that the trend has changed for real will occur in a panic with the center of wave ③ of C, essentially the same position it occurred in the opposite direction on the way up, as detailed in the first part of this chapter. Ultimately, the deeper the bear market goes, the more news-oriented "reasons" people will find to become bearish on their investments. The waxing bewilderment that will have characterized the mindset of the bulls up to that point will change to concern. Hope will melt into fear, and fear will ultimately give way to panic. At 90% down, buying weakness will not be in fashion. The old arguments about bears and bargains will eventually be thrown aside, right about the time both are actually true. At the bottom, there will be *no* discernible news-oriented reason to own stocks, precisely because news is produced by the same psychology that moves markets. With that small bit of profound knowledge, you can spend all the time that most people are in panic calmly making plans to take advantage of the historic buying opportunity that awaits us at the upcoming bottom. Do not let the gloom and doom books that will then be popular (as they were in 1980-1981) paralyze you when the time to commit funds to investment markets arrives several years hence. Their publication, and their appearance on *The New York Times* best-seller list, will be a sign of the bottom, just like the "How to Get Rich By Investing in the Stock Market" books of the past four years are a sign of a top.

Today's operative word is *hope*, one of only two "four letter words" in the world of investing. The professionals who own stock today on the assumption that the economy is in "the best of all possible worlds" of contained inflation and steady growth are going to be shocked to realize in retrospect that the economy was in fact *ending* exactly such a period. Small investors who "can't live on 5% interest" and are betting the farm on stocks because they see it as their only option against slipping into poverty will be stunned to discover that their investment only served to hasten the process.

The unthinking mindset of optimism and complacency so widespread today will be balanced by a period of correspondingly extreme pessimism in coming years. Throughout the bear market, you must keep in mind that all the technical information presented in this book has profound *long term* implications. In other words, the market is going to have to suffer the extensive dissipation of today's historically optimistic mood before it will present true bargains. Despite all short term events and market movements, today's level of optimism will be an overriding factor to consider every day the market trades, even next year, the year after, and for awhile beyond. The only value in observing the short term action will be to ascertain an opportunity to orient your investment or trading account to that inexorable long term trend. Staying out of a bear market requires just as much discipline as getting out in the first place. Just as high-conviction selling is typical investor behavior early in bull markets, so is high-conviction buying early in bear markets, a practice that is devastating to one's prosperity. The best antidote is a clear look at the big picture, which is the purpose of this book.

After the stock market has declined for awhile, financial, economic and social conditions, which now appear just fine to so many, will begin deteriorating rapidly. Bad news will begin to pour forth, often appearing as a surprise. At the bottom, despair will reign, and the trend will be projected further downward by the majority of economists. Financial professionals will counsel asset safety and conservation, not profit. Academics will issue scholarly studies to support the bearish mindset. The public will have very little money in investment markets, either because they withdrew it or because they failed to withdraw it. Investors will have slid to the bottom of the Slope of Hope, and the market will begin its new climb up the Wall of Worry.

So what is the right course of action? As *The Elliott Wave Theorist* cautioned in early 1986, "Once the craze really takes hold, just be aware of what is going on, and make sure you are not caught up in the amorphous feelings of confidence, complacency and love at the ultimate top." The reader of this book faces a difficult task, one that will put him in such an extreme minority that he will feel isolated and unsupported. By selling all of your stocks, you will take the maverick road, and you will take it alone. Perhaps the best words of wisdom were those offered back when the bull market was in its infancy, when it was possible to adopt a cool perspective, many years and many points away from today's frothy frenzy. A dozen years ago, on August 18, 1983, *The Elliott Wave Theorist* explained how the pressures would mount throughout the bull market to the point that psychology would be in diametric opposition to that of the early 1980s. We can now take this paragraph out of our wallets and gently unfold it, observing that the pressures we face are exactly those anticipated so long ago:

> I have no doubt that by the time this bull market is ending, our call for a huge crash and depression will be laughed off the street. In fact, that is exactly what we should expect if there is to be any chance that we're right. Do not lose your perspective when the time comes. It will take great courage to make money during this bull market, because in the early stages it will be easy to be too cautious. However, it will take even *greater* courage to get out near the top, because that's when the world will call you a damn fool for selling.

One thing I have learned is that if the majority does not laugh at or dismiss as worthless my long term market opinion, it is wrong. Given the fact that the market reflects the sum total of people's opinions, it must be ever thus. Whenever the world calls you a damn fool for doing anything involving investments, you know without a shadow of a doubt that it is they who are the fools. You are a fool only if you listen to them. Everyone *wants* to be a contrarian, but it takes many trials, tribulations and years of experience (i.e., mistakes) to learn when to act as a contrarian. If you have the courage to separate yourself from the herd because you suspect it might be stampeding over a cliff, the time to do it is before the herd reaches the cliff. That time is now.

Chapter 9

THE ROLE OF FUNDAMENTALS

Many people insist upon being given "reasons" for market action, both anticipated and actual, other than those derived from market analysis. However, conditions and events outside the market that are presumed to *cause* market trends in fact *lag* those trends. Price patterns, which reflect social psychological changes, are precisely what forecast a change in outside events. The true fundamental cause of market movements is the nature of social man, which in the aggregate is governed by unconscious forces that produce wave patterns. (These forces include the fight-or-flight and herding instincts, which are impulsive and unconscious as opposed to reasoned.) Thus, an armchair argument about why current extra-market conditions do or do not support the case for change is a waste of time and often counterproductive to reaching a correct conclusion. Since conventional theories misunderstand the relationship between the market and events, investors often allow such events to persuade them to join a market's trend after it has substantially progressed, or even after it has ended. This is the reason they are caught fully invested at the top and in cash at the bottom.

The false belief that government can affect trends, i.e., change a bear market to a bull market, often causes people to stay invested in a bear market. However, government does not act; it only reacts, and it is always the *last* institution to react, because it is the ultimate crowd, every decision being made by committee and as a result of pressure from the majority of voters. For example, the securities laws of 1934 were passed to prevent the crash that had already occurred and the depression that had already bottomed. Indeed, it was a lagging indicator that the bottom had passed. Similarly, the Monetary Control Act passed in December 1980 was designed to deal with the runaway inflation that had raged for a decade and had ended nearly a year before. Again, the passage of the act was a lagging indicator that the period of accelerating inflation was over.

While knowledge of current events and extramarket conditions has almost no value in predicting the stock market, knowledge about the position of the market can be used to predict changes in outside conditions. The Wave Principle provides a basis for speculating upon upcoming changes in market trends and therefore, the events that result from the social psychology that the trend changes represent. This ability provides an opportunity to prepare for possible events before they are realized or before their inevitability becomes obvious to the majority. It is worth knowing, for instance, that banks were closed by government decree in 1933 shortly after the low of Supercycle wave (IV), and that most of the banks in the country closed in 1857 as well, at the end of Supercycle wave (II). It is unlikely, therefore, that with regard to bank health, the current bear market will fail to produce similar results. Most analysts work the other way around. For example, they would wait until they observed widespread bank closings and then declare their bearish meaning for the market, which is precisely the opposite of their true implication.

Most people need favorable out-of-market news to give them the conviction to buy. However, it was the *real* good news, the mass psychological state reflected by the Wave Principle, that gave A.J. Frost and myself the conviction to counsel buying stocks at the bottom, way before what most people consider good news started coming out. Similarly, the bearish news today is the position of the wave structure. What most people consider bad news for the market will come out at the bottom.

Events always fall into place to reflect the trend of the market, and thus the social mood, whether we can describe them in advance or not. As an example, when we forecasted the great bull market of the 1980s, we had no idea where the vehicles for speculation would come from. In 1983, *The Elliott Wave Theorist* pointed out the emerging conditions that were becoming associated with the bull market:

> With sentiment, momentum, wave characteristics and social phenomena all supporting our original forecast, can we say that the environment on Wall Street is conducive to developing a full blown speculative mania? In 1978, an Elliott analyst had no way of knowing just what the mechanisms for a wild speculation would be. "Where is the 10% margin that made the 1920s possible?" was a common rebuttal. Well, to be honest, we didn't know. But now look! The entire structure is being built as if it were planned. Options on hundreds of stocks (and now stock indexes) allow the speculator to deal in thousands of shares of stock for a fraction of their value. Futures contracts on stock indexes, which promise to deliver nothing, have been created for the most part as speculative vehicles with huge leverage. Options *on* futures carry the

possibilities one step further. And it's not stopping there. Major financial newspapers are calling for the end of any margin requirements on stocks whatsoever. "Look-back" options are making a debut. S&Ls are leaping into the stock brokerage business, sending flyers to little old ladies. And New York City banks are already constructing kiosks for quote machines so that depositors can stop off at lunch and punch out their favorite stocks. Options exchanges are creating new and specialized speculative instruments — guess the CPI and win a bundle! In other words, the financial arena is becoming the *place to be*. And, as if by magic, the media are geometrically increasing coverage of financial news. Financial News Network is now broadcasting 12 hours a day, bringing up-to-the-minute quotations on stocks and commodities via satellite and cable into millions of homes.

At the same time, services that rate analysts and fund managers came into being, and the mutual fund industry began its greatest expansion in history. Not only did these market-oriented factors develop, but economic conditions improved as well. Interest rates declined, inflation receded, employment grew, unemployment fell, production expanded, and a business-friendly president was elected for two straight terms. In essence, if not in specifics, those conditions were forecasted years ahead of time by the simple prediction that wave V in stocks was due to take place. The projected size of the bull market, moreover, assured their continuation for a number of years. For instance, deep concern about the precariousness of financial institutions still characterized the investment environment in 1983-1984, but as *The Elliott Wave Theorist* said then, "we'll worry about the banks after [the top]."

The stock market pattern was the crucial tool in forecasting the great bull market, but the pattern in gold was additionally helpful in countering the arguments for hyperinflation and economic collapse that were so frequently voiced in the early 1980s. This excerpt from the March 7, 1983 issue was entitled, "What the Technical Outlook Means For the Fundamentals":

> The [Elliott Wave] outlook for gold says that the gold bugs are wrong on two counts: (1) that inflation will heat up again immediately to new high levels, and (2) that the big banks are on the verge of collapse due to the difficulties of the oil-producing nations. The Kondratieff cycle is bigger than either of these

arguments, and still calls for *mild deflation with no economic disaster* during the plateau period. It appears that the supply-siders will be vindicated, at least for a while, as a surge in economic production and lower interest rates takes care of inflation and deficit worries. As for the banks, what could be better for them than to have the world's capitalist countries, helped by lower oil prices, producing *real wealth*, some of which has to be deposited in banks?

From the time of its acceleration in 1982, Cycle wave V has been one exciting wave. It has spanned a time that people will look back upon with much fondness, similarly to the way they do the 1950s and early 1960s. The reason is that it encompassed a powerful bull market in social mood, which has had enjoyable *consequences*.

If extramarket conditions are the effect of social mood change, not the cause, then what conditions should we be seeing today, after years of a positive mood? One consequence is strong corporate earnings, and indeed the latest reports have been exceptional. Earnings have come through so strongly that it has become a common adage today that "The stock market is shifting from being interest rate driven to being driven by better corporate earnings." One article accurately describes this certainty as being "recognized by practically everyone." Even some technicians have been uttering it. Yet this classically conventional expectation is a nugget of nonsense. Earnings are the result of the human energy reflected by a bull market, which is why they lag stock price trends by as much as a year. Earnings do not "drive" stocks; the energy reflected by stock trends drives earnings.

What about the social consequences? Look around and witness how the results of this upswing in mood have become manifest. In only the past six years, in moves previously unimaginable, the forty year long Cold War has been pronounced officially over, the USSR has freed Eastern Europe, creating what *The Wall Street Journal* called "a period of euphoria unequaled in the postwar era," China is on the long term road to adopting capitalism and freedom, U.S. political leaders are promising a balanced Federal budget by constitutional amendment, and the U.S. has been basking in the afterglow of winning its first war in 46 years. In just the past year and a half, even more happy events, most previously considered impossible, have occurred: The Prime Minister of Israel and the Chairman of the Palestine Liberation Organization, enemies (symbolically speaking) for millennia, executed a historic peacekeeping handshake for the press; the South African government ended apartheid, three and a half centuries after the Dutch arrival in South Africa and 45 years after its adoption as official government policy; the U.S. adopted the North American Free Trade Agreement (NAFTA) and the General Agreement on Tariffs and Trade (GATT), which was signed by 117 nations; after decades of violence, the Irish Republican Army ceased military operations in Northern Ireland, and the English and Irish Prime Ministers signed a peace treaty; the Catholic Church entered into an accord with the Jewish state in which the Vatican and Israel, enemies for nearly 2000 years, officially recognized one another for the first time; Russia, Ukraine and the U.S., after 40 years of mutual nuclear threat, promised in a treaty to stop aiming warheads at each other; China and Russia, enemies for decades, signed a peace pact vowing not to use force against one another; Presidents Clinton and Yeltsin met in a summit that was described as a "virtual lovefest" by *USA Today*; Yeltsin stated flatly in a speech at the Library of Congress: "We will never fight the United States"; France even invited Germany to parade its soldiers down the Champs-Elysees in Paris on France's biggest national holiday in a symbol of postwar reconciliation!

As a result of all this wonderful news, the Consumer Confidence index stands near its highest levels of the past 25 years. The vast majority of citizens, public and private, are bullish on the market, the economy and the future, and express joy that a new golden age of world peace and prosperity has begun. No conventional economist or political analyst today is anticipating major trouble. The majority of pundits are saying that all these changes have created "favorable fundamentals" that are bullish for stocks. Understanding that "bullish" means that it is time to buy stocks because they will go higher from here, ask yourself, *are these "fundamentals" bullish or bearish?*

In forming our answer, let's compare today's conditions with those of the previous times this century that it was time to buy and sell stocks. The 1932-1937 bull market began in the depths of the deepest depression in nearly a hundred years and ended after four years of economic expansion on the hope that the worst was over. The 1942-1966 upwave began in the grimmest days of World War II and ended in an environment of peace, prosperity and cultural creativity. The current advance began in 1974 in the depths of recession, the highest inflation in thirty years, and shortly after the first time in U.S. history that a scandal forced a Presidential resignation. It has reached a point today at which factories are running at full capacity, and peace and global capitalism appear assured.

The difference at Supercycle degree is even clearer. Political events were *scary and dangerous* in the 1930s and 1940s. They included totalitarian takeovers of vast territory, war on an unprecedented scale, state directed murders of forty million people, countless atrocities, the invention and deployment of atomic bombs, and the annihilation of cities. These events reflected the negative social psychology of a Supercycle degree bear market. *That period also presented one of the greatest stock buying opportunities of all time.*

Events of *recent* years, as chronicled above, are the *opposite* of the social spectacle of the 1930s and 1940s. Are these events, deeply welcome as they are otherwise, reflective of a buying opportunity?

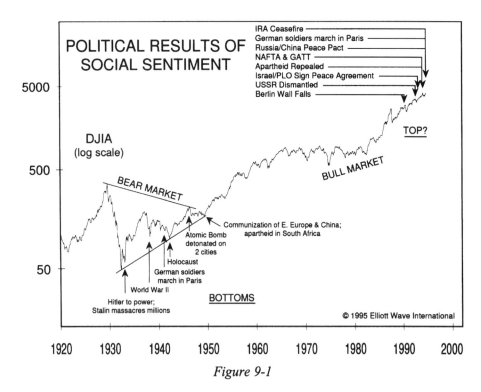

Figure 9-1

Well, if today's fundamental conditions are the opposite of what they were at previous buying opportunities, then is it not logical that the current juncture in the stock market is the opposite of a buying opportunity? During which set of conditions should you become fully invested and during which should you be selling out to the crowd? Buying stocks in which environment will make you rich? Understand that, and you will understand why *The Elliott Wave Theorist* was bullish in the late 1970s and early 1980s and today believes that the best of the advance is behind us, that a major top in stocks and mood-induced economic and political conditions is in evidence, and that what will be viewed retrospectively as a golden age consisting of fifty years of peace and prosperity is reaching a point of culmination. As noted on the graph in Figure 9-1, the stock market is at the opposite sociological juncture from that of the 1930s and 1940s. Social conditions inspire no fear. For that very reason, the public mood is poised to reverse, and the market is ready to decline.

Markets and Social Liberalism

Countless books today reflect optimism toward the long term trends for markets, the global economy, technology and everything else. "Futurists" of all stripes project today's trends decades ahead, unconcerned with possible interruption and convinced that any setbacks will be so minor as to be unnoticeable. Linear extrapolation is not confined to the professions of economics and market analysis, either, but permeates the social sciences. For example, a scholarly book published in 1992 entitled *The End of History and the Last Man* has been called "must reading" among intellectuals. It presents an argument in favor of, as one reviewer described it, "profound optimism" toward the future. I have no quarrel with any particular author, as all such books present classic cases of identifying a trend when it is nearly over and then projecting it into the future. However, the theme of this book is particularly instructive because it deals with long term history, which is so exquisitely the province of the Wave Principle. The author argues that the inexorable trend of history is toward worldwide liberal democracy. As evidence, he presents the increasing number of such democracies worldwide since 1790 (see Figure 9-2), when only three existed: the U.S., France and Switzerland (prior to 1780, Switzerland was the only one). The author does the same thing that most sociologists and financial analysts do: he extrapolates prior trends linearly into the future. Five years

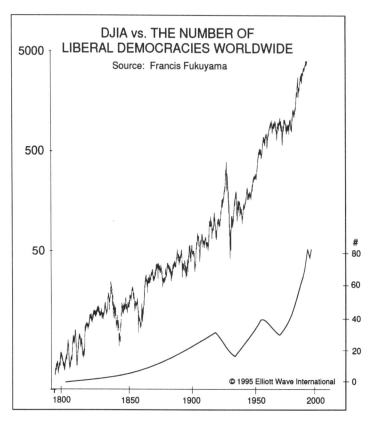

Figure 9-2

ago, had another historian listed the increasing number of people subjugated by Communist regimes since 1917, he might have projected worldwide takeover by Communists, when in fact the trend reversed in a crash. The numbers this author presents showing the rise of liberal democracy simply reflect the trend of the stock market, i.e., of positive social mood, from its Grand Supercycle degree low in 1784 to its current all-time high. In fact, the two "corrections" of the trend toward liberal democracy in the author's graph roughly coincide with bear phases in stocks, exactly reflecting the case that a negative trend in social mood has tangible results. The extent of worldwide liberality in politics has waxed and waned for millennia, so it is doubtful that an endless political New Age is dawning; more likely, one is cresting. While the Wave Principle does reveal that mankind's progress is ultimately ever upward, each advance is nevertheless interrupted by setbacks. As the worldwide decline in fortunes takes hold during the Grand Supercycle bear market, the number of liberal democracies will shrink. (Indeed, from a larger perspective, the next major wave of cultural advance might coincide with an even more liberal form of government, one that does not allow the majority to impose its whims upon everyone else.)

Books such as this are not written, much less widely read and recommended, when markets are presenting buying opportunities amid gloom and pessimism. They are written and read at tops, both of the trends they address and the social mood that produced them.

Using Fundamentals in a Technical Analysis

Because "fundamentals" are the *product* of the psychology that propels markets, their state of health as compared to that in previous waves should reflect the relative technical power of those waves. For example, as stated just before the start of Chapter 6, "the key to knowing whether a bull market advance is truly a fifth wave is to compare its quality, in action (technicals) and foundation (fundamentals), to that within the supposed third wave. If an improvement is clearly evident, it is probably not a fifth. If the wave is less impressive both technically and fundamentally, then a fifth it is." Chapter 6 showed that the bull market from 1974 displays the characteristics of a fifth wave from the standpoint of its technical aspects. Is the same thing true of the fundamentals? Let's compare wave V to wave III.

An objective contrast of the 1974-1995 period to the 1942-1965 period shows that wave III was built upon a more solid foundation in terms of interest rates (2%-4%), trade balance (flat to favorable), federal deficits (small), banking system soundness (no crises and few bankruptcies), and the overall level of outstanding debt (very small). Because background conditions since 1982 have been a great improvement over those of the *1970s*, people miss this very important comparison. Nor is this difference merely something observed in retrospect. *The Elliott Wave Theorist* specifically forecasted in 1982 that the bull market would be accompanied by *"moderately improving prosperity"* as compared to wave III. As every political party that is out of office has reminded us since, the economic expansion has not been as deep and broad as many in the past.

The same contrast can be made at the Grand Supercycle level. The bull market of 1932 to the present, wave (V), has not had the same powerful fundamental environment favoring business and production as did wave (III) from 1842/1857 to 1929. It is not coincidence that the period of laissez-faire capitalism from 1784 to 1929, when a low tax, regulation-free atmosphere prevailed, produced a rise in value of the productive capacity of the U.S. of over 11,000% measured in constant dollars, as revealed in Figure 3-3. Nor is it coincidence that the measly 45% gain (a mere 23% when adjusted by the CPI) from the 1929 high to today has accompanied the rise of the meddling American welfare state from that time to the present. The former fundamental environment was far more conducive to growth.

Despite demonstrably poorer *background* conditions in fifth waves, stock market *valuation* in a fifth wave, as discussed in Chapter 7, typically matches and often exceeds that seen at the peak of the corresponding third wave. Consider that in 1987/1995, U.S. stock prices reached an all-time record valuation with respect to dividend payout and value relative to bonds (see Figures 7-2 and 7-5). This extreme, achieved against relatively weak background conditions, provides a hint of why fifth waves end larger progressions: The rise in valuation to well above what an objective comparison of the background conditions would justify makes the market vulnerable to a relatively severe correction at the peak of the fifth wave. That is the situation today. From this weak and weakening foundation, a real crash can occur.

Surveying the Land From the Crest of the Wave

We have been enjoying a golden time in history. You should be happy that you have gotten to witness and experience it. It is time, though, to prepare for a change. The environment at the end of the next ten years will be the result of a mood trend in the opposite direction that will ultimately reach its own extreme. You should enjoy today's conditions emotionally, while in action preparing for the next phase. Man cannot change nature's physical laws, but he can master them through understanding and harness their power for his benefit. The same is true of the laws of human social behavior. Our only method of anticipating change is to discern the implications of the price patterns of markets, which reflect the patterns of social mood. Understanding the Wave Principle is the only method one can employ to stay in tune with the dynamics of human history and to be their master, not their pawn.

PART II:

OTHER AREAS

Chapter 10

THE ECONOMY

PERSPECTIVE

The first three years of the 1980s contained the most months of officially recognized economic contraction since the Great Depression bottomed out in March 1933. On November 8, 1982, right at the end of this period, *The Elliott Wave Theorist* announced on its front page, RECOVERY BEGINNING, commenting, "The stock market has given a powerful signal: the current very deep recession is ending." The January 10, 1983 issue announced RECOVERY UNDERWAY, which was amended to ECONOMIC BOOM on March 7. This forecast was based on one thing: an understanding of the *degree* of the upturn in the stock market. The start of a bull market of Cycle degree implied a long period of economic expansion. What indeed began the very next month was the longest uninterrupted economic expansion since 1961-1969.

This book is being published at what I believe is a juncture opposite that of mid-1982. At that time, the long term stock market pattern indicated RECOVERY AHEAD, but the actual start of the recovery was not signaled until stocks advanced on powerful upside momentum in August-October. Today, the long term pattern in the stock market emphatically indicates DEPRESSION AHEAD. When will it arrive? The signal will be the same as that of thirteen years ago: a change in the trend of the stock market, this time in the opposite direction. *The Elliott Wave Theorist* commented on this approach a decade ago, in December 1985:

> We should keep the ultimate probability of an economic crash and financial calamity in mind, but it is still *too early* to prepare for it. Legions of super bears have warned of impending monetary collapse, imminent full-scale banking crises, and so forth for years. Although they continue to warn that such events could occur "out of the blue," "at any time," and "without warning," history shows that a substantial decline in the stock market has always provided an early warning to such conditions. As long as the stock market is trending upward, there is no reason to harbor such fears.

So years ago, the Wave Principle answered concerns about the economy by saying, "Not yet," allowing us to prosper from the very start of the expansion. This approach is in direct contrast to those of the two main groups: the perennial doomsayers, who have for decades predicted another depression "just around the corner," and the far larger contingent of perennial optimists, who have neither the means nor the desire to identify signs of impending trouble.

As the above quotation indicates, the signal for the Grand Supercycle downturn will be given when the stock market begins falling in earnest. Then you will know that a new label will be added to our front page forecast: DEPRESSION BEGINNING.

Why *must* a depression occur? The answer is as simple as it is important: No Supercycle degree decline in stock prices on record has failed to produce a depression. The 1840s and 1850s during Supercycle wave (II) saw a depression. The 1930s during Supercycle wave (IV) saw a depression. Even under the mildest possible scenario, the next decline will be at least of Supercycle degree. Therefore, it must produce not simply a recession, but a depression. As for *why* economic contractions follow bear markets, see Chapter 9. Before discussing the coming depression itself, let's examine the buildup of events and forces, and then the current conditions, that support the conclusion that a major economic contraction is imminent.

ANALYSIS OF THE TOPPING PROCESS

At Grand Supercycle degree, the late 1960s and late 1980s/early 1990s are a great double top (see Chapter 3) in the fortunes of the United States. At Cycle degree, the second of those is itself a double top, with 1987-1990 marking the first peak in investments and the economy and 1995(6) due to mark the second. Throughout this time, indications of a long term trend change have been accumulating.

The Subtle Influence of the Larger Bear Market Since 1966

Inflation-adjusted stock prices, and therefore the fortunes of the nation, registered their all-time peaks in February 1966. As *The Elliott Wave Theorist* stated in January 1982 with reference to Figure 3-1, "Since stock prices are by far the best indicator of economic conditions, it follows that the late 1960s marked the end of a long era of economic progress and ushered in an extended phase of contraction in the standard of living for most Americans." Numerous

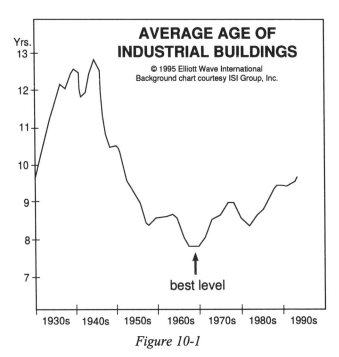

Figure 10-1

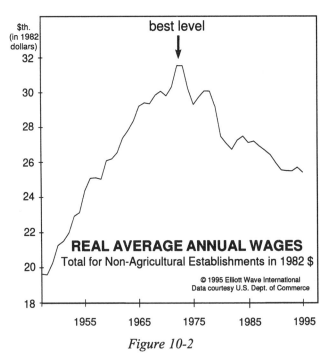

Figure 10-2

social mood indicators, such as crime and divorce rates, began to worsen in the late 1960s. The ongoing multi-decade bear market has exerted a subtle influence over the economic statistics as well. As an example, Figure 10-1 shows the average age of industrial buildings. During the last Supercycle bear market, which produced the Great Depression, people utilized older and older buildings because they could not afford to build new ones. Construction resumed in the mid-1940s and carried right up to the late 1960s, when the inflation-adjusted Dow signaled the end of the Supercycle degree bull market, as depicted in Chapter 3. The average age of buildings has been rising ever since, reflecting the underlying bear market in force at larger degree. Figure 10-2 depicts the purchasing power of the average wage, which has acted similarly. It climbed steadily for decades until 1972-1973, peaking with a normal lag time following the orthodox top of the inflation-adjusted bull market (on a test of the high in January 1973). Despite rebounding slightly at each peak rate of change in the business cycle since then, average wages have declined steadily ever since, reflecting the larger corrective forces.

The Increasing Dominance of Negative Forces Since 1987

The underlying bear market trend since 1966 has subtly influenced the breadth and sociology of Cycle wave V throughout its progress. This has been particularly true since 1987 despite the continuation of the bull market in stocks because subwave ④ was a corrective force and subwave ⑤, which began in 1987, has been the weakest advance among the three Primary degree impulse waves. As such, it has barely been able to maintain dominance over the forces of the larger bear market.

For this reason, social psychology has deteriorated substantially since late 1987. Reflecting upon one aspect of that change, an article in *The Denver Post* on February 27, 1994 investigated numerous measures of social well-being and concluded that after years of flat statistics, "1987 was the year that things started to go wrong, the year the United States social misery indexes began exploding." Those measures include the numbers of juvenile arrests, children in foster care, hospital cocaine episodes, out of wedlock births among black Americans, addicted mothers, and the teen birth rate. Government regulation, as measured by the number of federal employees and the number of pages of regulation, also began soaring again in 1987. In sum, while the Cycle degree bull market in mood did resume

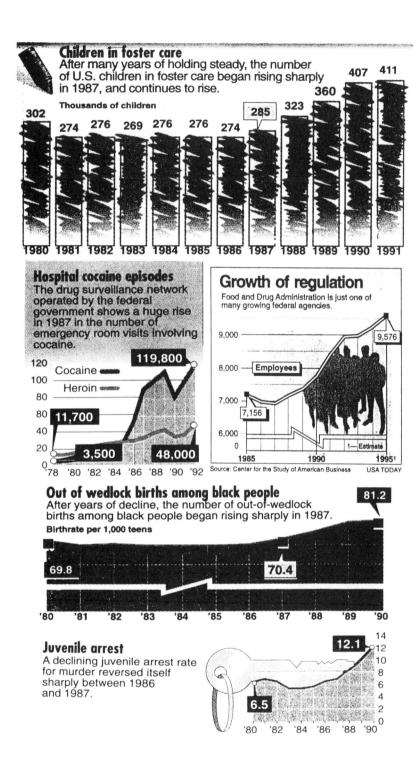

Children in foster care

After many years of holding steady, the number of U.S. children in foster care began rising sharply in 1987, and continues to rise.

Thousands of children

302 274 276 269 276 276 274 285 323 360 407 411

1980 1981 1982 1983 1984 1985 1986 1987 1988 1989 1990 1991

Hospital cocaine episodes

The drug surveillance network operated by the federal government shows a huge rise in 1987 in the number of emergency room visits involving cocaine.

120
100
80
80
40
20
0

Cocaine
Heroin

119,800
11,700
3,500
48,000

'78 '80 '82 '84 '86 '88 '90 '92

Growth of regulation

Food and Drug Administration is just one of many growing federal agencies.

9,000
8,000
7,000
6,000
0

Employees

9,576
7,156

1—Estimate

1985 1990 1995¹

Source: Center for the Study of American Business   USA TODAY

Out of wedlock births among black people

After years of decline, the number of out-of-wedlock births among black people began rising sharply in 1987.

Birthrate per 1,000 teens

81.2
69.8
70.4

'80 '81 '82 '83 '84 '85 '86 '87 '88 '89 '90

Juvenile arrest

A declining juvenile arrest rate for murder reversed itself sharply between 1986 and 1987.

14
12
10
8
6
4
2
0

12.1
6.5

'80 '82 '84 '86 '88 '90

Figures 10-3a-3e

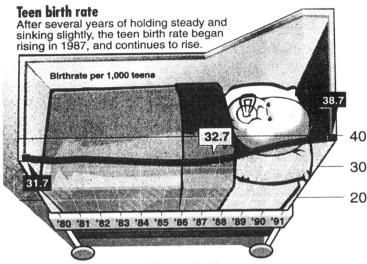

Teen birth rate
After several years of holding steady and
sinking slightly, the teen birth rate began
rising in 1987, and continues to rise.

Birthrate per 1,000 teens

38.7

32.7

40

30

31.7

20

'80 '81 '82 '83 '84 '85 '86 '87 '88 '89 '90 '91

Figure 10-3f

after the 1987 crash, it has been increasingly bedeviled by waxing
social chaos, as recorded in Figures 10-3a through 10-3f. These statistics are of particular interest given the Fibonacci time counts
published in *Elliott Wave Principle* and *The Elliott Wave Theorist*
that pointed years in advance to 1987 as the probable peak of the
Supercycle, as detailed in Chapter 4. Though the article cited above
states that "no social expert claims to understand" why the change
began happening then, it insightfully concludes that "perhaps the
only foreshadowing that 1987 held some bad seed occurred October
19, when the stock market crashed."

Thus, 1987 was the turning point from a broad upward trend in
social mood, which had been characterized as "the Ebullient
Eighties," to a fractured trend. This fractured trend is a *transition*
phase that will lead to a monolithic downward trend in social mood.
Though the consensus among economists was, and remains, that
the stock market crash of October 1987 was meaningless, it was in
fact a vitally important event: a high-volume, high-velocity announcement of the psychological kickoff for the long process of
slowing upside momentum in some social measures and outright
contraction in others.

Social indexes are not the only ones that changed in 1987. A
shift in the long term rate of economic expansion has been telegraphed subtly yet relentlessly both by markets and, with the usual
time lag, the economy. The stock market crash led to a Northeast-

ern real estate bust beginning in 1988, which rapidly sent New England diving headlong into a deep recession. In 1989-1990, the manic rise in California property values reversed to a downward trend, junk bonds crashed, and much of the savings and loan industry went bankrupt. In 1990, collector coins, art prices and the Japanese Nikkei stock index began falling. In 1990-1991, a recession occurred that, despite mild aggregate figures, sported many of the worst statistics since the Great Depression, including record job layoffs, record business failures, and a rare nationwide drop in real estate values. Over 100 of the Fortune 500 companies had negative earnings in this period, the greatest number in the history of the list. Dun & Bradstreet reported a record number of business failures in 1990. The recession saw the worst downturn in history for the hotel industry, with a 33% vacancy average. In 1991, the value of business failures as a percent of GDP was the highest on record. Cumulative layoffs were the worst since the Great Depression, with job eliminations announced by companies running at 2000 per day. In early 1991, the "big three" car makers lost a record amount of money for a single quarter, $2.6 billion. For the first time since the 1940s, total real after tax income declined for three straight quarters. By mid-1991, for the first time in half a century, the U.S. had not a single bank listed in the world's top ten for assets. In July and October 1991, employment, the average work week, and average hourly earnings all declined for the first time in the history of the figures. California, which in 1989 had been considered "recession-proof," suffered the most severe economic contraction of all. At the end of the contraction, the Federal Reserve Board of New York's Quarterly Review stated, "The Gross Domestic Product [has generated its second] weakest performance over any four-year period since the Great Depression." The contraction was worldwide, as Europe fell into its deepest recession since the Depression, and Japan's economy contracted. 1991 was the first year since 1945, four and a half decades earlier, that total world production and income declined.

Since the recession officially ended in 1991, subtle messages have been declaring that the recovery is anemic compared to the average postwar expansion. Indeed, through 1993, two years into the recovery, numerous indicators remained more compatible with continued contraction than with expansion. In 1992, business failures in the United States reached a record. Sears posted a 1992 loss of $3.9 billion, its first loss since 1933 at the bottom of the Great Depression. Ford reported a 1992 loss of $7.4 billion, setting a new U.S. company record, until it was eclipsed immediately thereafter by GM's announcement of a $23.5 billion loss. Rents and property prices in Los Angeles continued falling and were cut to as much as 50% from the 1989 high. A record number of Americans (26.6 million people, or $1/10$ of the population) received food stamps in December 1992. Layoffs not only continued into 1993, they *accelerated* and have continued high right through today. In Connecticut, a newspaper story from early 1993 recounted the fact that 14,000 people, responding to an announcement of employment opportunities, showed up to apply for 1000 jobs. Dunn & Bradstreet reported that 2000 companies per week were going under in the spring of 1993, and the year-end pace was still heavy at 1700 per week. IBM achieved an $8 billion loss, cut its dividend by 55%, laid off workers for the first time in 53 years, and lost its AAA credit rating by Standard & Poor's. No other U.S. economic recovery since the 1940s has produced such poor results. In the same way that a weak rally in the stock market signals that larger cycles are beginning to assert a depressive influence, this weak recovery in the economy has been a warning that the larger cycles of economic activity are rolling over and turning down.

Most economists see no connection among all the events discussed above. The conventional forecasting time horizon is only a few months, so these events are simply relegated to the past, as if irrelevant to forecasting. In fact, they are an intricate part of the present. How does the long term perspective provided by the Wave Principle help in understanding this progression of change?

A Short Term Peak Within a Long Term Slowdown

Figures 10-4 through 10-17 provide a brief tour of the economy's path in recent decades. An examination of these graphs will serve to make two points: (1) that the short term business cycle, which has been in expansion mode for four years now, is at levels compatible with a peak, and (2) more important, that the measures of expansion have traced out a series of *lower highs* over the two or three decades leading up to today. This lessening rate of economic progress indicates a *long term slowing* of the forward momentum of the economy.

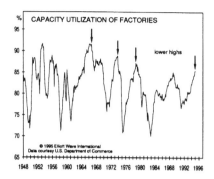

Figure 10-4

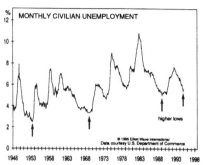

Figure 10-5

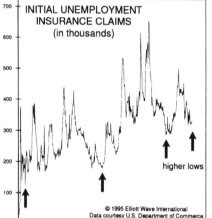

Figure 10-6

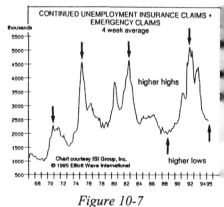

Figure 10-7

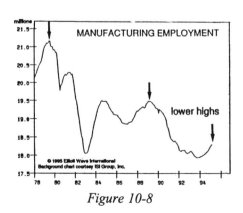

Figure 10-8

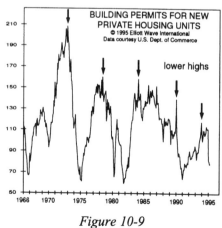

Figure 10-9

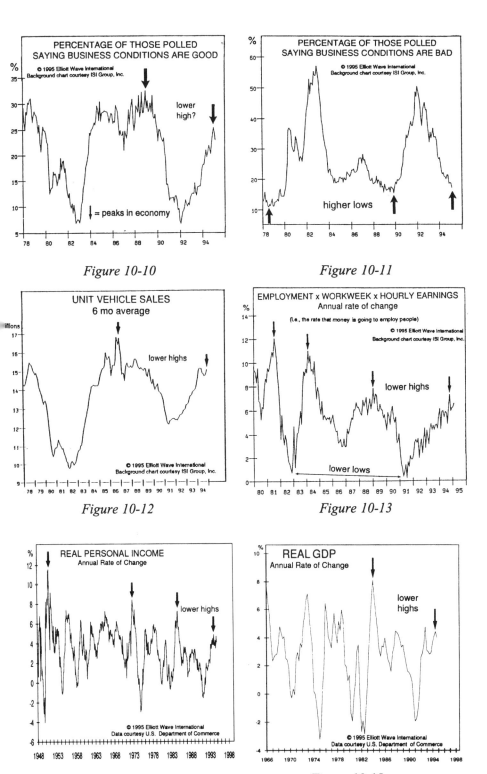

Figure 10-10

Figure 10-11

Figure 10-12

Figure 10-13

Figure 10-14

Figure 10-15

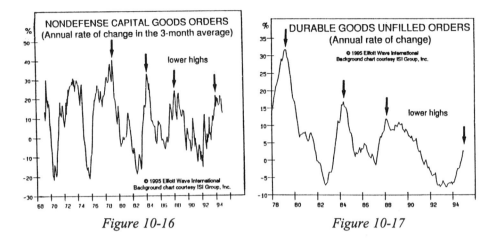

Figure 10-16   Figure 10-17

Figure 10-18 shows sales relative to business inventory, which is a highly sensitive reflection of economic activity. Notice the dates of the prior highest levels: 1955, 1959, 1966, 1973 and 1979-80. Every one of these times immediately preceded a downturn in stocks, which preceded a recession. In every case but one (1966), a recession hit the following year. As you can see, the ratio has just reached its highest level in at least forty years.

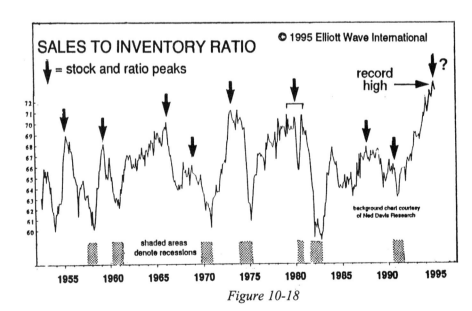

Figure 10-18

The Message Conveyed by These Graphs

Though the Dow is at new all-time highs in nominal terms, reflecting powerful social *emotion*, many of the current levels among the various components of economic activity are lower than the peaks of the 1960s and 1970s, reflecting a deterioration in the *tangible results* of such emotion. This fundamental change in the health of the economy says that what is approaching is not just the end of a four-year business cycle expansion, but one of much larger degree.

As discussed in Chapter 6, a fifth wave in the stock market is weaker than the corresponding third wave. In other words, even though prices reach a new high, the rate of change is less and the breadth is not as good. As explained in Chapter 9, the same thing is true of the accompanying fundamentals, which include economic performance. The period from 1974 to 1995 has been productive, *but economic performance today does not reflect the stock market's high valuation as strongly as did the economic performance from 1942 that culminated in 1968/73*. The overall picture since then has been one of declining peaks, revealing a long term slowing of upside momentum. Rarely does a trend enjoy more than two lower momentum peaks (the stock market since 1983 being a notable exception). If these were stock charts, they would be saying "sell." The fact that indicators of economic endeavor peaked in the 1960s-1970s fits the Elliott Wave thesis that what occurred at that time was not the ultimate extreme in psychology, which occurs in the fifth wave, but the extreme in the ability to *render real* the bullish psychology of the time, i.e., to translate ebullience into actual capital production, which is accomplished most effectively in a third wave.

New Highs in Some Measures

Charts of a few selected industries appear to reflect a very ebullient economy, but with those, one must be alert for special situations. Drug company earnings, for instance, have continued to break all records, as shown in Figure 10-19. The pharmaceutical industry is in a boom because of government health care giveaways. When government withdraws its support or imposes price controls and supply restrictions or takes its role to the point of socialized medicine, this line will turn down dramatically. Similarly, Figure 10-20 shows that auto company earnings are at their highest levels in decades. Take

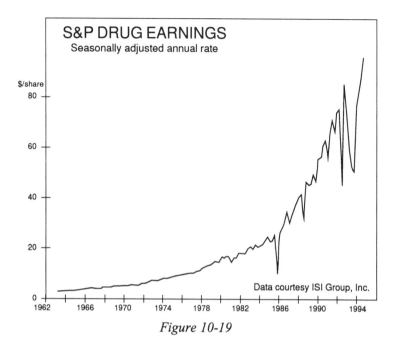

Figure 10-19

a look at Figure 10-21 and you will see why. The soaring yen and sliding dollar have cut U.S. purchases of foreign vehicles in half in seven years! These currency trends are a gift to Detroit that will disappear when the dollar rises. (Even then, though, protectionist measures slowing or preventing auto imports might serve to keep the U.S. auto industry in the "special situation" category for a bit longer, though ultimately, it will succumb.)

A Past Resolution of Long Term Economic Slowing

History provides an excellent guide to the importance of a long term slowing in upside economic momentum. If the Elliott Wave interpretation is correct that a fifth wave of Cycle degree has been in force for the past two decades, then the previous fifth wave of Cycle degree, which lasted through the 1920s, should have behaved similarly. Not only were social mood and the behavior of the stock market extremely similar, but the lessening rates of expansion in the economy painted the same picture as well.

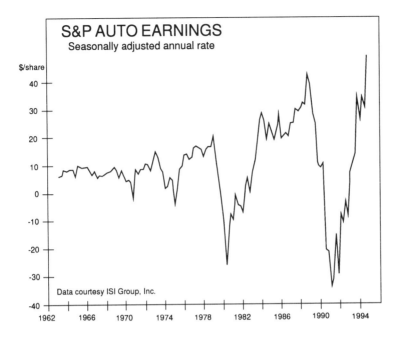

Figure 10-20

Figure 10-21

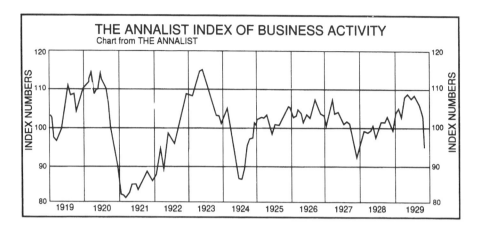

Figure 10-22

Figure 10-22 is a chart of business activity from 1919 (two years before the bull market began) to 1929 (the year of the high). It shows the same phenomenon that has occurred from 1972 (two years before the bull market began) to 1995 (our scheduled year for the top). Specifically, the peak in economic activity at the end of wave V in stocks in 1929 was *lower* than previous ones. The time element is spread out in the modern example because of the "mixed" monetary environment that will be discussed in Chapter 11 and because this peak is one degree higher (Grand Supercycle instead of Supercycle), but the *form* of the pattern is the same. Thus, while the expansion of 1928-1929 represented the last gasp of a tiring advance that had lasted seventy years, the anemic rise in so many of these measures over the past two to four years represents the last gasp of a tiring advance that has lasted over two centuries.

An Elliott Wave Analysis of Economic Statistics

Figures 10-23 through 10-25 show the pattern in economic statistics from the low in the 1974 (through January 1975) recession. Charts include coincident economic indicators, retail sales and durable goods sales. All show excellent five-wave advances that are nearing termination.

The sequence of lower highs shown earlier in Figures 10-4 through 10-18 reflect the *momentum* character of the Primary waves within Cycle wave V. Wave ① had a strong rate of change, wave ③

Figure 10-23

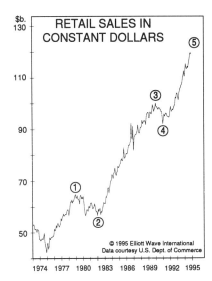

Figure 10-24

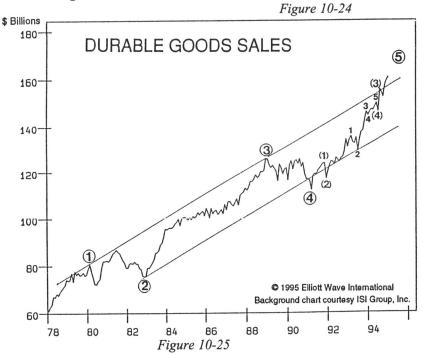

Figure 10-25

a lesser rate of change, and wave ⑤ since 1991 a weak rate of change that has set up a classic divergence against the new highs in the economic aggregates.

Copper Prices: An Excellent Economic Indicator

The price of copper always rises during an economic expansion, and a peak in its price almost always precedes an economic contraction. Figure 10-26 presents a 145-year history of the price of copper as it relates to expansions and contractions in the U.S. economy. The correlation is striking on the short term, but also on the long term. During the major bear market of 1864-1933, there were many recessions, while in the bull market that has been in force since then, there have been very few. Notice that even during its long bear market, copper's few advances came during economic expansions.

The performance of this indicator has remained true in recent years. From its high in February 1980 at $129.16, copper fell sharply, and the recessions of 1980/1982 followed. From the mid-1980s low, copper ran to a new high, and in February 1989, *The Elliott Wave Theorist* noted, "Copper in recent months has been in a spectacular advance typical of all its prior pre-recession/depression spikes. The current spike is also occurring when it is possible to count five waves up from 1933." Copper fell sharply again, and, though with more

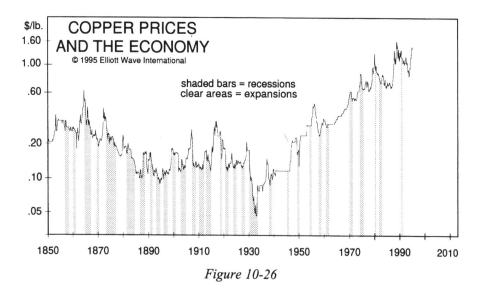

Figure 10-26

time lag than usual, the recession of 1990-1991 followed. Figure 10-26 depicts that recession as being brief, but the discussion earlier in this chapter reveals that copper was actually a more accurate indication of the continuing economic hardship as it trended lower into January 1992. From that low, copper has been moving upward again.

The pattern in copper over the past fifteen years has been similar to, but slightly different from, that of 1916-1929, which preceded the last depression. While the inflationary peak of 1916 led to a drop and a two-step rise to a *lower* high in 1929, the inflationary peak of 1980 has led to a drop and a two-stop rise that may end at a *higher* high. Regardless of this difference, the recessions that accompanied the two pullbacks of 1920-1921 and 1927 in the previous

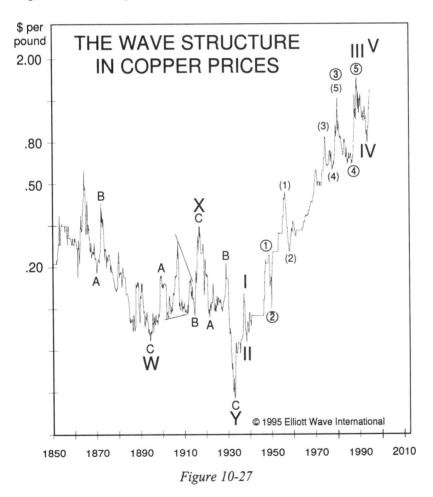

Figure 10-27

era correspond to the recessions that accompanied the pullbacks of 1980-1982 and 1989-1992 in the current era. In the previous era, wave B culminated in 1929, the final year of the great stock market mania and disinflationary economic recovery of the Roaring 'Twenties. The culmination of the current advance should similarly coincide with the end of the Great Asset Mania and the disinflationary economic recovery of the past thirteen years. The difference this time will be one of degree. Figure 10-27 shows that the current rise will complete a five-wave pattern from the depression low of $.0471 per pound in February 1933. When copper reaches the top of wave V, probably this year or early next, it will not be in the same position as it was at the 1929 high, but at a more important juncture: the end of a Supercycle degree advance. Copper is therefore due for its furthest fall in over six decades, which portends not just recession, but depression.

Professional and Public Psychology

Recall from Chapter 8 that throughout the early years of the 1980s bull market, many economists remained concerned about a renewed recession. The previous back-to-back recessions of 1980 and 1982 made caution ingrained. By June 1990, after eight years of expansion, that psychology had changed to the point that a month before the worst recession in decades began, 88% of economists polled forecasted economic growth "for at least the next twelve months."

Today there is once again no indication from the profession that there is any danger of a recession on the horizon. If linear projection of trends were a valid method of forecasting, the current economic environment would undeniably support an optimistic stance. The rate of commercial bank failures is the lowest in fourteen years. The level of delinquent payments owed to banks by consumers is the lowest in twenty years. Mortgage delinquencies are the lowest in 21 years. Corporate return on equity for the S&P 500 companies is near 20%, the highest *ever*. The bond market is rebounding, the stock market is making new all-time highs month after month, the economy is still expanding, inflation is "under control," and the Fed appears to be engineering its interest rates brilliantly to keep the economy on an even keel. In January 1995, Republicans gained control of Congress for the first time since 1954, and their promises to present a balanced budget amendment, cut the size of government spending, and especially to reduce the capital gains tax, have helped heighten the mood of optimism that has increased steadily among economists, financial commentators and the public for the past four years. There is no phrase that has been repeated to the media as often by economists, analysts, and even the Federal Reserve Board as this one: *"It is the best of all possible worlds* for stocks and the economy."

Headlines today reflect the extension of this mood: "The American Economy Back on Top," "The Evidence: Glowing Numbers and More to Come," "The U.S. Economy Back in the Driver's Seat," "Business Is Expected to Boom in 1995," "Pros [Say] Economy to Keep Perking," "No Recession in Forecast For '95," "Economy May Not Dip Significantly Until 2000," "Greenspan Says Foundations of Economic Expansion Increasingly Well Entrenched," "All Signs Point to Soft Landing," and "Clinton Team Predicts Steady Growth." The latest reports show that 82% of economists predict continued expansion until at least 1997, while 40% predict no recession until 1998 or beyond. The President's Council of Economic Advisors says, "we don't see any scenario that generates a recession in the next *five years*." "Many private economists," says an article, "agree there's a good chance the economy will escape a recession *for the rest of the decade*." Alan Greenspan's recent testimony before Congress has crystallized the consensus opinion already in place that the economy will slow gently into a "soft landing," i.e., not go into recession, and then continue expanding without pause for five years or more. Certainly there is no concern among these forecasters over the economy's move over the past fourteen years from historically high inflation to no inflation, the same trend that preceded the 1929-1932 stock market collapse and ensuing deflationary depression. The general expectation of continued growth is so pervasive that a recent study of such references in *Barron's* shows that 1995 is already on the way to setting a record in terms of references to a "soft landing," the last record having been set in 1989, the year before the worst recession by some measures since the 1940s. Optimism would persist forever if the economy never changed, as all conventional "forecasts" are simply a reflection of present conditions and the trends that led to them.

The level of public optimism has edged even higher as well. As this book goes to press, the Consumer Confidence index is at a level commensurate with previous tops in the economy. Economists always assert that consumer optimism is bullish, when in fact, extremes in psychology in both directions signal that the trend is likely to reverse, as it has in every instance on record. For instance,

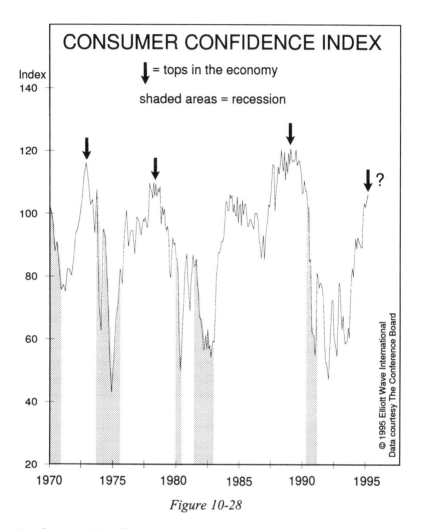

Figure 10-28

notice that in 1982, the average consumer had little confidence about the future. To have correctly anticipated the future, the reading should have been on the ceiling. It is *consumer pessimism* that is bullish, as you can see by the coincidence of low confidence with recession lows in Figure 10-28.

Today, after a long bull market in stocks and a resumption of the economic expansion, the average consumer is again optimistic. The last times that consumers were approximately this bold in their willingness to bet on a rosy economic future were in 1969, 1973, 1978 and 1989, all of which were good times to begin preparing for an economic contraction. The fact that the readings so far are below the 1989 high puts the indicator in a position similar to that of 1978, when it was in between two related contractions. Given the uneven economic performance of 1992-1995, the current reading is especially reflective of psychology outrunning reality, and is therefore particularly bearish for the stock market and the economy.

The Purchasing Managers Index and the Conference Board Index of Business Confidence, which is a quarterly survey of 500 to 600 U.S. chief executives, reflect the outlook of a group of business people more sensitive to advance warnings of change than the average consumer. Study Figures 10-29 and 10-30 and notice that these measures turn earlier and more sharply than the Consumer Confidence index. They turn up dramatically right at the bottom of recessions and peak way early in recoveries. These business people seem, to a degree, to factor into their thinking the cyclical nature of the ups and downs of business rather than simply extrapolating current trends. It is noteworthy, therefore, that in the recent recovery, these indexes have not only failed to exceed their previous extremes, but have begun trending lower in recent months, ahead of the crowd. Despite this trend, however, the indexes are still on the side of optimism. This group, the only informed one, is antici-

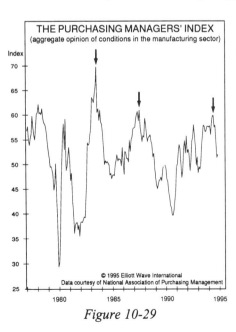

Figure 10-29

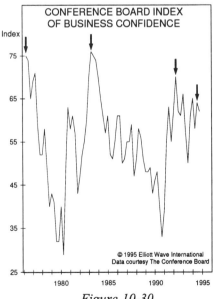

Figure 10-30

pating a slowdown, while the public and most other professionals, who extrapolate linearly and reflect the mood of the moment, see only blue sky ahead.

To summarize the psychological situation, economists, government, the public and most businessmen all express optimism, from moderate to unprecedented, toward the long term trend of the economy. That condition is bearish for stocks, as it leaves little room for an increase in optimism to support further buying. It is also bearish for the economy, as extremes in sentiment usually are.

OUTLOOK

The economy may remain expansive for a few more months, but it will thereafter be vulnerable to a dramatic contraction on the heels of a decline in investment values nearly across the board. Panels of economists have recently asserted that the chances of a recession are one in ten. Given the Elliott Wave outlook, I would say that the chances of a *depression* are nine in ten, so one might say that I agree with the consensus. A recently published book well reflects the breadth of this optimism. *The Great Boom Ahead* is endorsed by three authors, four CEOs, five corporate presidents, three economists/investment planners, one Group Chairman and a professor. The thesis of this book would have been well-timed in 1982; 1993 is another question. The author states flatly, "We are going to scream out of this recession." This statement may yet prove accurate, though not in the way the author intends.

The events and conditions chronicled in this chapter are subtle precursors of a trend change of very large degree, in this case Grand Supercycle. This fact is of paramount importance to understanding why the next contraction will not merely be an expression of what economists call "the business cycle." It will unfold very differently from the typical recessions of the past fifty years. Despite today's favorable reports and the linearly extrapolated bullish outlook by economists, the patterns shown in this chapter indicate that the economy is at the crest of a major cycle.

This fact explains why the current recovery is so weak. Previous business cycle upturns in the 48 years preceding 1990 were reinforced by the larger uptrend. With the longer economic cycle now pointing *down*, the shorter business cycle has been fighting

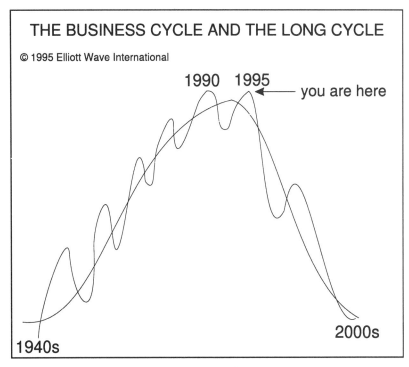

THE BUSINESS CYCLE AND THE LONG CYCLE

© 1995 Elliott Wave International

1990 1995

you are here

1940s

2000s

Figure 10-31

that backdrop for the past four years, thus producing mixed economic figures within a struggling, fragile, selective recovery. Ever since the business cycle turned up in early 1991, economists have repeatedly kindled hopes that a major boom is developing. The true situation is better expressed by the schematic in Figure 10-31, which places the recent expression of the business cycle in the context of the larger picture. If my analysis is correct, the contraction of 1990-1991(3) separated two highs within a major cyclic top in economic activity, and the second of those tops is due quite soon. This year should mark the final high in the stronger measures and a secondary high in the weaker ones, preceding the onset of economic collapse. I also believe that some historians will look back years from now and conclude that the trend toward depression actually began in 1990 in many measures, and that the post-1991 recovery was simply a temporary interruption of the forces of contraction.

Depth of the Contraction

The Elliott Wave Theorist made this unequivocal statement fifteen years ago on July 7, 1980: "After Cycle wave V peaks out, we should see a depression like never before in our history." As opposed to the dual depressions of the 1840s and 1850s and the Great Depression of the 1930s, a Grand Supercycle contraction in economic activity will definitely be deeper and will probably last longer. The last time the stock market ended a bear pattern of Grand Supercycle degree was 1784. The following year saw the beginning of a deflationary depression of corresponding degree that took place throughout the Western world and lasted nearly six years, from 1785 through the first quarter of 1791. Given the magnitude of the expected contraction in the U.S. and the fact that countless charts of economic activity in various foreign countries show the same general profiles as those shown in this chapter, the depression will not be confined to this country, but will be a worldwide affair. In the process, not only will hundreds of moderately sized corporations listed on the stock exchanges declare bankruptcy, but many national and international blue chip companies that are seemingly permanent fixtures, that are decades and even centuries old, will fold under the pressure of the coming depression.

Form of the Contraction

If the stock market outlook described in Chapter 5 is accurate, the next depression will be only the first of two, or perhaps three, deep depressions over the coming century. The first depression will be the result of wave (A) down in the Grand Supercycle (see Figure 5-4). Given the few years it has to unfold according to our time studies in Chapter 5, wave (A) is likely to be a unidirectional slide like that of 1929-1933. Even that relentless contraction enjoyed many months of optimism and hope for recovery that ultimately were dashed. Though less likely, the slide into depression could be interrupted by one or more periods of temporarily improving conditions, as suggested by the schematic in Figure 10-31. If such "bear market rallies" in the economy do occur, they may look like the real thing, but will ultimately give way to the next downward wave to significantly lower depths until the larger trend is exhausted. The first depression should reach its nadir between zero and six years after stocks bottom. If stocks bottom in or near 2003, its effects could last through most of the first decade of the next century.

Wave (C) down, which is ideally due to end in the 2050s, will usher in a second depression and, regardless of its relative depth, greater social unrest. If there is a wave (E) decades later, it will accompany a point of great lethargy in some parts of the world and unrest and revolution in others.

Maintaining Perspective

Keep in mind as events unfold that even as the economy overall begins to sink relentlessly, economists will not call it a depression for quite some time. The record optimism of today will maintain a hold on the majority, dissipating slowly. There will be hope; there will be pep talks; there will be learned commentary. On the way down, economists and government will first deny it, then call it a mild setback, then assure the country every quarter or so that "the recession is ending." Most of the way down, through every passing month, observers will be expecting an almost immediate upturn. Optimism will dissolve only when events force its last remnants out of the collective consciousness. The slide into depression will accompany a long process from optimism through denial, lagging recognition and worry, and finally to panic and despair. Remember this: The consensus will recognize the depression as such only when it finally hits bottom. When the low is reached, pessimism will reign. The majority of investors will project the trend further downward. Economists, who in the aggregate do not recognize depressions until bread lines, bank closings and camps of homeless are on the front page of the newspaper, will be making bearish forecasts. Each will say sternly, in the most erudite prose, "While I would like to be optimistic, I must be realistic, and all the data says that there is no end in sight to our miseries." Psychology will have turned 180 degrees, and the media will reflect and support the widespread fear. Government spokesmen will finally admit the severity of conditions. At that point, not only will it be far too late to take protective measures, it will be time to turn bullish.

The good news is that despite their extreme depths, depressions are relatively swift events compared to the booms that characterize the long periods between them. If you are positioned properly, the downdraft need not hurt you, and the next upswing will, for its duration, return the world to "normal." You can employ the Wave Principle to recognize the turning point a few years hence. If you arrange your business affairs to be properly positioned for the upturn, you can place yourself in the extreme minority of people who will be charting the course of future business empires, and build your fortune.

Chapter 11

THE MONETARY OUTLOOK

The most widely held beliefs with regard to the future course of national monetary affairs are (1) that inflation is the number one economic threat and (2) that the Federal Reserve Board is in full control of the rate of monetary expansion and contraction. The studies in this book challenge those assumptions. The first assumption is a case of fighting the last war. This chapter will demonstrate that the true threat today is not inflation, but deflation. The second assumption is pure mythology. A close study of short term interest rate trends reveals that the Fed is reactive, not proactive. It does not determine interest rate levels; it reacts to changes set by the mechanism truly in charge: the *market*. If central banks could control monetary trends, then why, despite all "efforts," is the Japanese government unable to change the course of its collapsing investment prices and soaring yen, the early byproducts of a raging deflation? If the U.S. Fed could control interest rates, then why did they explode to double digit levels in the 1970s and early 1980s, and why did they soar again in 1994? Does anyone claim these trends are what the monetary authorities truly desired?

If history does not make the Fed's powerlessness obvious, the next trend in rates will. Readers of *Elliott Wave Principle* will recall Charles Collins' words with respect to coming events:

> My thought is that the end of Supercycle V will probably also witness a crisis in all the world's monetary high-jinks and Keynesian tomfoolery of the past four and one-half decades and, since wave V ends a Grand Supercycle, we then had better take to the hurricane shelters until the storm blows over.

By conventional methods, there is no hint of any such crisis on the horizon. Indeed, economists are unanimous in their identification of the slowing money supply expansion and moderated price index gains as the best imaginable news for long term economic growth. Before we describe what the Wave Principle and history suggest about the monetary outlook, let's review *The Elliott Wave Theorist's* position at the last tidal wave juncture, another time when our outlook differed mightily from that offered by conventional approaches.

PERSPECTIVE

1966-1968 was a time of ebullience about long term financial and economic conditions. Interest rates were low and the stock market was registering what stands today as its all-time high in CPI-adjusted terms in the DJIA (1966) and Value Line (1968) indexes. Beginning in the center of this period, in 1967, two years after silver was removed from the country's coinage, the prices of gold and silver began to edge upward for the first time in 33 years. That price movement reflected the beginning of a period of increasing inflation that developed in three upward phases, each more dramatic than the last.

The spiraling inflation, after weathering two setbacks, finally culminated in January 1980 in an atmosphere of long term financial panic. The month before, in December 1979, *The Elliott Wave Theorist* spelled out its expectations for the major sea change that was at hand. *Commodities* (now *Futures)* magazine published EWT's comments in its January 1980 issue. Here is an excerpt:

> The incredible conjunction of "fives" in different markets [gold, silver, interest rates, bonds, and commodities] all seem to point to the same conclusion: *The world is about to begin a phase of general disinflation* [i.e., decelerating inflation]. As I see it, a pattern of several disinflationary years leading to a deflationary trend later on would be a perfect scenario for the Elliott outlook for stocks. A gradual disinflation would create an optimistic mood in the country and lead to the conclusion that we may have finally licked the inflation problem. This sentiment would support a bull market in stocks for several years until the snowballing forces of deflation began to take over. At that point, a major deflationary crash would be impossible to avert, and the Grand Supercycle correction would be underway.

The inflationary trend that had accelerated for a Fibonacci 13 years ended abruptly that very month. Indeed, the above paragraph spelled out, just weeks before the reversal of trend, the experience of the last fifteen years.

The onset of the new trend was as exciting as the termination of the old one. The 1980 peak was followed by a brief two-year period of extremely rapid disinflation that shocked the markets. From a peak of $850/oz. in January 1980, gold collapsed to $296.75 (basis London fix) in June 1982. From its long time resistance area just above 1000, the Dow fell back to 777 in August 1982, reaching its lowest real value since World War II. The bond market was scraping bottom, having been ravaged by both the inflationary period, which stoked fears of ever-rising interest rates, and the recessions of 1980 to 1982, which kindled default worries. The next monetary event appeared to be anyone's guess. The most popular competing opinions were (1) that inflation would accelerate into hyperinflation, and (2) that deflation and economic contraction would bring about financial collapse. These opinions were so popular that they were called "The Great Debate" at financial conferences.

In contrast to the two prevailing opinions, the September 13, 1982 issue of *The Elliott Wave Theorist* offered ten points supporting the super bullish forecast for the Dow to soar 3000 points to 3885. (For details, see Appendix A of *Elliott Wave Principle*.) Two of those points pertained to the expected monetary environment:

> — Fits the idea that the Kondratieff cycle plateau has just begun, [supporting] a period of economic stability and soaring stock prices. Parallel with late 1921.
> — Celebrates the end of the inflationary era [and] accompanies a stable reflation.

Specifically, then, *The Elliott Wave Theorist* forecasted a mild *reflation* relative to the crunch of 1980-1982 that would occur within the longer term trend of *disinflation*. Monetary stability was the last thing on most people's forecast list. Yet, the period of stability and reflation began right then. That the Wave Principle could be applied to recognize the onset of such a period was of immense value to investors, particularly in the stock and bond markets, which began historic advances.

Four months later, in January 1983, *The Elliott Wave Theorist* added to its case as follows: "Quietly behind the scenes, despite all the return-of-inflation rhetoric, the utility stocks have scored a major breakout, providing [another] strong foundation for the 'continuing disinflation' argument." That November, EWT further bolstered the case that the slackening in the rate of inflation was not just a brief respite, but was of multi-year significance:

> Two years ago, I used the percent change in the PPI to show a massive momentum divergence against new highs in the index in 1980. That lower peak in the rate of change was essentially a "sell signal" on inflation. Since then, the inflation rate has not only declined substantially, but its rate of change has fallen be-

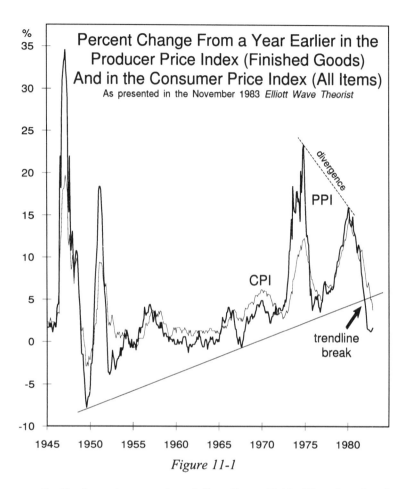

Figure 11-1

neath the long term uptrend line from 1949. That break...does seem to support the claim that there has been a change over the last three years that is larger than just a cyclical disinflation due to recession.

Figure 11-1 shows the divergence (see Chapter 6 for a full discussion of this term) between the peak rate of change in 1974 and that of 1980, indicating a reversal at hand, and the trendline break, confirming the large degree of the reversal. As the long period of disinflation since then has proved, the turn in 1980 was indeed of major degree.

Originally, *The Elliott Wave Theorist* expected the period of disinflation to last as briefly as five years. Circumstances developed to extend the time element, as described in Chapter 4. The disinflationary trend has continued right up to this day. Where do we stand with respect to the next monetary trend change?

The final sentence from the December 1979 analysis quoted at the outset of this chapter should prove to describe the experience of the next event as well as it did the last one. That "a major deflationary crash" now lies dead ahead is the whole point of this book (perhaps following one last brief inflationary scare in coming months). While the timing of the event is once again the least certain aspect of the forecast, the event itself is *highly* probable. As with so many past Elliott Wave forecasts, you are welcome to stop reading now, as the outlook presented those many years ago remains exactly as stated then. The rest of this chapter is simply an elaboration of a long-held opinion.

ANALYSIS

Is a tidal wave turn due in monetary phenomena once again? Before we examine the last two decades' trends in the money supply, credit, prices and markets, it must be understood that the case for a tidal wave trend change in the monetary environment cannot be made solely by an examination of monetary trends or their effects. The question would remain, "What if those trends change tomorrow?" The only evidence that is *predictive* is that pertaining to the Wave Principle. Our forecast, then, relies upon the fact that stocks, gold, commodities and the economy are all in the process of completing major upward Elliott Wave patterns of 13 or 21 years' duration. The only difference in these trends is that stocks and the economy are completing *impulsive* waves, while gold and commodities are completing upward *corrective* patterns. The high probability of a major decline thereafter in all four areas sends a strong one-word message: deflation. The extent of the deflation should be far greater than that of 1980-1982 and not unlike that of 1929-1932. It should break records in many markets, and maybe all markets. The rates of change in money growth, prices, investment markets and debt accumulation have no predictive value apart from this analysis, but are powerfully *compatible* with this outlook, as will now be demonstrated.

Change in the Money Supply

The single most important indicator of inflation is the rate of change in the money supply, as money supply growth is what inflation *is*. Figure 11-2 shows the rate of change in M-2 over this century.

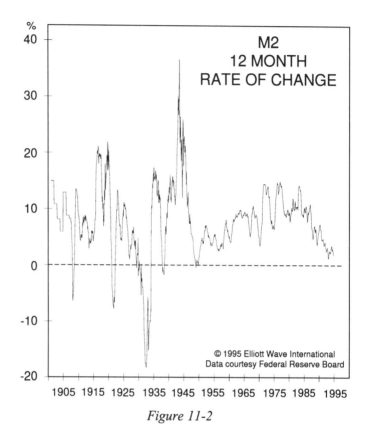

Figure 11-2

The 13-year period from 1970 to 1983 contained three bursts of money supply growth in percentage double digits. Such high rates of change have not been seen since, as disinflation has reigned, exactly as forecast in *The Elliott Wave Theorist*. The persistent drop in the rate of expansion in the money supply since then has had *consequences*. Let's see if we can spot some of them.

Price Trends Reflect Liquidity Flows

Prices for goods overall ebb and flow with both the level of production and the money supply, the latter being the greater influence. How have prices behaved? Figure 11-3 shows an index of prices for industrial materials; Figure 11-4 shows the GDP deflator, a price index used to adjust the Gross Domestic Product for changes in the prices of a broad array of goods and services included in GDP; Fig-

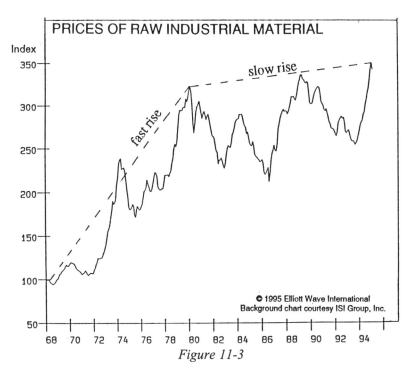

Figure 11-3

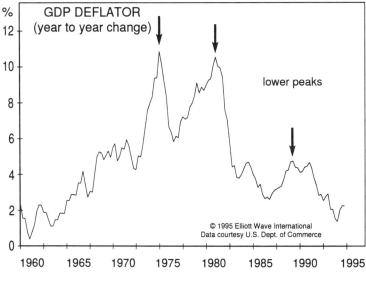

Figure 11-4

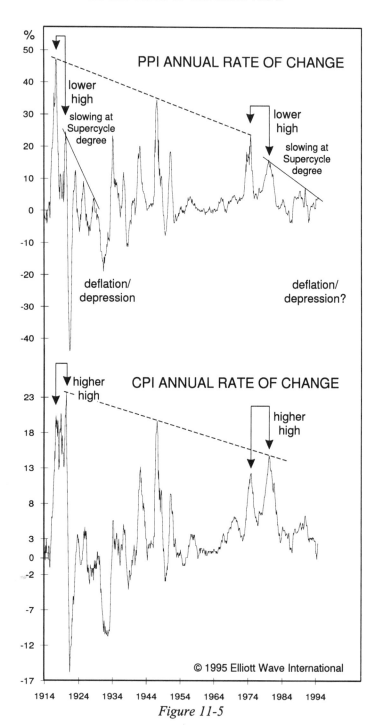

Figure 11-5

ure 11-5 shows the rate of change in the Producer Price Index and the Consumer Price index updated to the present. These three graphs show that the lesser rate of money supply growth since the early 1980s has slowed the trend of rising prices. These charts reveal that each burst of reflationary pressure since 1982 has been *less intense*. Lessening intensity is a classic precursor to trend change, as discussed in Chapter 6.

A study of Figure 11-5 is particularly instructive in revealing that the same action in the rate of price change in the PPI that occurred from 1917 to 1929 has occurred from 1974 to the present. Both periods began at a peak rate of change for the PPI. After a decline, the rate returned to a lower peak at the same time that the rate of change on the CPI reached a higher peak. (The difference came about because retailers, having "learned" what happened last time, adjusted their prices rapidly upward. That response was not only inappropriate, but deflationary as well.) The divergence between the two measures ushered in a period of slackening in the upside rate of change of prices, which in the last few years of both periods fluctuated around the zero line. The slowing of rise in the first period ended in 1929 and rapidly gave way to deflation and depression. Although precise timing is not necessarily implied, the rate of change indicator stands today exactly where it did in 1929. Once again, the money supply and prices are poised for a trend reversal of at least Supercycle degree.

Now for one last crucial point. Not only is it true that uptrends in the stock market, monetary phenomena and the economy slow before they reverse, but the degree of the slowing reflects the degree of the coming reversal. Is it not then potentially of great importance that the upside rate of change achieved in 1974/1980 is less than those achieved in 1947 and 1917/1920? The dashed lines in Figure 11-5 indicate a slowing of the peak rates of price change over this entire century. This long term slowing implies a trend reversal not just of Supercycle degree, then, but of Grand Supercycle degree.

Investment Markets Reflect Liquidity Flows

This lessening rate of growth in the money supply has had consequences not only for the prices of industrial and consumer *goods*, but for the prices of *investments* as well. Review Figure 6-3 and recall that in the stock market, each advance following the 1983 kickoff generated a *lesser upside momentum*. Starting in 1980 when the disinflation began, each peak in gold (and silver as well) was *lower* than the previous peak. Like the prices for goods, then, the prices for investment markets, both physical and paper, subtly reveal the effects of the lessening infusions of liquidity, which ultimately drives the markets.

Debt/Credit Trends

Now let's examine Figures 11-6 through 11-12, which reflect trends in the *cause* of inflation and deflation in a debt-based (as opposed to currency-based) economy: trends in the creation of credit, and its inverse, the assumption of debt, which are at root psychological phenomena. The first four graphs reveal that the aggregate trends shown in the three ensuing graphs are not due to one sector of debt growth but are revealed by all sorts of measures of consumer and commercial debt. These figures present the composite picture of the great financial and economic tidal wave that began cresting in the 1986 to 1990 period and speak eloquently of the magnitude of the change in trend of (and attitude toward) debt that has taken place since.

The real estate decline, the junk bond collapse, the sluggish economy, meandering aggregate investment market prices, and all the rest are in great part simply manifestations of the underlying change in trend *from the expansion of debt/credit to its unwinding*. The change in attitude toward debt has progressed so far that it is on the verge of forcing a change from disinflation to deflation that will ultimately impact all markets, all prices, all debtors, and ultimately all creditors as well.

The Message From the Indicators

The charts discussed in this chapter and others show that over the past thirteen years, the rate of money supply growth has steadily fallen to zero, the rate of price increases for goods has slowed to near zero, the upside rates of change in the aggregate investment markets have fallen to near zero, and the rate of debt increase and the level of debt service peaked in 1986-1990. Total debt is still expanding, but at an ever-slower rate.

The charts of the money supply, goods prices, investment markets and debt/credit trends together convey a message about the reflation that began in 1982: it is becoming exhausted. The stock market's reaction to a temporary *deflation* in 1987, moreover, was

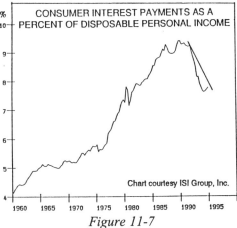

Figure 11-7

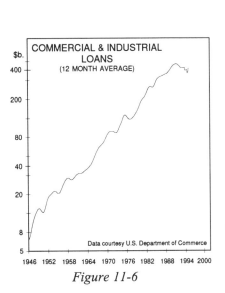

Figure 11-6

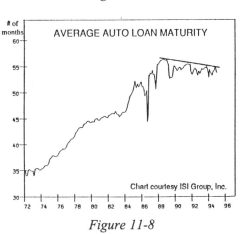

Figure 11-8

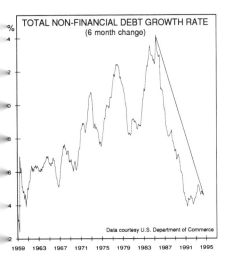

Figure 11-9

Figure 11-10

Figure 11-11

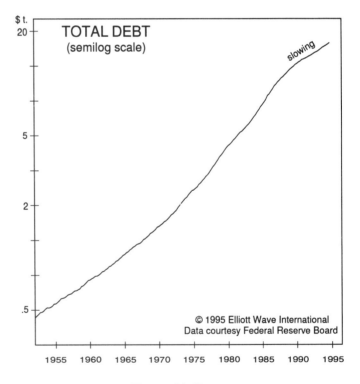

Figure 11-12

the *most violent yet*. The economy's reaction in 1990-1991 was the *most severe yet*. While each new reflationary push has been weaker and weaker, these responses indicate that each new disinflationary setback has been wielding increasing destructive power. In the past year and a half, stocks, gold, the money supply and goods prices have all been rising at their *slowest pace yet* within Cycle wave V. In the meantime, bonds and bills in recent months have been recovering only partially in a new bear market. These weak advances reflect the last gasp of the trend toward increasing liquidity.

Substantial evidence points to the conclusion that the re-liquefaction of the markets and the economy that began thirteen years ago, as well as the disinflationary trend that began fifteen years ago, are terminating. The new forces of deflation have wrestled the old forces of inflation nearly to a standstill. What's more, all these trends are slowing on the same scale that they did in the late 1920s, leading up to the start of the Great Depression. The 1980s are *abnormal* monetary times when compared to the rest of the post-WWII environment; they are *normal* times if they are a transition phase between inflationary and deflationary trends. If the overall analysis presented in this book is correct, deflation will win this match. Evidence of that victory will be announced by a downturn in the line reflecting total debt, shown in Figure 11-12.

Creditor and Debtor Psychology

Not only the widespread *assumption* of debt, but its *issuance* as well, are consequences of an overly optimistic mood. Those who lend are confident they will be paid back, just as those who borrow in good conscience are confident they will be able to service and pay back their debts. On both sides, that attitude reflects a belief that the economy will remain strong enough to complete the transaction.

Today, consumers, businesses and government express this mood in many ways. For instance, for the first time ever, sellers are willing to lend and consumers are willing to borrow nearly half the equity in a home and 94% of the value of a new car, paying interest for the privilege, as shown in Figures 11-13 and 11-14. Household debt, which had been forever below 70% of annual disposable personal income until 1985, has soared in the last ten years to reach 93%, as shown in Figure 11-15. The Federal National Mortgage Association has been so aggressive in its lending policies that it has purchased or securitized one *trillion* dollars worth of mortgages for low- and middle-income families *just since 1990*. That is twice the

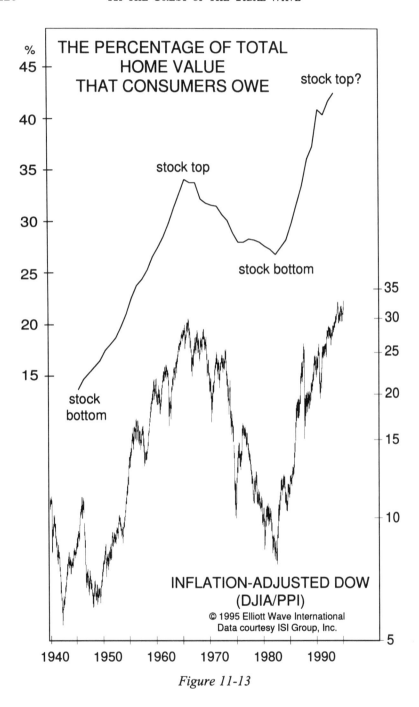

Figure 11-13

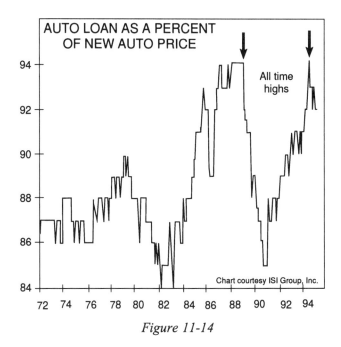

Figure 11-14

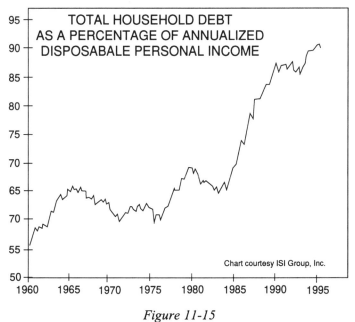

Figure 11-15

amount lent in its previous five decades of existence, which means that its lending rate over the past five years has been running at *twenty times* its previous historical average. This government-guaranteed gift to the construction and real estate sales industries will end abruptly when home owners begin to default. Investors currently rate any such risk as absolutely nonexistent. As proof, FNMA stock is up nearly 1000% in 7½ years and currently pushing toward yet another all-time high. The creditors, debtors and investors in all these transactions are obviously complacent to a record degree with respect to the job security of the debtors.

The link of debt/credit growth to confidence is clarified by the coincidence of peaks and valleys in the general percentage of home equity with major turns in the stock market, as shown in Figure 11-13. Stock buying is certainly a measure of confidence in future economic activity, and the coincident trend in debt shows that *rates of borrowing and lending are a measure of this same confidence.* If the wave structure and valuation in the stock market have a message, it is that confidence is at a record high. The fact that borrowing of all kinds around the world is at an all-time record in the history of man supports the Elliott Wave case that the top in stocks is of Grand Supercycle degree. When that trend reverses, the contraction will set new records as well.

Professional Psychology Toward Inflation and Deflation

The first thing to note with respect to professional sentiment is that forecasts for deflation are nonexistent. In 1991, a spokesman for a famous think tank stated that the chances for deflation were "1 in 10,000." Some variation of that opinion is held by all mainstream economists.

The second point to note is that observers today, almost to a man, fear inflation the most and believe that the recent signs of low or nonexistent inflation are *bullish*. Indeed, countless times in the media, analysts have called the low inflation rate of the past two years "the best of all possible worlds" for investments and the economy. Actually, the trend toward deflation carries precisely the *opposite* of a bullish message, and that message will be delivered as soon as the coming deflation continues past the point normally seen in a moderate business cycle.

One tribute to the extent of professional and public optimism over "the containment of inflation," and thus lower interest rates and continued economic expansion, is a recent innovative offer from

$1t. in S&L and finance company loans to business, is *$17.1 trillion*. This total does not include mob loans, loan shark loans, money owed to bookies, drug dealers, friends and family, unfunded Social Security obligations (which total $2.8t. to $10t., depending upon one's definitions), or Federal deposit insurance obligations to banks, S&Ls and credit unions (which total another $2.8t.). These latter items add between $6t. and $14t. to the total debt. This amount might be offset somewhat by the value of tax receipts that will be available to meet at least some of the government's insurance obligations, so we might very conservatively estimate the total debt at approximately **$20 trillion**. This amount compares to the total value of privately held U.S. real estate, which stands at $12.9 trillion, and the total value of U.S. equities, which stands at $6.1 trillion, for *a total value of privately held non-debt based investment assets of* **$19 trillion**, approximately the same figure. To put the value of the total debt in perspective, to pay it off tomorrow would require the sale, *at today's high prices*, of the entire land mass of the fifty United States and its territories and all publicly owned U.S. companies in existence (after which would still be owed a trifling trillion dollars). The problem with even contemplating that fanciful solution is that the debtors do not own much in the way of those assets. We can say that in essence, the country's debtors have borrowed, and to a great degree consumed, the entire investment value of the United States of America.

The growing level of debt and its decreasing quality are not limited to U.S. issues, either; it is a worldwide phenomenon. The richest country per capita in the world, Japan, in the late 1980s went as far as to develop "two generation" mortgages of fifty years' duration, ultimately to be paid off by the children of the borrower. The World Bank has reached so far down the creditworthiness scale in issuing its loans that it must have achieved an unbreachable low. Although the bank had seldom made loans of less than $5 million before, two years ago it began lending $50 and less to the world's poor individuals, none of whom have any collateral. It is as if the bank is *trying* to destroy money. In 1993, it lent $18 billion in this fashion, and in 1994 $16 billion, mostly of U.S. taxpayers' money. Would you want to hold these IOUs as an investment? The World Bank does. With poor individuals of the Third World now in hock, is there anyone left unmortgaged? We cannot even exclude the Roman Catholic Church. The Vatican has amassed a multi-billion dollar debt and continuously operates at a deficit that is becoming acute. Is Mother Theresa next?

The Coming Debt/Credit Contraction

If there is one fundamental event that will result from a major bear market in social mood, it is a collapse in the bloated debt structure, a devastating event that not one citizen in ten thousand knows is coming. All this debt will have to be liquidated, and the process is unlikely to be serene.

The only thing holding today's debt pyramid together is *confidence*, one of those amorphous mental states suited to analysis under the Wave Principle. It is confidence that creates credit, and thus a kind of fictional money that is not a real asset but the promise to pay a real asset, which often means the promise to produce a real asset that at present does not exist. Owed money is as valuable as actual assets if in the aggregate, creditors' mental processes say it is valuable, and only then. If their opinion on that point changes, that form of money is no longer on an equal footing with real assets. The danger to a monetary system comes when the outstanding credit far outstrips the pool of assets and the productive capacity that back it up. That is when a real deflationary crisis, a severe drop in the total money supply caused by a collapse in the portion that is credit (which in our economy is most of it), can occur. It will *actually* occur when the confidence that supports it erodes and then dissolves. The timing of that event is the province of market analysis.

The coming psychological change among the populace from an expansionary mood to a mood of retrenchment will initially cause an actual net debt retirement to take place. The retirement of debt will cause a contraction in the money supply, which is deflation. A reduction in the volume of outstanding credit will remove purchasing power from the financial system, so investors and consumers will reduce purchases. Sellers will react by lowering prices, first in investment markets, then in the market for goods, services and labor. As people begin to sense that prices are declining, they will defer purchases even longer, waiting for even lower prices. The postponement of purchases will induce sellers to lower prices further, which will reinforce decisions to postpone purchases. The spiraling forces of falling prices and curtailed spending will cause precarious businesses to fold. Those failures will create a further contraction in business (as well as more unpaid debts), and cause otherwise marginally successful businesses to follow suit.

As the money supply and economy contract, all classes of debtors and creditors will be affected. Many individuals, who in the aggregate owe a record amount of money on credit cards and installment plans and who have taken out second mortgages on their homes to buy new cars, will have to sell assets to pay off debt. Variable mortgage payments and credit card interest rates will rise, devouring a greater percentage of income. Many corporations, some of whom have billions of dollars of debt outstanding, will experience a drop in profits, and will have to sell assets to pay interest. As the trend continues, local, state, federal and foreign governments will experience a drop in tax receipts, and will have to curtail spending.

Events associated with a debt collapse will provide continual justification for creditors to call in loans. Banks will call in houses, property and other collateral. As debtors sell everything they *can* to raise cash in a mad rush to stay solvent, unpaid creditors will sell everything they *must* to make up for the shortfall due to defaults. Raising cash by all parties will require the selling of stocks, real estate, commodities and bonds. The problem with selling assets is that *net selling reduces the overall value of the assets*. Thus, while the total value of U.S. property and public companies may be $19 trillion today, this very value will be shrinking relentlessly as the deflationary process unfolds. In the deflation of the 1930s, stocks, real estate and commodities fell 90% in value, and questionable bonds fell 20% to 50%. Many stocks went to zero, and the companies were never heard from again. Many parcels of land were placed on the auction block. Many bonds went to zero as their issuers defaulted. The Elliott Wave outlook calls for a decline in asset values of at least that magnitude. At the end of the process, the current 1:1 ratio between total debt and real assets could change to 10:1 or worse.

As the plight of debtors worsens, the selling of bonds based upon fear of default will begin to reinforce the selling being done for cash-raising purposes. This part of the spiral will be of devastating importance because the world's wealth, and thus its presumed purchasing power, is tied up more in IOUs today than at any time in history. As the value of IOUs falls, the value of bond investors' portfolios will fall, and their wealth will disappear. Disappearing wealth is disappearing money. This will not be money "withdrawn," but money *evaporating*. Evaporating money threatens the value of the remaining IOUs, as it is money that services them and money that is ultimately required to pay them off. That threat will cause a further fall in the value of IOUs. The monetary result will be more deflation. Thus, the initial debt-contraction psychology of retrenchment will be reinforced with every downtick in prices and every notch downward in economic activity. The spiraling effect of these forces will destroy what many creditors today believe are their stores of value.

Eventually, selling assets will prove fruitless for most debtors. Many individuals will default as they turn their energies away from maintaining their credit ratings and toward obtaining the basic necessities of life. The weakest corporate sectors, led by issuers of junk bonds, will default. The next weakest sectors will be forced to pay huge rates to borrow just to compensate for the risk that the investor will assume he is taking with his principal. As each newly weak sector falls, thereby proving such fears correct, the rate rise will extend to more and more issues that were previously highly regarded but whose prices will be falling because of the need to raise cash and whose safety ratings will be falling because of the contracting economy. Every strong issuer will become a victim of the weak. Banks under such conditions will be foundering in a sea of red ink as borrowers default and their collateral slides in value. When the trend becomes global, Eastern European countries, despite the current euphoria over their future, will default on their loans; Russia will default on its loans; Central and South American countries will default on their loans; the Third World will default on its loans. Many First World governments will default on their guarantees to support Third World debt, then on their promises to bank depositors, retirees, the ill, the poor, and finally on their direct obligations to bondholders. The few remaining financially strong governments will be left holding the nearly worthless debt of weak ones. By the end of the crisis, the total issue value of bonds that have gone to zero could well be substantially more than the value of those that have not. Creditors will lose much of their principal, and the more incautious among them will go bankrupt.

The Role of Debt/Credit in Deflation and Depression

Mechanics of mood reinforcement such as those described above propel economic expansions as well as contractions, inflations as well as deflations. The dynamic is less recognized in expansions because, due to their relative longevity, people view them as normal. That is why economists sometimes refer to depressions as "spirals," but do not so refer to booms. Yet they are both processes involving mood and a reinforcing feedback loop of result and new cause. Expansions begin with a psychological change that produces initial

positive results, which then feed the psychology anew. This reinforcement continues until the participants are exhausted. Booms
last longer because optimism is fed by slowly rising emotions involving hope and greed, which, because they are tempered by caution,
can reach maximum intensity only over a long period of time and
fulfillment only after prolonged effort. Busts are swifter because
pessimism is fed by fast-flaming emotions such as fear and anger,
which can be realized in a flash of destructive action. According to
our Elliott Wave clock, the long, spiraling, self-reinforcing expansion of the past two centuries has finally slowed enough to reach a
point of stasis, and from a point of stasis, it can only reverse the
process and start a spiral in the other direction.

The late A. Hamilton Bolton was well aware of the risks associated with excessive credit. His studies of how credit relates to
depressions were summarized in a personal letter to Charles Collins
in 1957, as follows:

> In reading a history of major depressions in the U.S. from
> 1830 on, I was impressed with the following:
> (a) All were set off by a deflation of excess credit. This was the
> one factor in common.
> (b) Sometimes the excess-of-credit situation seemed to last
> years before the bubble broke.
> (c) Some outside event, such as a major failure, brought the
> thing to a head, but the signs were visible many months, and in
> some cases years, in advance.
> (d) None was ever quite like the last, so that the public was
> always fooled thereby.
> (e) Some panics occurred under great government surpluses
> of revenue (1837, for instance) and some under great government
> deficits.
> (f) Credit is credit, whether non-self-liquidating or self-liqui-
> dating.*
> (g) Deflation of non-self-liquidating credit usually produces
> the greater slumps.
> *[This term may mean collateralized, but he gives no definition.]

Major deflations are ultimately extremely destructive, and the
next one should be no exception. That we are in the midst (and apparently near the end) of the greatest debt buildup in world history
suggests that the resulting deflation and depression will be correspondingly severe. Against that backdrop, the Elliott Wave outlook
for the deepest depression in two centuries hardly appears radical.

OUTLOOK

The brief deflationary crunch of 1919-1921 was an advance warning of what the 1930s would bring after an intervening paper asset boom. In the same way, the deflationary crunch of 1980-1982 was an advance warning of what the next ten years will bring now that the intervening paper asset boom is ending. From the first half of 1980 to the summer of 1982, a dramatic decline occurred in all three major markets: stocks, bonds and gold. As the previously *strong* markets (gold and silver) fell sharply in the initial declines of their new bear trends, the previously *weak* markets (stocks and bonds) plunged to final bottoms in their old bear trends. This across-the-board tumble was a foreshadowing of the coming difficulty, as the same phenomenon is scheduled to recur, but more severely. This time, the previously *strong* markets (stocks and bonds) will initiate Grand Supercycle bear markets, while the previously *weak* markets (precious metals) will plunge to final bottoms in their old bear trends.

As long as gold remains below the peak of wave Ⓒ at $502.30, as long as breadth and the rates of change in the broadest stock market indexes do not indicate an upside acceleration (see Chapter 6), and as long as commodity indexes remain below their 1981 highs, the markets will continue to confirm a slowing of the long term upside momentum in the reflationary trend. When the uptrend ceases, a crushing bout of deflation will be unavoidable. As explained in Chapter 10, a reversal in the long term uptrend in the stock market will be the sign that the confidence bubble has burst. Proof that deflation and depression are the bond market's true concerns will be given when the PPI and the CPI begin falling, yet bonds are unable to exceed their previous highs.

While most prices will be falling during the coming deflation, there might be a few items that enjoy rising prices. However, any price rises are likely to be the product of temporary and selective forces. Contrary to the popular idea that any rising prices indicate "inflation" or are "inflationary," rising prices, which when broadly based can reflect underlying inflation, actually contribute to the forces of deflation by diminishing the purchasing power of the consumer.

Timing the End of the Deflation

Elliott's guideline of alternation recognizes that markets alternate their patterns. This is particularly true of corrective waves

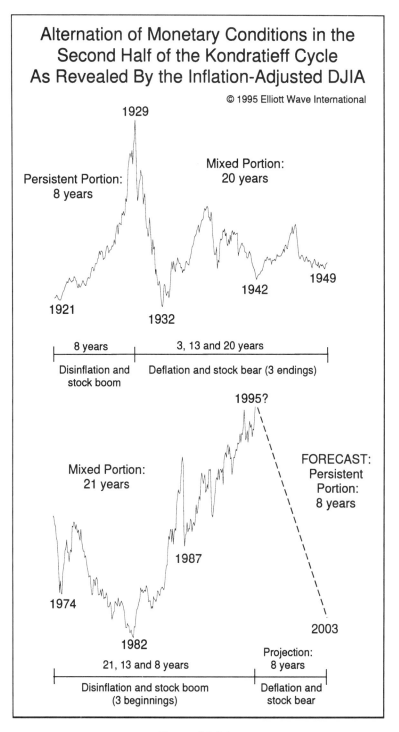

Figure 11-16

two and four, as the labels in so many charts in Chapter 2 commu-
nicate. The guideline is also of general utility and may apply to the
question of how long the coming deflation may last.

In the previous inflation-deflation cycle, the inflationary boom
(as signaled by stock prices) began in 1896 (see Appendix B) and
reached its peak rate of change (as measured by the PPI) in 1919. It
was 25 years after its beginning, in 1921, that the stock market
began rising in a disinflationary boom that lasted 8 years.

The current cycle began the same way, as the inflationary boom
(as signaled by CPI-adjusted stock prices) began in 1949 and reached
its peak rate of change in 1974. It was 25 years after the cycle's
beginning, in 1974, that the stock market began rising. Rather than
lead to 8 years of disinflation, however, 1974 was followed, after a
pause, by continued high inflation. This difference has affected the
shape of the disinflationary and deflationary phases, but not
randomly.

The disinflationary stock market boom that began in 1921 was
persistent. It lasted **8** years, from 1921 to 1929. The deflation that
followed was *mixed*. It had three endings: one after **3** years, in 1932,
one after **13** years, in 1942, and one after 20 (just shy of a Fibonacci
21) years, in 1949. This time, it is the disinflationary stock market
boom that has been mixed. It had two major beginnings and one
resumption, for a total of three lows: 1974 (when the stock market
bottomed and the rate of PPI inflation peaked), 1982 (when the inflation-adjusted Dow bottomed and inflation died), and 1987. If the
bull market ends in 1995, it will have lasted **21, 13** and **8** years from
those starting points, similarly to the way the deflationary portion
of the last cycle lasted **3, 13** and **20** years to its ending points. The
deflation was the mixed portion of the cycle last time, so the disinflation has been the mixed portion this time, reflecting Elliott's
guideline of alternation. The disinflation was the persistent portion
of the cycle last time, so *the deflation should be the persistent portion this time*, as depicted in Figure 11-16. If the duration of the
entire process remains comparable, the deflation will last **8** years,
balancing the 8-year boom of the 1920s. Thus, it should carry into
the year **2003**. While that year should mark the deflationary low in
prices for financial assets, economic depression could easily last a
few years beyond that time, as discussed in Chapter 10.

Notice also that if the reversal occurs in 1995, a major stock
market turning point will have subdivided both inflation-deflation
cycles at the .618 point if the current cycle ends in 2003. The **53-**

year period from 1896 to 1949 was divided by the major top of 1929 into periods of **33** and **20** years. A **54**-year period from 1949 to 2003 will be divided by the major low of 1982 into periods of **33** and **21** years. 3, 8, 21, 34 and 55, of course, are all Fibonacci numbers.

The Outlook for the Dollar

The falling value of the U.S. dollar since 1933 has reflected the expansion of credit that has fueled Supercycle wave (V). The coming contraction in credit will cause a rise in the value of all dollars that are not destroyed in the process. How will this happen? When a corporation's junk bonds are declared worthless, when a government's bonds drop in value, when a stock portfolio falls, when real estate becomes illiquid, dollar-based purchasing power is rapidly removed from the system. Classically, when the stock of any item is depleted, the value of the remaining supply rises. The *demand* for dollars will increase, as debtors facing insolvency will sell anything and everything, even strong assets, at fire sale prices to raise cash to keep from going bankrupt. At the same time, the *supply* of dollars will decrease, as creditors stressed by nonpayment from debtors and falling values for their own real assets will constrict their lending. This two-sided dynamic will be reinforced by creditors' demands for higher interest rates, which will accelerate the need for dollars on the part of debtors. Higher rates will also depress bond prices, causing a further shrinking of the money supply. These forces will propel higher the value of all dollars that are in a form that cannot face immediate or direct default, such as currency and perhaps Eurodollars (short term dollar-denominated debt of European companies and governments) issued by strong debtors. Dollar-based debt that is initially *believed* to be equally safe (such as Treasury bills and notes) may (but may not) rise in value concurrently for a time as part of a "flight to quality" until it, too, is perceived or understood to be too risky to hold.

A corollary of deflation, then, will be a *soaring value for the U.S. dollar*, contrary to virtually all current expectations. Today the persistently climbing Japanese yen appears as a complete mystery to currency watchers, but the reason for the rise is simply that the Japanese economy is deflating. It has been deflating since the start of 1990. Japan is the only major industrial country experiencing deflation, so their currency is climbing against all others. When the U.S. financial system begins to deflate, most countries around the world will join in the process, so currency trends will be far more chaotic than they are today. Traders will jump from one currency to another, trying to figure out which trend is real, when in fact by the end of the process, most major currencies will have risen in value relative to things. Which one ultimately rises the most is anyone's guess.

Figure 11-17 shows that the U.S. dollar is nearing the end of a five wave decline from the early days of this century. An upward correction of Supercycle degree, the largest since the start of the decline, is due to begin when wave V ends. It will be a temporary and only partial recovery, but a strong one. The 1929-1932 period provides a very minor precedent for this development. Locate in Figure 11-17 the brief jump in the dollar at that time, and you will see how swiftly the trend can appear and then reverse. The rally of

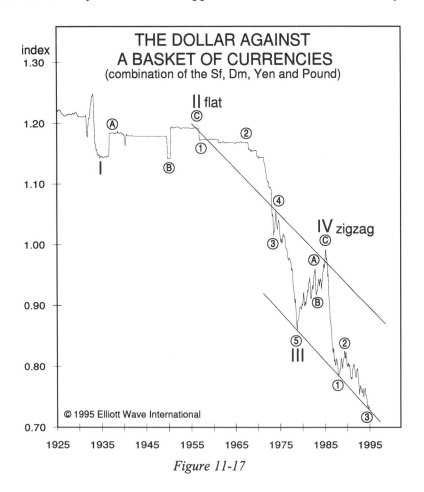

Figure 11-17

that time occurred under conditions similar to those forecasted by the current wave counts for stocks, gold and commodities, but that trend change was of one smaller degree than the one we currently face.

Is the potential for a huge rise in the dollar bullish for stocks, bonds and the economy, as conventional wisdom would hold? An article from the March 13, 1995 *Wall Street Journal* assures us that the converse is true, as "history shows that a wheezing dollar is sometimes followed by a sickly stock market." The truth is that there is little correlation, and if there is any at all, it is quite the opposite. During powerfully inflationary times such as the 1970s, the stock market is typically weak. Yet stocks have been rising most of the time since the 'teens, when the dollar began its relentless slide of 90%-95%, as measured against gold, goods and stable foreign currencies. Moreover, in 1929-1932, as the DJIA underwent its biggest collapse, the dollar soared. As usual, the conventional wisdom is based on a falsehood accepted as an unassailable truism. The falling dollar has not been bearish for stocks as so many contend; it has in fact been a secondary consequence of the relentlessly expanding liquidity bubble in the United States. Credit expansion is a major reason why stocks have kept rising and the dollar has kept falling. When the bubble begins to deflate, the investment markets will go down and the dollar will start up. So when stocks begin to fall and commentators talk about how bullish the rising dollar is, do not believe it.

While holding "safe" dollars could prove immensely profitable during the deflation, attempting to dispose of them at the right time could prove tricky at the extreme in the deflationary crisis, so choose your investment vehicles carefully. Disposing of those dollars will be imperative, however, because the coming rise will almost certainly be the final rebound in the value of the dollar, as discussed after the next section.

Can Deflation Be Stopped or Avoided?

Despite a nearly unanimous opinion to the contrary, government cannot impose inflation to solve the deflation threat. Deflation in a credit economy results from a *collective state of mind*. It is not a mechanical phenomenon, as it is to a far greater degree in currency based economies. This is particularly true in today's economy in the U.S. While the Fed and the government might have had some power to control interest rates temporarily in the past, they have created and fostered so much debt that they no longer control the market. The power to determine interest rates is entirely in the hands of *creditors* in what is now a multi-trillion dollar debt market. Because *their* collective state of mind is susceptible to a loss of confidence in government paper, the Fed has no choice but to tailor its actions to please them. Soon, the government will have to plead for bond owners' confidence as well, and act to keep it. Although many inflationists continue to claim that "all the government has to do is fire up the printing press," it simply cannot be done without destroying the bond market. If the government and the Fed were to collude in an attempt to inflate the money supply, that very act would panic bond investors, who would sell. Any attempted inflation would be more than offset by the disappearance of purchasing power that is currently being held in the form of bonds, notes and bills. Whatever liquidity the government tries to add to the system will come at the cost of falling prices for debt instruments, resulting in a net destruction of presumed wealth. The government, then, *cannot* combat deflation, which will run its course regardless of actions taken or not taken.

To be sure, *the government may eventually choose to inflate the currency and abandon the bond market*, but if history is a guide, that decision will not come when times are comfortable. It will come years from now, when the markets have fallen a long way, deflation and depression are raging, and a political response is demanded. At the ultimate point of crisis, the government will have used up all available funds, and at the same time, the sources that have satisfied its demand for loans in the past will refuse to lend. At that point, the government *de facto* will have gone broke. As discussed in more detail in Chapter 12, it will have little recourse but (1) to cancel the national debt and return to a system of sound money, or (2) to order the Treasury to print the currency it needs to fulfill its promises, launching a runaway inflation. The great irony is that paper money printing cannot result in inflation until the deflation is over, and at that point, it is not needed.

Possible Hyperinflation After the Deflation

As far back as its first publication year in 1979, *The Elliott Wave Theorist* aggressively argued against the immediate return of accelerating inflation, but nevertheless addressed the question of when that return might come. As the December 9, 1979 issue stated, "The period *after the market crash* will be the most vulnerable in terms of the potential for hyperinflation." That remains my opinion today.

The Federal Reserve System was set up with the passage of the Federal Reserve Act in December 1913. That is approximately when the value of the U.S. dollar began its amazing slide that according to the American Institute for Economic Research has since erased well over 90% of its purchasing power. In 1965, the U.S. changed the basis of its coinage from silver to base metal, and in August 1971, the Federal government ceased paying gold, even to foreigners, in exchange for dollars. The trend in this Grand Supercycle bear market, then, has been toward dollar destruction. Whether that destruction will become total or be halted at some point is little more than a guess. However, there are some signs that readers of this volume might wish to look for in coming to a conclusion later about this question.

The history of politically managed paper currencies suggests little chance of avoiding the ultimate destruction of the dollar. There are countless examples of currency hyperinflation, so it would be prudent to be aware of what political forces typically impact a currency following several years of severe deflation. Because deflation devastates financial markets and the economy, the populace often demands a solution. One option is to return to a state of fiscal stability based upon a system of sound money, i.e., gold. Indeed, that decision is recurrently forced upon human beings regardless of their efforts to avoid it. If that path is not *chosen*, however, the threat of hyperinflation will loom large. If politicians decide to "get the country moving again" via currency inflation, the monetary trend will not simply reverse, but reverse dramatically.

It would take a tremendous amount of knowledge, short-run sacrifice and moral courage to allow a deflationary depression to dissipate naturally. Unfortunately, given the choice between honest default ("Sorry, we can't pay, we're bankrupt") and dishonest inflation, government typically chooses the latter, thus ultimately bankrupting virtually all citizens rather than hurt a comparatively few bondholders. The Treasury and the Federal Reserve may decide to cooperate with politicians who vow to "restore liquidity to the system" by shipping truckloads of currency to banks to satisfy the demands of depositors and bondholders. Once an "emergency" currency inflation has begun, every incentive will exist over the ensuing years for politicians to continue inflating.

The mechanism for a runaway inflation is already in place, in the form of the Monetary Control Act, which gives the U.S. government the power to monetize any institution's debt. The implications of this power are staggering. In fact, the very existence of the Act itself virtually insures that it will be implemented. It is crucial to understand, though, that the government cannot *prevent* bankruptcy. All it can do is transfer the *cost* of bankruptcies from the investors in those businesses *to all people who are holding assets denominated in dollars*. From welfare to the FDIC to the minimum wage, it is extremely difficult to name a single government program designed to help people that has failed to bring about precisely the opposite result of what was intended. The Monetary Control Act is no exception; it will bring about monetary chaos. The initial response of the bond market to monetization might be positive, but any rally would be short-lived, lasting only until it becomes understood that the printing presses will not stop rolling. Currency inflation in a credit-poor economy has *never* been restrained. If it merely begins, it will assuredly lead to hyperinflation. The ultimate result will be the destruction of any value remaining in bonds and the wipe-out of all dollar-denominated paper assets. Thus, while many bonds will become worthless first, there is a fairly good chance that the dollar itself will become worthless thereafter. With the potential duration of the Grand Supercycle bear market as long as a century, however, it may be a long time before this final monetary event takes place or is concluded.

Investors today face the terrible task of dealing with the deflation of the biggest credit bubble in world history, which is quite enough to be concerned about for the time being. Perhaps the analysis in this chapter will give you an overall view of the tropical forest as it is hit by the hurricane. Most people will be in the middle of it, frantically dodging the falling trees.

Chapter 12

HIGH GRADE BONDS

The first five pages of this section are for those who are interested in some of the details of previous forecasts. Others may skip to the section entitled **ANALYSIS**.

PERSPECTIVE
The Tidal Wave Bottom in Bond Prices

From 1977 to March 24, 1980, short term interest rates rose in a five-wave structure that was contained in a parallel channel, as shown in Figure 12-2. The fourth wave was a contracting triangle, typical of the fourth wave position, and gave the call for a top added reliability. *The Elliott Wave Theorist* recognized the orthodox peak in short term debt yields in the April 6, 1980 issue, with this emphatic statement:

> For several months, I have been anticipating this burst in short term interest rates, expecting it to be the final rise to new highs. Elliott Wave analysis now suggests that U.S. short term interest rates, after a prolonged advance lasting over three years, are registering their final peak. The chart shows the long ascent of the return on 90-day Treasury bills in a clear five-wave pattern with an extended first wave.

Figure 12-1 is the chart shown at the time. That juncture marked the orthodox *top* for interest rates and the orthodox *bottom* for Treasury bond prices.

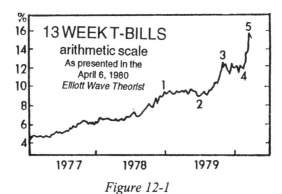

Figure 12-1

For four months thereafter, debt yields collapsed and prices soared. The violent reaction in 90-day T-bill yields from the highs at 16.69% ended at 6.38%, which was exactly 38.2% of their peak level. That relationship and the clear pattern of the decline combined to indicate an imminent bottom. In August, *The Elliott Wave Theorist* showed Figure 12-2, identifying the low of wave A.

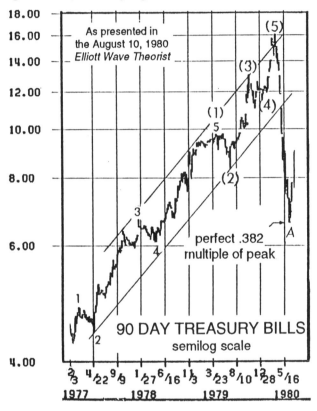

Figure 12-2

From there, rates soared again, and prices fell to new lows. The key to a proper analysis was to recognize that this move was part of a corrective pattern from the orthodox turning point that had taken place in March 1980. Ten days after the B-wave high in yield and low in prices in September 1981 (keep in mind that a plot of prices, such as shown in Figure 12-3, is the inverse of a plot of yields, such as shown in Figures 12-1 and 12-2), *The Elliott Wave Theorist* issued this assessment of bond prices on October 5:

We may be on the verge of the best bond market rally since the June 1980 advance. My long term bond count, showing the orthodox low in March 1980 and an A wave top in June, last appeared in the March 6, 1981 issue. The difficulty since then has been waiting for a satisfactory B wave to finish itself on the downside so a C wave advance could begin. *As I see it, such a point may have been reached at last week's low.*

So *The Elliott Wave Theorist* again called for a change in trend, this time at the bottom of a sixteen month decline, a five year decline, and a 35-year decline in bond prices, as shown in Figure 12-3. The rally carried into May 1983.

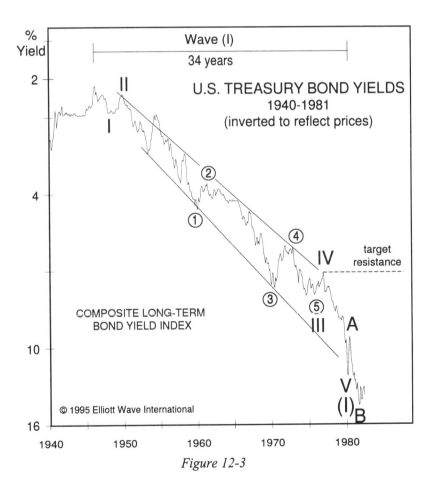

Figure 12-3

A forthcoming book will recount the forecast made for the ensuing one-year pullback, which was met with precision on May 30,
1984. That low presented the last great opportunity to buy for the
great bond price recovery. For a closer look at the 1980, 1981 and
1984 lows, see Figure 12-5.

As shown in Figure 12-3, U.S. 30-year Treasury bonds had declined in a five wave pattern from their peak value in 1946 to their
low in 1980. It is the essence of the Wave Principle that the direction of a five-wave impulse is the direction of the one-degree-larger
trend. In this case, the impulsive trend of prices was down and is
labeled accordingly as wave (I). Although the labeling of the starting waves of the advance (A and B) were changed as shown in Figure
12-5, *The Elliott Wave Theorist* continually reiterated that the advance would ultimately prove to be a *partial* retracement, i.e., a
bear market rally, not a new bull market. The distinction is crucial
to understanding why the advance took the shape of a countertrend
pattern, not a five-wave impulse, and more important, why the
market now faces another multi-year declining impulse, as will be
discussed under the section entitled **Outlook**.

The Path to the Peak of Wave (II)

Recognizing the buying opportunities of 1980 through 1984 was
relatively easy compared to forecasting the path of the ensuing advance. From 1985 forward, *The Elliott Wave Theorist* experienced
substantial difficulty in assessing the path of bond prices as they
chopped their way through a complex upward corrective pattern.
First, the direction of the triangle labeled wave X in Figure 12-5
was incorrectly assessed. Then wave Y ended at **1.618** times the
length of wave W (see Figure 12-5), a relationship that made the
1986 high appear to mark the end of the advance. The ultimate structure, a "triple zigzag," finally became clear in late 1991, about two
years before the final high. By the end of 1992, the time element
came into focus. *The Elliott Wave Theorist* concluded that "prices
will probably hold up until **1993** to reach a total of **13** years from the
1980 low," thus completing an impressive web of Fibonacci time intervals that had marked all key elements of the pattern. After several
attempts to identify the peak, on October 1, 1993, Elliott Wave
International's bond market specialist David Lockwood penned this
unequivocal outlook for *The Elliott Wave Theorist*:

The accompanying charts provide strong evidence that prices have just reached a significant point of reversal. The long term objective on the [10-year note] cash yield chart was achieved recently at 5.22%. A fall to as low as 5% cannot be ruled out, but it is not expected. Regardless, *a final low in yield is due in October*.

In the Bond Buyer 20-Bond Index of widely held municipal bonds, the clear five wave decline from 1946 to 1981 required a corrective rally to near the level of the wave IV triangle apex of July 1979. The advance so far has carried to slightly above that level and retraced a bit less than .382 of the decline from 1946, so this index is right at a point of maximum resistance [see updated Figure 12-6]. Good news for bonds has been more than fully discounted, and the next focus for the market will be on bad news.

The top occurred two weeks later on October 15. The October 29 issue added this final footnote: "The advance in futures prices ended in a diagonal triangle, a pattern that typically terminates longer trends. As you can see, the decline from here appears impulsive." Figure 12-4 shows the hourly chart published at that time. The longer term charts, updated to the present, are presented in the next section.

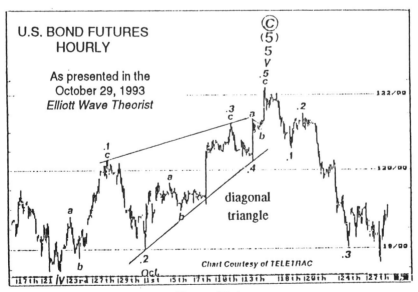

Figure 12-4

ANALYSIS

Pattern

The complex advance from 1980 in the 30-year Treasury bond formed a triple zigzag, labeled W-X-Y-X-Z, with contracting triangles in both "X" wave positions, as shown in Figure 12-5. This labeling, with variations and adjustments along the way, was developed in *The Elliott Wave Theorist* as it unfolded. Despite difficulties in current time interpretation, at no time was there any question that the advance might be a "new bull market." The three-wave structure of the initial advances (and all subsequent ones as well) eliminated this interpretation at the outset. Because there is no such thing as a quadruple zigzag, we are justified in concluding that the bear market rally ended with wave Z.

Fibonacci Time Spans

The time element in the bond market has nicely reflected Fibonacci mathematics. Critical to a proper time analysis is the fact that the orthodox low for 30-year U.S. Treasury bonds occurred in March 1980. "Prices fell to a new low in 1981," *The Elliott Wave Theorist* repeatedly explained for a dozen years, "but that low was part of an upward corrective pattern called a contracting triangle."

As you can see in Figure 12-11, the Supercycle degree bear market dating from 1946 lasted exactly a Fibonacci **34** years if it *ended* at the 1980 low, while the recovery that carried into 1993 lasted exactly a Fibonacci **13** years if it *started* at the 1980 low. Figure 12-5 shows that internally, wave W lasted **3** months in 1980, the wave X triangles covered **5** years (1980 to 1985) and **5** years (1986 to 1991), the intervening wave Y took **1** year, and wave Z took **2** years.

The fact that the entire pattern lasted **13** years, from 1980 to 1993 in 30-year Treasuries, and from 1981 (the price low) to the peak in junk bond prices in February 1994 in other issues, mirrors what should be a **13**-year rise in *stocks* from 1982 to 1995. Also, as with stocks from 1982 to 1987, the bulk of the bull market in bonds took place in **5** years, from 1981 to 1986.

Price Resistance

Throughout the advance, the guiding light for the ultimate upside target burned brightly. There was never any question that the level of the peak of wave IV, which was also the level of a Fibonacci .382 retracement of the 1946-1981 decline, marked a classic

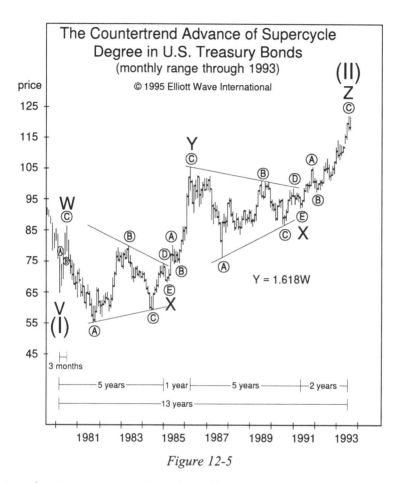

The Countertrend Advance of Supercycle
Degree in U.S. Treasury Bonds
(monthly range through 1993)
© 1995 Elliott Wave International

Y = 1.618W

Figure 12-5

point of resistance, as explained in *Elliott Wave Principle*. The dashed line in Figure 12-3 was drawn back in the early 1980s as the best estimate for the ultimate peak.

The final months of advance in the 30-year Treasury bond slightly exceeded this target (see Figure 12-11) as wave Z exceeded its ideal length of equality with wave W. However, 10-year Treasury notes and the Bond Buyer index of twenty municipal bonds stopped exactly at this classic point of resistance, as *The Elliott Wave Theorist* noted at the time in the last quotation cited above. Figure 12-6 shows the outcome, revealing a textbook example of five waves down followed by three waves up, stopping right at the top of the previous fourth wave. (Note: in this and other measures, the orthodox low occurred in 1981 and preceded a *double* zigzag, labeled A-B-C-X-A-B-C.) This form makes the wave structure from 1946 to

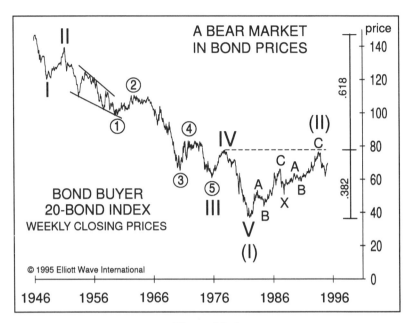

Figure 12-6

1993 a classic depiction of first and second waves of large degree to the downside.

Although the percentage gain in bonds from the 1981 low to the 1993 peak was the biggest in U.S. history, it retraced only half of the percentage damage done in the previous decline! This fact provides some perspective on how much price erosion had occurred from 1946 to 1981 and supports the case that the direction of the true underlying trend is down.

A Bull Market in Interest Rates

For those more comfortable with viewing charts of *bull* markets, Figure 12-7 shows the long term picture from 1941 in short term Treasury bill yields. Notice how wave (II) has bottomed near the .382 retracement level and the low of wave IV in the early 1970s, just as most bond yields did. All the charts in this chapter convey the same message: A long term bull market in interest rates (and bear market in IOU prices) was interrupted for twelve to thirteen years and has just resumed its multi-decade rise.

Remaining charts in this chapter will depict bond *prices*, as that is the investment that most people own and on which they are likely to lose money. This book, in contrast to the prevailing consen-

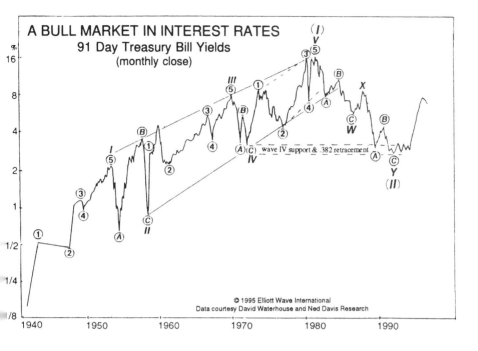

Figure 12-7

sus, recommends in Chapter 13 the shortest term yield bearing in-struments. By "rolling over" to new paper every thirty days, we will be positioned to *make* money on rising yields, not lose it.

The Start of Wave (III)

The behavior since the top in bond prices has been exquisitely consistent with the thesis that a new bear market wave of Super-cycle degree is underway. From the 1993 high, bonds traced out a textbook five waves down into last year's low. It has been labeled accordingly as wave ①, as shown in Figure 12-8. Believe it or not, wave ① ranks as the worst 13-month period of this century for bond returns. It caught the financial establishment and economists com-pletely off guard. The rally since then is wave ②, which should carry ideally to a .618 retracement near 112 basis 30-year T-bond futures (which is equivalent to a 30-year bond yield of 6.70), although sec-ond waves sometimes have deeper retracements. T-bill and Eurodollar prices have hardly budged, so may peak closer to a .382 retracement. This approaching high should coincide with a peak in the bullish fever toward stocks.

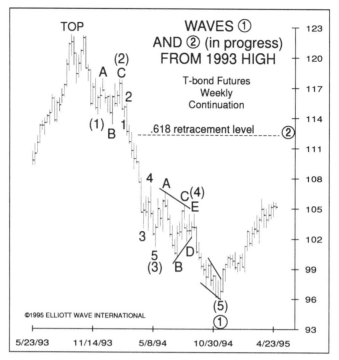

Figure 12-8

OUTLOOK

The powerful combination of factors cited above, including a triple zigzag pattern for the advance, the meeting of price resistance, the fulfillment of Fibonacci time intervals, and the five-wave kickoff of a new downtrend, argue emphatically that the 13-year recovery is over, that a major turn to the downside has taken place. Despite today's widespread opinion that bonds offer an unprecedented buying opportunity as a result of the 1994 decline, the Elliott Wave pattern requires that bond prices fall to new lows for the century in wave (III). Third waves tend to be powerful and/or lengthy, so downside potential is tremendous. Interest rates underwent a nearly nonstop rise from 1946 to 1981, doubling three times. If the bond market rally of 1981-1993 and the rebound into 1995 have done anything, they have lulled investors into thinking that there is no more long term risk, right when long term risk is its greatest.

On a shorter term basis, wave ② should peak soon. Wave ③ down is next and will be longer and more emotional than wave ①. A preview of its likely behavior is depicted in Figure 12-9, a chart of the Dow-Jones 20 bond index from 1915 to 1933. The "You Are Here" label shows today's approximate position in the unfolding long term decline. Because the current environment is that of a Grand Supercycle peak, not a Supercycle peak as in 1929, the two bear markets will differ in some ways. The current one will take longer, fall further, and recover less, if at all. So use this chart as a guide to general form and direction, not a map implying specific timing.

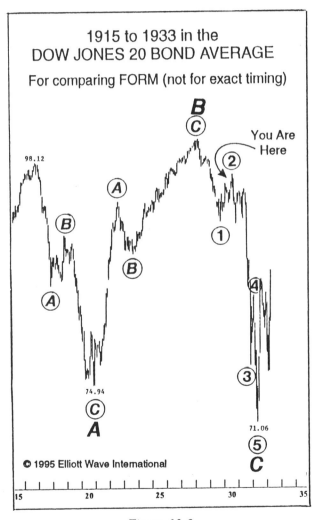

Figure 12-9

The Next Best Count

If the 1980/1981 low and 1993 high are not waves (I) and (II) but wave (A) and (B), then the current bear market will be wave (C). By this count (not illustrated), there is just one major debt crisis ahead, not several.

There is a slim possibility that the rally from 1981 is wave A of a larger wave (II), as depicted in Figure 12-10. This less bearish outlook still requires bond prices to fall to or below their 1981 lows. One could imagine the market returning to 1993 levels after the deflation has run its course and confidence returns for a decade or so. Thereafter, wave (III) would carry bond prices far lower in what could be a post-deflation response by government to inflate the currency. They would probably bottom with the next Supercycle low in stocks due mid-century. If this count proves correct, bonds at best appear to offer zero net capital appreciation potential from the 1993 peak through the end of wave (II) and will fall substantially in the meantime.

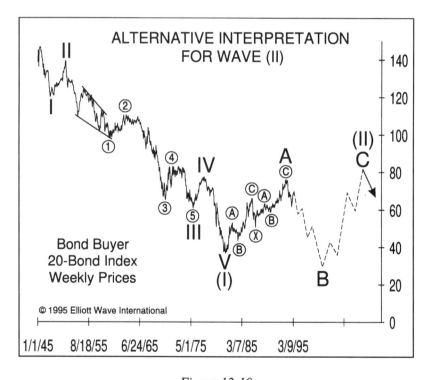

Figure 12-10

Price Forecast For the Next Tidal Wave Turn

The level of the ultimate bottom is impossible to predict. We can get a general idea of the market's potential from the fact that wave (I) from 1946 to 1980/81 brought 30-year bond yields from 2.15% to 15.77%, chopping bond prices to one-fourth of their starting value. Cycle analyst Martin Armstrong of Princeton Economics calculates a theoretical futures price at the 1946 high of 225 (near a Fibonacci **233**), while the 1981 low was a Fibonacci **55**. If wave (III) is equal in percentage terms to wave (I), it will bring bonds down to ¼ of their value at the 1993 peak of 122-10, to 30-18. If the decline is .618 times as long in point terms as the first, it will cover .618 of 170 points, or 105 points from 122-10, bringing the price to 17-10. A range of 17-10 to 30-18 equates to an interest rate on a 30-year Treasury bond of 27% to 46%. These conservative estimates provide at least a hint of the downside potential of the current bear market. The low for wave (III) can be forecast with more confidence once its subwaves through wave ④ are complete.

Time Forecast For the Next Tidal Wave Turn

When might the bear market that has just begun find a bottom? This question was addressed in December 31, 1992, nearly a year before bonds finally topped out, based upon the conclusion that the recovery would end after a Fibonacci 13 years, in 1993. That conclusion now appears to be confirmed, so the forecast from that time stands as quoted below:

> As you can see, the all-time high in Treasury bond prices occurred in **1946** and the orthodox low of the nearly nonstop decline in **1980**. These turns are a Fibonacci **34** years apart. If the upward correction ends after **13** years, the next decline should last **8** years, to **2001 + or - 1 year**, for a total bear market of **55** years from 1946, divided into a **34/21** Fibonacci section at the 1980 low.

Figure 12-11, updated to present prices, was shown in that issue, projecting a high in 1993 and a low in 2001. The projected time for a low is particularly satisfying because stocks typically lag the bond market by a year or two, and the ideal year for a final low in stocks based on Fibonacci time counts (see Chapter 4) and fixed-time cycles (see Appendix B) is 2003.

It must be stated once again that the only reliability of a Fibonacci time cluster this far in advance is that it should mark a

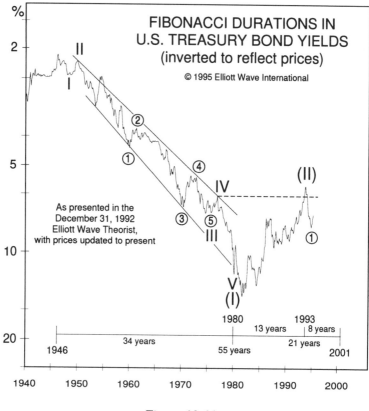

Figure 12-11

turning point. Whether that turn will be a bottom or top is little better than a guess. Usually the condition of the market at the time will clarify the direction of the probable trend change. However, for the reasons cited, the odds heavily favor 2001 ± 1 year marking a *low*.

INVESTOR PSYCHOLOGY

The area of finance that is most extended, most vulnerable, most hyped, and most widespread in its reach is the market for debt. The rush to buy bonds over the past one and a half decades has quite simply been a mania. In terms of volume and geographical breadth, it is an unprecedented mania. Up through February 1994, bond mutual funds in the United States enjoyed their biggest capital inflow in history, as summarized in Figure 12-12.

Not only did the mutual fund industry put all the new money it received during the mania into bonds, but it put in even more. According to the Investment Company Institute, bond funds' average cash percentage dropped from 20.8% of assets in 1980 to a record low 2.2% in 1993. In other words, bond funds embraced the mania, becoming 97.8% invested, their biggest commitment *ever*. As shown in Figure 12-13, their cash level in 1993 was *half* the percentage they held at the previous

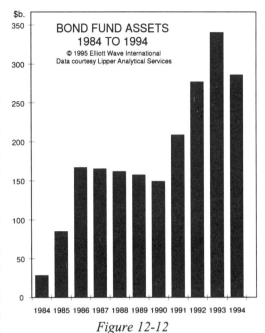

Figure 12-12

record low of 4.3% set in 1977, from which year bond prices took a drubbing that made the history books. As *The Elliott Wave Theorist* said in 1993, "That percentage represents a conviction among fund managers that bonds are utterly without risk." View this figure along with Figure 8-12 to see the combined results among fund managers of the psychological imperative to own paper investments.

The 1994 decline in bond prices caused enough concern to have brought funds' cash levels back to 5% today, but as that was the reading at the 1986 top, it is hardly a conservative position. Because the percentage of cash remains low and the public remains heavily invested, the long term decline that began in October 1993 is almost certainly not over.

As this is written, the wave ② rally is rekindling the atmosphere of hope and confidence toward the market for debt, keeping long term bullish opinion at fever pitch. Repeated reports that the bond market's total return of minus 20.92% for the 13-month decline ending in November 1994 was the greatest in U.S. history for any equivalent period has made bond investors believe that they have already suffered a bear market that cannot be repeated for a century. Today's "wave two" psychology is a Primary degree version of the larger "wave two" mania that culminated in 1993 at the top of Supercycle wave (II). Investors view the market as a compelling buying opportunity that will lead to substantial new highs in bond prices and have adopted the mental posture that focuses on good news and denies the existence of bad news. They contend that the Fed has succeeded in reining in inflation, the government has become fiscally conservative, and the economy is "under control" and due for a "soft landing," making lower rates assured. Even the falling dollar is bullish, they say, because when it finally stops, as it must somewhere, bonds will soar. That bond yields are way above the rate of inflation is taken as a sign that the market is *wrong* and will soon come to its senses. We will soon see how this conventional wisdom fares.

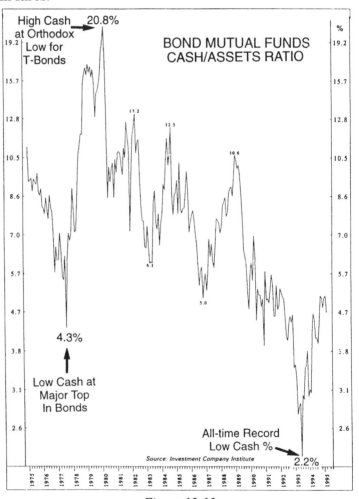

Figure 12-13

Evidence of Complacency

Investors consider bonds at today's prices a "gift." If they are a gift, it resembles the one the Queen gave to Snow White, and today's Snow Whites are no less naive. Their lack of concern is revealed by the strength of the belief that the trend of rates is down, the types of debt that people are buying, the narrow spread between healthy and unhealthy issuers, the length of maturities that people are willing to own, and the level of safety that investors erroneously believe that they enjoy. Let's examine each of these areas briefly.

The record buying of bonds in the early 1990s is all the proof needed to show that the public became convinced that interest rates will be trending lower over the indefinite future. Supporting this conclusion are two observations on the public's choice of mortgage financing. In 1994, two thirds of all mortgages issued were variable rate mortgages. People only choose the variable rate option when they believe that rates are more likely to fall than rise. In a similar vein, "balloon" mortgages have soared in popularity over the past three years. With a balloon mortgage, the borrower pays some interest for five to seven years, then has to pay off the whole mortgage or refinance the loan. In other words, to save ⅓% on his mortgage rate, the home buyer bets that rates will be lower or unchanged when it comes time to refinance and agrees to pay the difference if they go up. The popularity of this method of financing became widespread in the early 1990s because borrowers were extrapolating the multi-year decline in interest rates indefinitely into the future. With the latest easing in rates, that sentiment is no doubt still strong.

In the past ten years, investors have even been buying U.S. Savings Bonds in volumes not seen since fifty years ago. To understand the significance of this trend, just find 1945 on the long term bond chart. Another sign of a major top is the rapid growth of international bond funds. Why bother to discriminate among borrowers? You can now own a piece of the debt of the whole world!

Investors are also focusing so exclusively on the promised rate of interest that they are taking for granted the safety of their principal. For instance, the bonds and bills of government home loan institutions such as the Federal National Mortgage Association and the Federal Home Loan Bank in 1993 briefly had yields below the rate of Treasuries, implying that buyers rated them the safest debt in the world. The narrow spread between high and low grade bonds is similarly reflective of utter complacency with respect to any question of safety.

Investors are taking long term monetary and economic stability for granted as well, to a degree unthinkable just ten years ago. For example, two of the USA's biggest corporations (Disney and Coca-Cola) issued *100-year bonds* in 1993, the first such issues since 1954. Investors who own these bonds are demonstrating the same degree of conviction that interest rates will remain low as their counterparts did in the early 1950s after two decades of decline to an all-time record low for long term government bond yields of 2.15%! From that psychological state of the bond market, interest rates began a nearly nonstop rise that lasted three decades.

This blank state of thoughtless complacency extends beyond refusing to consider negatives to assuming positives that are not there. The survey by the Securities and Exchange Commission referenced in Chapter 8 also reveals that a shocking 66% of respondents are under the impression that the federal government insures money market mutual funds sold by banks. 50% think that even money market funds sold by stock brokers are federally insured. All these beliefs and attitudes will be shattered in coming years.

WINDS OF DEFAULT

If there is one conviction on Wall Street, it is that bonds are a safe investment. If stocks are good, goes the argument, then bonds are good, and if stocks are bad because of a recession, bonds are even better, because a recession will bring about lower interest rates. As the depression unfolds, then, what is the one thing that almost no one will be expecting (besides the depression itself)? The answer is, *higher interest rates*. How might such a trend come about?

Economists argue that recessions are always bullish for bonds. This prevailing professional view is ultimately nonsensical. It is not good for bond values if a deteriorating economy produces a drop in production so severe that the issuers of bonds, i.e., the borrowers, are unable to earn enough money to pay interest or principal. A few billion dollars worth of bond defaults over the past thirteen years clearly reveal this point. More generally, if all the economy ever did was stand still or contract, no one could justify lending or borrowing, as there would be no production to pay off the obligations. Then why do economists, almost to a man, believe that economic contraction is good for bonds?

The reason for this view is that in the post-WWII period, an expanding economy has coincided with rising rates of inflation and falling bond prices. Economists typically begin their studies of history at that point, ignoring all else, as previous economic history took place before government presumably learned to "manage" the economy and the money supply and is therefore irrelevant (until the next depression, anyway). As a result, economists have studied only the behavior of bonds and the economy during the rising portion of a long term economic and monetary cycle (see Appendix B). It is indeed true that (1) in an environment of general growth and inflation, (2) when only a recession occurs, bonds typically rise in price as the economy contracts because the inflation component of the bonds' interest rate falls. When the *long* term economic trend turns down, however, the relationship between the economy and the bond market is dramatically different.

How Bonds Behave In a Depression

It is a confusing paradox that a depression produces trends toward both higher *and* lower interest rates, the trend determinant being perceived default risk. While interest rates rise on weak debt, they fall on guaranteed strong debt (except for a brief time when the crisis temporarily forces strapped investors to raise cash). As previously stated, the ultimate true capital return of a bond is the value of the interest payment times the number of payments made, plus whatever principal is recovered. As the chances of a borrower's survival is perceived to worsen, credit-providing investors demand higher rates in an attempt to get back as much of their investment as possible. As interest rates paid by issuers of questionable reliability soar, those paid by borrowers of perceived impeccable reliability fall to extremely low levels as investors search not for income but for a safe haven. This movement is classically termed a "flight to quality." High and rising interest rates in evidence for many issues reflect not inflation or a desire to borrow, but people's increasing fear of losing their principal. Any debt that is perceived to be risky falls in price along with the contraction in the economy, and the greater the contraction, the further the fall. In the 1930s depression, many bond prices collapsed significantly on such fears, and some issuers did indeed ultimately default. As the contraction worsened, even completely safe Federal government bonds experienced a brief, sharp selloff, as some investors sold even good bonds just to raise cash. So while today bondholders are convinced that a poor economy means rising prices, history will reveal that on a larger scale, a poor economy means *default*.

In the bear market of 1929-1932, the percentage of bonds outstanding that were at risk of default was relatively low. The next depression, however, will cause countless bond issuers to default, even ones that today sport impeccable ratings and appear unquestionably sound. How could bond defaults surprise even the rating services? Consider that the Orange County (CA) bankruptcy in December 1994 was the largest municipal bankruptcy ever. Bondholders are stuck with $1.5b. worth of paper. In all the ink spilled over the event, one sentence (from *USA Today*) stands out as being of quintessential importance to practical planning: "The nation's premier bond ratings services, Standard & Poor's and Moody's, had described the county fund as one of the best-run in the nation." In other words, the fund went from AAA-rated to bankrupt, with no intervening rating. Regardless of what the rating services might say in their defense, the fact is that they are not taking into account many crucial factors. In the Orange County case, it was a high percentage of leveraged derivatives. In upcoming cases, it will be the developing depression. The ideal service for investors would rate bonds risky at a top, when it is the best time to sell, and attractive at a bottom, when it is time to buy. Bonds were at a top in 1993 and should have been at their lowest rating *then*. However, services base their ratings not on market analysis, but on fundamentals, which lag prices. Because of this practice, they are doomed to announce changes far behind the market, a result that rarely fails to produce the largest number of upgrades as the market recovers and a dramatic culmination of downgrades as the market approaches a bottom. The forces that will soon propel the U.S. into depression will devastate bond prices, and along the way, bond ratings.

Rising interest rates in a deteriorating economy will be a complete mystery to most investors. Consider that for two years, economists have uniformly applauded the environment of moderate economic growth with low inflation, *yet bonds had their worst thirteen month decline of the century last year anyway*. Labor Secretary Robert Reich said on January 3, 1994, "There is no basis, either in meaningfully higher inflation or in much greater credit demand, to expect that interest rates would rise in a sustained way this year." Interest rates promptly rose a record percentage for *any* single year. The fact that bond prices fell so hard even though everyone can see that inflation is not a problem and that runaway credit demand is not a problem *means that there is another problem*. The bear market in bonds will develop not on fear of inflation, but on fear of deflation and depression, which is precisely why so many will err in the coming environment. The scramble for cash by desperate borrowers will ultimately push interest rates higher, not despite deflation, but because of it. Yet the worse the economy gets and the less inflation is in evidence, the more many analysts will be escalating their bullish opinions on the basis that it is the best possible environment for bondholders. Most will view bonds in a slowing economic environment with no inflation as a bargain and will stay invested in anticipation of the turnaround that must surely be "just around the corner." This retained optimism toward bonds, based on a false premise, will take place despite a falling market, one of the rarest of events.

THE OUTLOOK FOR VARIOUS CLASSES OF BONDS

The few analysts who have even considered the question of deflation and have looked up the performance of AAA-rated bonds in the 1930s see the picture of an investment that held its own through the crisis. They conclude, therefore, that "If deflation is likely, high quality bonds are the best long term investment." On this point I find widespread assurance and no dissent. However, it is hardly the certainty that people assume. Before answering the question of which bonds might be safe, it is crucial to understand that charts depicting AAA bond yields during the 1930s show only the action of those bonds that *stayed* AAA. Those whose ratings fell below AAA were *removed from the list*. That means that investors who bought certain AAA bonds in 1929 that subsequently were defaulted upon could have lost everything, and it would not have shown up in the index. The successful investors of that time, then, were not those who bought AAA bonds, but those who bought bonds that remained AAA. The unreliability of bond ratings, as discussed above, compounds the task of finding a safe bond in which to invest.

The only accurate conclusion with respect to investing in bonds in the coming environment, then, is that any bond that is rated AAA before the depression and remains AAA throughout the depression will be an acceptable long term investment. Even instruments such as these will experience temporary declines when investors are forced to raise cash, so they must be considered safe only for investors who will not be perturbed by a sharp temporary setback and who will not need to sell them during the crisis.

Now that we have narrowed the group of potentially acceptable debt-based investments, let's ask the question that matters most: How easy will it be to determine which bonds will stay AAA? Keep in mind that the larger the bear market, the greater the percentage of issues that will fail. The 1930s crisis reflected a social mood swing of only Supercycle degree, and its attendant problems were only of that magnitude. The coming mood swing will be of Grand Supercycle degree, and problems will be correspondingly severe. How many corporate or government issues will you be confident enough to own in such an environment? It might be prudent to go down the list and explore the outlook for the various classes of bonds.

Municipal Bonds

After the 1990-1991 recession, confidence returned to the bond market, and state and local governments have taken advantage of the renewed demand (and their typically tax-exempt status) by issuing securities in an unprecedented borrowing binge. States and cities have sold an average of $260 billion worth of bonds in the past four years, over triple the 1980-1981 rate. The all-time annual record was $338.8 billion worth in 1993. Local government borrowing has continued right through early 1995 despite higher rates because investors have continued to pour money into municipal bond funds, oblivious to risk. Many municipalities have invented big new projects as if there is no end in sight to prosperity and production to pay for the new debt on top of the old, while others are on the brink of insolvency and are selling bonds because they are in trouble.

The complete lack of fear in the market for these bonds is revealed by the extremely small difference between muni bond yields and Treasury bond yields. Investors clearly view state and local governments and the federal government as *equally safe* issuers of debt. Yet the number of potential disaster cases among municipalities is greater than people realize. In the 1990s, they have been operating at a total annual deficit of $30b.-$50b. according to figures published by the International Strategy and Investment Group (see Figure 12-14), and an economic contraction will swell that figure substantially. The fact that half of the states' unemployment funds have only several months' reserve underscores that opinion. Local governments are the most precarious issuers of debt, and one of the most prolific. When the depression arrives, municipalities will have their backs to the wall, and many will default.

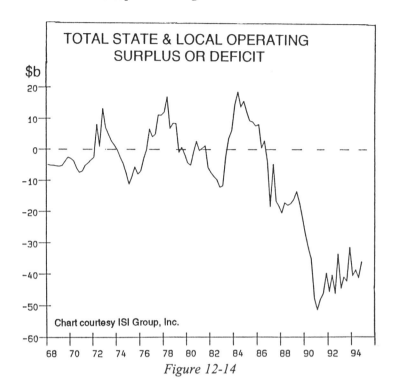

Figure 12-14

One of the most dangerous classes of tax-exempt municipal bonds are so-called "certificates of participation," or COPs. Investors have purchased billions of dollars worth of these instruments, which now amount to 6% of all municipal debt. The attraction was yet a higher yield. However, a simple vote by county residents can stop "lease payments" on these debts. Insurance companies might be able to pay off a few such defaults, but their resources are limited and will not withstand a general trend toward taxpayer refusal to honor politicians' promises. When the economic contraction begins in earnest, this paper will be considered risky-to-worthless by the market, and prices will plummet.

Municipal bonds, treasured by retirees and others who like to save on interest income taxes, are a trap. Investors may save on their taxes, but it will be at the cost of their principal. In coming years, watch not only for a dramatic increase in muni bond defaults, but also for numerous stories of reckless negligence and corruption involving municipal and state government bond issues.

Zero Coupon Bonds

For years, investors, spurred on by brokerage firms, have been loading up on "zero coupon bonds." "Zeros," as they are called (perhaps unconsciously in reference to their ultimate value), are bonds that pay no interest until they mature. For waiting, investors are promised a bit more yield.

These bonds are tops on my list for bad purchases. For one thing, every year the government charges you tax on the interest even though you are not collecting any. This fact has prompted many people to buy zeros for their IRAs and pension plans, which makes the nonexistent income temporarily tax-exempt. However, all that this "advantage" has done is to decrease further the level of caution among buyers. Assuredly, if there were ever an attractive way for a marginal (or doomed) enterprise to borrow money, it would be zeros. Imagine not having to pay out a cent of interest for ten years! You could issue tons of the stuff. The lender takes all the risk.

Purchases of zero coupon bonds are an aggressive bet on falling long term interest rates and a steadily expanding economy with little inflation, just what we are all assured will continue. The huge risk of loss if the bet is wrong is not even being considered. Who knows if the issuer will be in business when the bonds are due to be paid off? Who can guarantee that inflation will not return to devastate these bonds' value? At least when you collect interest, you are getting *some* money back, money that has retained some of its purchasing power, thus reducing the ultimate loss if there is to be one. Given the Elliott Wave scenario from here on out, zeros are one of the worst imaginable investments.

Federal Government Bonds

What about Federal government bonds, which except for a brief drop in 1931, held their value during the Great Depression? Could bonds backed by the full faith and credit of the U.S. government really be considered risky someday? *The Elliott Wave Theorist* has prepared readers for its current opinion for years. In discussing the ultimate resolution of the Grand Supercycle bear market fourteen years ago, in May 1981, EWT painted this picture:

> Government will not be collecting sufficient taxes from a country deep in depression, and the social programs that have created

a sea of red ink on government ledgers during *prosperous* times will cause total bankruptcy during an economic depression. Government won't even be meeting the *interest payments* on its colossal debt.

The U.S. government today is in disastrous shape financially compared to its condition prior to the Great Depression. For a century the most respected debtor in the world, the U.S. government now owes too much money and continues to borrow at a feverish pace. It is also a potential disaster as a creditor, which further weakens its position as a debtor. The government continues to lend to weak debtors through student loans, farm loans and loans to foreign governments, while borrowing at a frenetic pace to keep the whole operation going. It is therefore extremely vulnerable to a collapse in other financial sectors.

Perhaps most important, government has encouraged profligate, unsound banking practices for sixty years via a simple blanket "guarantee" of virtually all bank deposits. This guarantee is taken seriously by the nation's depositors. On March 14, 1995, the last failed Savings & Loan institution was closed out by the Resolution Trust Corp., which itself will expire on July 1, 1995. There has been a collective sigh of relief that the problem has been solved. Says one interviewee, "No one feels threatened any more. As long as you have less than $100,000 in the bank, it's government insured." Few realize that the insurance fund has enough money in it to rescue about three banks. The FDIC, relative to its promises, is broke. In a depression, it will be called upon to pay off depositors in banks that hold worthless obligations and severely devalued collateral such as real estate. The next round of bankruptcies among savings institutions will be unmanageable.

The government's promises to foreign governments, banks, other institutions and individual bondholders are so great that a depression will surely lead to a massive increase in its obligations, while at the same time, tax receipts will plummet. The government's debt load, deficits and interest payments even after twelve years of economic expansion out of thirteen are monstrously high. If the economy enters a severe contraction, the Treasury will be hard pressed just to pay the interest on the national debt, much less any of the principal.

The simplest yet most profoundly indicative measure of the federal government's fiscal health is its interest expense as a percent of total receipts. Notice in Figure 12-15 that the steady and relatively manageable payout level of 11-12% ended in the late 1960s, at the orthodox Elliott Wave peak for the inflation-adjusted Dow Jones Industrial Average (1966) and Value Line index (1968). As explained in Chapters 3 and 10, those few years marked the long term cultural, financial and economic peak for the United States. The applicable observation today is one made nearly a decade ago by Earl Hadady of the *Bullish Consensus*, who developed the indicator: "With almost 40 cents of every non-trust fund dollar being used to pay Lawful Interest Expense, the situation is out of control... Uncle Sam could eventually go bankrupt." That amount rose to 54.8 cents in 1992, and has since fallen back to 47 cents. While the retreat may appear to be good news, the reasons for it are not all good. Falling rates into early 1994 were partly responsible, but the bigger factor was the government's deliberate decision to shorten

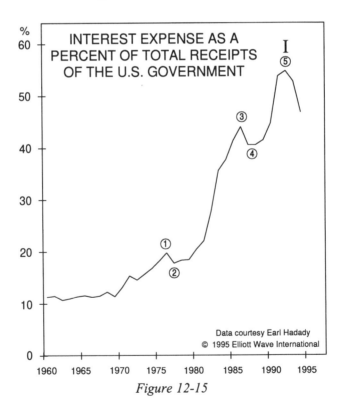

Figure 12-15

maturities, a near term expediency that is set up to backfire. Because interest rates turned higher in 1993, the government will have to begin paying higher interest rates sooner than otherwise as the shorter maturities come due. The five-wave count in Figure 12-15 suggests a drop for wave II back to the 40% level as tax receipts improve over the near term and the rollback to short term maturities continues. When rates rise again, though, this line should accelerate upward in wave III.

This chart is important in that it reflects the *results* of the higher interest rates of the past two decades and shows that the government's high and rising interest cost will be part of the *cause* of still higher rates for government debt. While any further increase in rates will force up this percentage, ultimately a rising percentage will heighten creditors' perception of the coming crisis. They will demand a higher compensation for the risk, which will force interest rates up even further. When the world begins to doubt U.S. solvency and moral resolve, nothing will halt the relentless trend of eroding confidence. These factors will constitute a self-reinforcing spiral until a point of panic and crisis is reached.

The prospect for a depression, and therefore a severe drop in the total tax take with which governments pay the interest they owe, suggests that most issues of government debt, local and national, will eventually be valued at or near zero. A *de facto* default will take place if the depression lowers tax receipts so much that governments must stop interest payments on debt. Local governments have defaulted before with only moderate remorse, but the U.S. government is in the unique position of having issued the world's "reserve currency," a fact that will make it want to maintain its credibility with foreign creditors as long as conceivably possible. After all, foreign central banks own one-fourth of all U.S. government debt, and if they were to sell in a panic, the Treasury's bonds would be smashed. The government's first option in the crisis might be to declare a moratorium on *domestically* owned U.S. bonds, notes and ultimately even bills. The moratorium may be effected by a declaration that the maturity dates have been "temporarily extended" and interest payments "temporarily reduced" to "reasonable levels" or even suspended due to the "national emergency," but by whatever means, interest payments to U.S. creditors will probably cease or be drastically cut. Bondholders, it will be pointed out, are mostly rich and can afford to wait. It is doubtful that foreign bondholders will continue to lend under such circumstances, and unlikely that they will refrain from identifying any such situation as a golden opportunity to sell. Whether or not the term is used, the Federal government will be bankrupt by the end of the process.

Today there is no shortage of people who believe that the U.S. government's promises are as good as gold. Anyone who is confident that its debt will survive unaffected in a depression is welcome to take the risk of buying the Treasury's bonds. There is no way I will risk being one of the government's long term creditors, though, and neither should you.

Derivatives

Some derivative debt instruments are fairly straightforward. Others are so complex that it takes half an hour to understand what they are. I was having breakfast in New York in 1986 (at the peak of wave Y) and overheard a feverish pitch for — get this — puts and calls...on zero coupon bonds...which were tax deferred...through an insurance policy!

A few of these exotic debt instruments will cause losses of greater than 100%. How is that possible? To give you just a taste of the intricate nature of some of the debt instruments available, read this description of just one exotic derivative, from a March 1993 article in *The Wall Street Journal* (emphasis added):

Heavyweights such as Dreyfus and Putnam mutual funds are making big bets in a little known corner of the municipal bond market. To spice up returns, some muni funds have put 5% to 15% of their money into inverse floaters. Never heard of them? You have plenty of company. But sales of municipal inverse floaters have exploded during the past three years, to $4.8 billion in 1992 from just $100 million in 1990. Sales this year may set another record. Underwriters say that municipal bond funds buy more than 90% of all inverse floaters. To make an inverse floater, underwriters take a regular bond issue—for example, a 30-year bond with a coupon of 6%—and split it into two parts. Half the issue pays a low money-market rate (say, around 2%) that "floats" in line with other short-term interest rates. The other part—the "inverse floater"—gets all the rest of the bond's interest payments. So, when short-term rates fall, yields on garden-variety floaters fall right along with them, but yields on "inverse floaters" rise because there is more interest left over for them. Inverse floaters offer higher yields in exchange for greater risk. Price gains for an inverse floater can be twice as large as those for a standard municipal bond during a bull market. *But in a bear market, the losses can also be twice as large.*

In March 1993, Merrill Lynch & Co. began marketing inverse floaters directly to individual investors with $25,000 or more. *The*

Wall Street Journal noted that because the Merrill brochure "teems with warnings about the securities" (as well it should), "they are known at Merrill as Teems." The bear market in bonds predicted in this book is expected to carry short term rates well into double digits. If it happens, the losses in inverse floaters will turn out to be greater than the underlying principal, as the payer of the "low money market rate" on the guaranteed half of the issue may find himself paying out 20% or more per year on a 30-year bond.

High Grade Corporate Bonds

A depression will impact the ability of debt-leveraged companies to earn the income required to service and even ultimately to pay off their debt. The less debt-laden a company, the greater its potential ability to honor its obligations. Of all classes of bonds discussed so far, those of cash-rich corporations with the least outstanding debt have the best chance of proving safe through the coming depression. It will still be prudent to assess the nature of each company's business to determine if it is likely to maintain an acceptable level of sales under such conditions. Bonds of such companies will prove safer than those issued by the majority of governments.

Foreign Government Bonds

The criteria for choosing bonds, notes and bills issued by foreign governments are similar to those for selecting bonds issued by corporations. The depression will negatively impact tax receipts around the world, so most governments will be under intense scrutiny, and for awhile at least, will experience skepticism over their ability to service and pay back debt. The safest foreign debt paper will be that issued by countries with the least debt, the most solid economic bases, and the soundest political structures.

These criteria leave very few candidates, but there are some. I decline to make a list for the same reason I decline to list corporate issues for safe investing: fortunes of companies and nations change, and that is never more the case than in the volatile environment of a worldwide depression. If you decide to go this route, you will have to choose your investments carefully and monitor the political environment of the issuing country, switching positions as events require.

Safe Debt Issues

The most important question bondholders can, and must, ask themselves is, "Is this issuer really safe?" By the end of the bear market, the list of those that ultimately default will be far longer than anyone today remotely suspects. Prospects for a contraction of Grand Supercycle degree make it questionable whether *any* safe debt can be identified in advance. Indeed, at the worst point in the bear market half a century from now, there may be no top grade debt except that backed by gold, a fiscally sound government, or a cash-rich international corporation whose business is such that it stays financially healthy in a time of depression and social conflict.

If throughout the crisis, a borrower is able unquestionably to guarantee a bond issue, either by depositing collateral gold in a trust account at a safe bank, presenting a picture of impeccable corporate health, or by pledging a strong tax base, then the interest rate on that issue will be near zero. However, those who would be able to guarantee their debt to that degree in the coming environment will have the least need to borrow money. Thus, there will not be large issues available of whatever guaranteed debt there is. Due to short-ages of such investments, a perceived store of value could actually command a *zero* or even *negative* interest rate. For instance, the short term debt or currency of a sound foreign government might be in such demand for safety reasons that investors would pay for the privilege of owning it, as they did for owning Swiss francs in the late 1970s. In a debt crisis, if you knew that another government's bonds and bills would maintain or even improve their value as demand caused its currency to rise, would you balk at paying to own them? Judging which issues will survive is out of my field. Suffice it to say that one might do well investigating debt issued by and in countries with less outstanding debt than the United States.

THE APPROACHING CRISIS

While debt securities are currently enjoying a rally, they will ultimately be the scene of staggering losses for institutional portfolios, including those of banks, corporations, pension funds, insurance companies and universities. Too many of these institutions have participated in buying every issue, even down to the lowest grade imaginable consumer IOUs for houses, cars, boats and mobile homes, which has been packaged by Wall Street and sold as investments.

The slightest breeze of depression will begin to topple this inverted pyramid of confidence-sensitive promissory notes. At the end of the process, the public's beloved bond mutual funds will be devastated. A loss in values among all grades of debt securities is likely to occur whether the culmination of the slide into depression is inflationary or (as I expect) deflationary. Either way, the bond market will have to face the reality that trillions of dollars worth of long term debt cannot be serviced at interest rates over 3%, no matter what the government or the economy does. In fact, not just domestic debt, but currently outstanding *worldwide* debt cannot be supported, no matter how powerfully the economies of the world produce.

The next serious breakdown in bonds is likely to precipitate a collapse of the global debt structure. What exists today is not merely risk but the recipe for an unprecedented financial disaster. Needless to say, the Elliott Wave outlook presented in this chapter is in stark contrast to prevailing opinion. People have no idea of the magnitude of the tidal change that is about to occur. One by one, investors will be confronted with the reality that the ocean of dollar-denominated debt currently outstanding cannot and will not be paid off. While a crisis is ultimately guaranteed, only deteriorating investor confidence will precipitate it. According to the Elliott Wave patterns, that change in psychology is very near at hand.

Chapter 13

HOW TO HANDLE
THE COMING ENVIRONMENT

The outlook for the stock market and the economy currently communicated by the market's pattern has been anticipated in the general sense by every Wave Principle practitioner since R.N. Elliott. Bolton, Collins and Frost knew that when wave (V) topped out, a great bear market would be due, but in their times, that was an event far in the future. *Elliott Wave Principle* was the first book written as that day came close enough to address. It described the environment after the expected wave V bull market this way:

> O.K., what next? Are we in for another 1929 to 1932 period of chaos? Situations of this nature that have happened over the last two hundred years usually have been followed by three or four years of chaotic conditions in the economy and the markets.

The investment-related conditions of the past few years have been serene compared to what is coming. The few hints of the approaching chaos have appeared in the context of a slowly curling tidal wave that has yet to break. The rate of debt growth was at the front of the curl when it stopped accelerating in 1986. In 1987, the bond/stock yield spread topped and the stock market crashed. From there followed the real estate downturn in the Northeast that rapidly spread across the country. Then came the fall in junk bonds, the collapse in coins, art and collectibles, the bear market in Japanese stocks, and a slowdown in the overall rate of economic growth. More recently came the drops in utility stocks, high grade bonds, and the advance-decline line. Many of the markets that slipped early are in a "wave two" rebound, joining in the overall culmination in the upward force of the tidal wave. The irony is that the stock market, which was near the front of the curl, is also at the rear of the curl, as illustrated in Figure 13-1. The last of the upward energy in the tidal wave, which is concentrated in the major stock averages, prices for goods, and aggregate economic figures, will soon succumb to the force of the downward curl. This spacing out of the tops, crashes and partial recoveries among all the investment markets reflects a frenzied shuffling of money from one asset to another, a phenom-

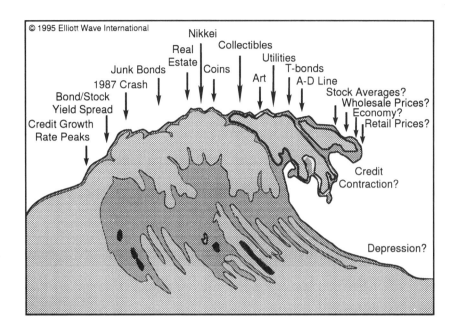

enon similar to the increasingly nervous animal activity that takes place in the hours before an earthquake.

Completed wave patterns, slowing long term upside momentum, euphoric investor psychology, the expanding economy, and the state of political calm all support the case that a major top in mood, on a scale equivalent to those of 1720, 1835-1836, 1929 and 1966-1968, is forming. The next several years should be the resolution phase, beginning with net debt retirement and ending with depression. With the body of the tidal wave will fall all investment markets around the world. Markets that began declining early will continue their descent to depths currently inconceivable to conventional observers. The giant wash will take with it wholesale prices, consumer prices, employment, profits and tax receipts, as well as the fortunes of banks, manufacturers, insurance companies and pension funds. Ultimately, the process will devastate the debt balloon, the welfare state, the solvency of municipal and federal governments, and the political status quo.

If you attended financial conferences and read financial books and newsletters in the late 1970s and early 1980s, you will vividly remember hearing this kind of talk from virtually every source. At that time, the investing public was in intense agreement with such sentiments as I am now expressing because during recessions and at major stock market bottoms such as then, fear is rampant. Naturally, at the time, it was exactly the wrong thing to believe. Now almost no one believes that anything like it can happen. Investors today are deeply convinced that stocks and bonds are desirable investments, and that at minimum, they always go up long term, so there is no reason to be concerned. Once again, the popular belief is wrong. In reality, a sociofinancial turning point of major dimension is at hand.

This turning point can be understood only with a knowledge of centuries of economic, social and political history, and most important, stock market history. The Wave Principle alone is able to integrate the massive growth of credit, the increasing complexity of the investment marketplace, the climate of speculation, the long but slowing economic expansion, the political atmosphere of conciliation, as well as the patterns that produced this background, into a meaningful whole. These conditions have appeared in a few rare instances throughout history and have always led to a substantial crisis in the financial system.

The only statements I am willing to make categorically are that (1) the stock market is near the end of Cycle wave V from 1932, (2) the Dow Jones Industrial Average will fall at least back to 1000, and (3) when the stock market falls that far, we will have a depression. If at any time daily advance-decline ratios for several weeks become larger than those of any equivalent period since the 1974 low (i.e., something akin to those of the 1940s and 1950s), it will demonstrate the behavior of a third wave up, and the most essential analysis in this book will have been proved flat-out wrong. While I place the chance of such an event at zero, everything else in this book with respect to Elliott Wave analysis and the resulting projections involve a clearly stated probability, sometimes very high, but sometimes barely better than 50%.

Regardless of uncertainties, it is a fact of life that success demands the assessment of risk and decisive action based upon probability. Indeed, to survive, sometimes one must act merely on *possibility*. If there were a 1-in-10 chance that grizzly bears were nearby, wouldn't you move camp? In contrast, the evidence indicates that the odds of a coming financial and social calamity are far greater than 1-in-10. Delaying defensive action will almost certainly cause substantial anxiety later. Insurance was invented because there are few guarantees in life or about the future. If this book contains any advice, it is simply to arrange for some insurance. Let's recap the reasons why doing so may be a good idea.

When *Elliott Wave Principle* said in 1978 that a great bull market in stocks and economic boom lay dead ahead, it was extremely difficult to convince still cautious investors that financial and economic trends were positive and that they should do everything they could to establish their businesses, invest in stocks, make their fortunes and put money away for the future. Ten years ago, in June 1985, *The Elliott Wave Theorist* was still delaying further elaboration on what to expect after the bull market had run its course:

> Some subscribers have urged me to write about what the crash, due several years hence, will be like. I haven't wanted to do so, because it has taken all my energy to convince subscribers to remain fully invested. As for strategy with regard to the Grand Supercycle wave, the label on the front page table says it all. It has read the same since the first month of publication in April 1979: "NO ACTION WARRANTED." We will have plenty of time to explore that theme a couple of years from now. Unfortunately, at that time, few will want to hear about it.

Today, action *is* warranted, so I face the opposite task: to help investors to become safe and liquid and avoid the losses that the markets are poised to inflict. Back then, the majority was defensive and worried about how *low* prices should go, while now the majority is focusing only on how *high* prices will go, confidently predicting a continuation of the 1982-1995 experience well into the next decade. Indeed, the forecast that "few will want to hear about it" is true to a degree that I hardly imagined when I wrote the above paragraph. As with the bullish opinion expressed in *Elliott Wave Principle*, this attitude will change as the new trend progresses.

The general attitude toward market timing will change as well. Today's investors have countless "stock pickers," "bond analyzers" and "portfolio allocators" to choose from, but no market timers. Money managers pooh-pooh market timing almost to a man. Statistics show that in 1994, 2800 equity mutual funds lost money, 400 had some gain, and only 35 had a double digit gain. Even worse, of 3233 bond funds, only 25 had a gain. These results are generated by the people who tell you that market timing is worthless. Obviously, *their* method, which is to "select" stocks and bonds while staying fully invested, offers no advantage or protection whatsoever even in a sideways market, much less a decline. This book is a remedy for the absence of an alternative money management approach.

Why do professionals disdain market timing so? I received some insight in May 1987, three months before the start of the record-breaking 1000-point drop in the Dow. That month, I was invited to participate on a panel of stock market academics, one of whom argued that money managers should never attempt to time the market, but should remain fully invested always. Why? Because timing is difficult, he said. Shouldn't one investigate ways to prepare for repeats of 1968-1974, when stock averages lost 45%-75%, or 1929-1932 when the averages lost 89%? Don't worry, came the response. The stock market will always eventually rise to new highs after bear markets.

Needless to say, I do not consider this view a proper investment strategy. It "works" as long as the relevant trend degree is up. Otherwise, this kind of thinking will ruin you. One major problem is that in response to a bear market, the economy slides, jobs become scarce, and people find that they need the money they thought they could leave invested. Few can survive a drawdown of 50%-90% and wait two decades just to get even again. Yes, "90%" and "twenty years," and I am *not* referring only to the aftermath of 1929. When the Dow fell 42.6% from 1968 to 1974, the average stock, as reflected by the Value Line index, fell 74%. From 1966, the inflation-adjusted Dow fell 75%. During this time, many stocks fell 90% and even 99%. Even using the mildest measure of decline, the Dow Jones Industrial Average, it took until June 1986 for an investor in the DJIA to catch up with someone who bought Treasury bills in February 1966. If the buyer of Treasury bills had any market timing sense at all, moreover, he would have bought *some* stocks at lower levels, so the stock investor of 1966, presuming equal stock selecting ability, will *never* catch him.

Even this analysis understates the case. The buy-and-hold contingent tells us that even people who bought stocks in 1929 would be fabulously wealthy today. Yet claiming that the Dow Jones Industrial Average, or even the S&P 500, represents the average investor's loss in a bear market of that magnitude is false advertising. Their conclusion would be accurate if the investor had the good fortune to buy stocks of companies that survived and prospered through the Great Depression. However, as one subscriber points out, "A really typical 1929 portfolio included Auburn, Cord, Missouri Pacific, New York Central, Pierce-Arrow and Stutz." The Dow and S&P averages do not factor in stocks of companies that go out of business, and in Supercycle declines, there are quite a few of them.

There were so many in 1929-1932, in fact, that a number of *mutual funds* (then called investment trusts) even went to zero. As detailed in Chapter 5, wave (A) of the last Grand Supercycle decline, from 1720 to 1722, forced *91%* of the issues traded in London off the board in a brief two years! The averages normally published for the period show a mild 66% decline because besides reflecting only year-end figures, *they omit the ruined companies.* Needless to say, the DJIA and reconstructed S&P averages for 1929-1942 do the same thing. But real people buy real stocks, and many become wallpaper. Does a single academic study or buy-and-hold thesis tell its readers what to do about such holdings in a real bear market? Do any of them take this reality into account? Many of today's hot stocks and even "aggressive growth" mutual funds face ruination in the coming bear market. To assume blithely that most investors and fund managers will magically choose only issues that will still be on the New York Stock Exchange twenty years from now is to adopt a rose-colored outlook, to say the least.

Disregarding all these facts for a moment, even if it *were* true that you would "eventually get even," why should you set yourself up for such a wait when tools exist to provide warnings of bear markets? More important, why should you endure a bear market in stocks when in most cases, such as in the 1970s, *other investments may provide profitable bull markets*?

Upon reflection, there are two reasons why someone can hold such an opinion and recommend that course of action. The first is psychological. For 200 years, the stock market has been in a Grand Supercycle uptrend, and just like technicians who follow the trend, such "philosophies" simply reflect a mental adjustment to what has been. The long term version offered by my fellow panelist merely reflects trend following on a large time frame. This opinion has had other periods of widespread acceptance that always turned out to be the latter years of extended uptrends. Had you attended a stock market panel in London in the year 1784, undoubtedly more than one participant would have argued that common stocks are worthless as a long term investment, that rallies were always temporary, that prices always return to a low level eventually. A 64-year bear market would have taught them that, and they would have been just as wrong as present day champions of buy-and-hold-'em-forever will soon prove to be.

The second reason why so many professionals advise never selling is the one repeated by every stock selecting money manager who has reached guru status: "No one can time the markets." What this sentiment truly means is, "*I* can't time the markets." It is not uncommon for people to think so highly of themselves that an inability on their part means an impossibility on everyone else's part. Yet to raise such an inability to the status of an investment philosophy has the potential to be devastating not only to its practitioners' portfolios, but to those of every individual investor who swallows this line of thinking.

Logically, while timing may be difficult, no investor *can avoid having an opinion on the market*, even if he claims otherwise. Every investment requires a market opinion. Those who say they have no opinion are merely expressing, by their action of purchasing or holding stocks, a bullish outlook at some degree of trend. If you are going to invest your money in any market, you must have an opinion, you must justify it, you must decide in advance either the grounds for deciding you must exit the position or that you will write off the entire amount if necessary, and finally, you must live with your decision.

Truly successful professional traders and market timers usually end up cultivating a *preference* for bear markets. One reason is that bear markets are swifter, and the reward for being right comes more quickly. A second reason, justifiable or not, is ego gratification. Any novice can luck into a profit in a bull market, but it takes a knowledgeable player to profit from a bear. Most people are perfectly happy to become invested in a bull market, but those willing to hold 100% cash (or to go short) in a bear market are few and far between. (For some money managers, 20% cash is a "maximum bearish" position.) Thus, a bear market most clearly separates the accomplished speculator from the rest. If you have not joined this select group already, maybe it is time for you to do so. The first major stock market move I personally followed closely was the 1973-1974 bear market, and I can tell you, it was substantially more exhilarating than all but seven years (1975-1976 and 1982-1987) of the 21-year bull market that has followed. Of course, the real key to a well-rounded investment strategy is learning to appreciate and handle *both*. Each has its day, and each will bring joys and gains if you are on the right side of it.

It is a curious fact of psychology that most investors, money managers and analysts hate bear markets even when they are bearish. It may stem from the fact that customers disappear in bear markets. Indeed, if the main goal of a portfolio manager is to retain his job or his customers, he will fear missing an uptrend more than losing all his clients' money in a downtrend. In an uptrend, the big winners get all the customers. In a downtrend, the customers disappear anyway. The public's bias in this regard is based upon an illusion that "up" is good and "down" is bad, indeed, that there even *is* an "up" and "down." However, a market chart merely shows a *ratio*. If one item is going down, the other is going up. If stocks and bonds are in a bear market, *then dollars in terms of stocks and bonds are in a bull market*. Flip the ratio, and you can show any bear market in stocks and bonds as a bull market in dollars. Why aren't investors happy to see *that* bull market? The psychological bias against bear markets produces a very negative result among professionals: Not 1% of the effort that goes into analysis and strategy for bull markets is spent to make money from a bear. I am not so biased, nor do I have a customer base that thinks only one way. Today, we are buying dollars with our stocks. Furthermore, if a speculator is willing to buy stocks and real estate with borrowed dollars (i.e., on margin and with a mortgage), doesn't it make sense to buy dollars with borrowed stocks and property? You can do it, in the stock market at least, by selling short.

Though an entirely reasonable thing to do at the right time, short selling entails risk. One must recognize such facts and say so, unlike most of today's investment advisors. For example, an *Elliott Wave Theorist* subscriber in 1994 wrote to a major stock fund group in the U.S. to ask if they offered a short selling fund. He was informed that management "preferred long term investment to speculation." *All investment is speculation*, and there is no more risky speculation than one that is confidently viewed by a majority of portfolio managers and the public as an investment.

WHAT TO DO (AND WHAT NOT TO DO)

Forecasts are made for a reason. To be successful in investing and in life, one must take advantage of high probability scenarios when they indicate opportunity and defend against high probability scenarios when they indicate danger. Followers of wave patterns took full advantage of the opportunity presented in 1982 when *The Elliott Wave Theorist* announced (a bit dramatically, perhaps) "SUPER BULL MARKET UNDERWAY!" and urged subscribers as follows:

Make no mistake about it. The next few years will be profitable beyond your wildest imagination. Make sure you make it while the making is good. Tune your mind to 1924. Plan during these five years to make your fortune. Then be prepared to lock it up safely for the bad years that are sure to follow.

Back then, taking risk in anticipation of a bullish scenario was warranted. The current juncture, in contrast, is providing us an opportunity to prepare for danger.

How might you go about surviving, and perhaps even prospering, in the approaching financial environment? Whatever your ultimate objective, you must think first of conserving what you have made during the good times. Take steps immediately to position yourself for maximum safety. Your first goal should be to get out of debt. Next, liquidate any assets that are likely to suffer in the depression. These include stocks, investment real estate, long term U.S. bonds and notes, corporate bonds, municipal bonds, "emerging market" debt and equity, overpriced collectibles and even your business, if it suits you.

Avoid having long term funds tied up in currently popular investment strategies. Eschew the now too popular exercise of selectively picking stocks and high yield debt instruments in an attempt to outperform the averages. Outperforming the traditional investment markets by buying the right issues is no longer a rational goal, as these markets will be falling, and outperforming (even if it is successful, which is a rare feat) will simply mean losing less money. Neither will "contrarian" stock market mutual funds be profitable in a bear market, as the only thing most contrarians are contrary about is *what stocks to own*, not whether to own them at all.

Given the high odds of a persistent decline in real estate values and the drying up of liquidity, readers of this book should avoid ownership of real estate for investment purposes unless you are a professional who genuinely knows something about a property that everyone else does not. The evidence of a change in trend for real estate prices in the late 1980s demanded only one change in your thinking: Consider your home only as a *consumption* item, no longer as an *investment* item. If you want to consume it, if you can afford it, and if it is situated to provide convenience, safety (in the case of social unrest) and the amenities you enjoy, then keep it. If you cannot afford it, or will not be able to afford it if you or your spouse loses a job, or if you consider it an investment and do not mind renting, then it is probably best to sell it. Since 1989, office rents in New

one road to riches. Unfortunately, there is not one person in a thousand who can perform it properly. Even for those who can, there will be unforeseen pitfalls.

For example, while short sales today appear to be a relatively safe speculation, the projected depth of the bear market is such that it may be a viable approach for only so long. There is an excellent chance that at some point the markets will be shut down. What are the odds that the New York Stock Exchange will close? Perhaps not very high, but neither is such an event impossible. A lot of people recall that on October 20, 1987, the bottom day of the crash, there were rumors, and evidence to back them, that the Federal Reserve was financing purchases of stock index futures and stocks to prop up the market. If that is true, today the Fed must look back on that experience as a dramatic success, as the market reversed and has not seen that level since. Its members will be confident of succeeding again if they decide to attempt to stop the upcoming bear market. Unfortunately, this one will be three degrees larger than that of 1987, and any success will be only temporary. An attempt to forestall the inevitable will ultimately prove to be a very expensive proposition, as were the government's repeated sales of gold in the 1970s, made in an attempt to halt the metal's runaway bull market. Such plans always fail in the end for lack of funds. Thus, if any authority, no matter how wealthy, tries to buy back the bull market, at some point it will realize that the tactic isn't working. When people who run a game realize that they are lined up for losses, they do what comes naturally, which is to protect themselves. In this case, they might choose to close the exchange. They might close it only to sell orders, just as the COMEX closed its exchange to buy orders in 1980 when the Hunt Brothers were helping push silver up to $50 an ounce. In January of that year, the exchange members, who were rumored to be heavily short, suddenly limited investors to buying and selling *only to liquidate existing positions*, which meant that if you were long, you could sell, and if you were short, as the exchange members presumably were, you could cover. Talk about a market rigged in favor of the shorts! In 1979, total trading volume in silver was 34 billion ounces. In 1980, volume dropped to 7 billion ounces, and prices collapsed. The message from this event is that the very smart market timers who are long puts or short futures might wake up one Saturday to find that the exchange will be selectively closed, or closed, period. They might be stuck for awhile wondering if they will ever see the money they rightfully earned.

Another wild card is the potential for the outright outlawing of certain markets. Government authorities, who proudly take credit for bull markets, will require a scapegoat for the decline. They will desperately order investigations to determine who (omitting themselves, of course) are to blame. The good news is that while the scapegoat is usually certain groups of *people* (speculators, short sellers, pool operators, you name it), this time it will probably be inanimate trading and arbitrage vehicles. The perfect candidate is derivatives, because so few people understand their role in providing risk reduction and market liquidity and will accept whatever blame is assigned to them. Though they are now seemingly permanently entrenched in the investment landscape, a dozen years from now, futures and options will be banned.

The point of these examples is that there may well be hidden pitfalls in terms of how you can prosper, or even survive, during the coming bear market. Some of them, despite the immense foreknowledge we do have, will be completely unforeseen. Do your best to avoid getting caught in an investment you cannot liquidate. If you are of that rare breed of trader who can move at lightning speed and stay alert for all contingencies, you should do extremely well.

If you are among the other 99.9% of the population, you should focus primarily on preserving your assets in what over the next several years may well be the most challenging investment environment in the history of the world. If you are successful, you will be able to scoop up bargains of historic proportion in stocks, property and gold at the ultimate bottom. More than one famous financier has built a dynasty by waiting patiently and then buying sold-out investments or near-bankrupt businesses at depressed prices.

One reason that the preservation of your savings is so important is that even the integrity of retirement plans and insurance policies is likely to be adversely affected by the coming crisis. Pensions are generally considered 100% safe, but today they are not. First, their assets are in investments that will fall a long way in the deflation. Second, they are not even fully funded in many cases. Among single-employer pension plans insured by the Pension Benefit Guaranty Corporation, the shortfall, i.e., the amount these corporations *should* have on hand to pay promised liabilities but do not, stood at $31 billion at the end of 1994. Companies' raids on assets are excused by the assumption that "everything is fine; we can fund it later." It does not help that the Pension Benefit Guaranty Corporation itself, which is a quasi-government agency that insures private pension plans, currently faces a $1.2 billion *deficit*. Even that is only a minor shocker compared to the fact that the U.S. government's own retirement programs are underfunded by *more than $1 trillion*. "Relax," they must be saying, "we can pay as we go with tax money and more bond issues, like we do with all our other promises." That game is about to end. When the deflation hits, countless pension plans will run dry of assets, and workers counting on them for retirement will find they have no value at the worst possible time: when the economy is in depression and their jobs are lost or at risk.

Unfortunately, your funds may prove to be at risk even if you have your own corporate plan or an IRA. These structures are government-granted and government-restricted. Several government spokesmen have lately made it clear that they have their eyes on this giant pool of money. How would you feel if someday the government announced, "Due to the obvious risks of stock investing, we will now forbid by law any pension plan from investing in anything other than safe U.S. or local government bonds"? At least you should be aware of the fact that your money can be confiscated without it ever leaving your account.

Insurance is considered most people's backup plan in case of disaster. Unfortunately, insurance companies in general are as caught up in the Great Asset Mania as anyone. As noted in Chapter 8, at least one company has already failed because it issued Guaranteed Investment Contracts (GICs) promising a return that the company could not meet. Most insurance companies hold a great portion of their assets in real estate, which is a highly illiquid investment in a bear market. Stocks and bonds, though liquid, also face bear markets, so will not be strongholds of value either. Few insurance companies have assets in high quality short term interest-bearing paper. When the markets fall and liquidity dries up, insurance companies will find themselves underfunded, and claims will go unfilled. Many will collapse under the weight of increasingly worthless portfolios. If you run an insurance company, get your portfolio liquid now. If you are an individual who can provide your own insurance, do so. At present, Swiss annuity certificates appear to offer the most attractive alternative.

The one and only place to put your money to insure that it will hold *some* purchasing power relative to goods and services is into money itself: physical gold. I do not include gold among a list of investments because gold is not an investment; it is *money*. Sad to

say, hoarding money does not add to productive capacity or prosperity. But in times of government currency and credit mismanage-
ment, there is little choice but to hold savings in a form that will
retain value. Unfortunately, gold is likely to fall precipitously during the deflation, in fact as much as 55%-80% from its 1995 high. So
even the gold bugs will lose money initially. If you want to accumu-
late gold now for the sake of capital safety, you can lock in its current
dollar value by selling futures contracts against it. If gold falls below $200 per ounce, though, it will be time to plan a major move into
real money, as it is unlikely ever to see the $100s again after it
bottoms in that area.

At the ultimate bottom, gold mining shares and collector coins,
though very inexpensive, will probably be less attractive than bullion and bullion style coins, for several reasons. First, in the next
multi-decade recovery, prosperity will return, but not to the best
levels of the 19th and 20th centuries. The premium that most people
will be able to pay for rarity or collectibility in coins will therefore
be far less than in the 1980s. Second, throughout most of the Grand
Supercycle bear market, even during its countertrend advances, global social conditions will be relatively unstable. Mining shares are
pieces of paper, the value of which is dependent upon corporate
health and the sanctity of private property. During difficult times,
governments become increasingly willing to confiscate assets, and
both the mines themselves and paper assets such as domestic stock
certificates might offer easy targets. Strikes and even foreign con-
quest could present risks. Indeed, the more difficult the situation
becomes for mines, the greater will be the probability, and therefore the fear, of a constriction of supply, which will raise the relative
value of existing bullion. Therefore, when the time comes to convert
cash to real money, non-numismatic gold coins will probably be the
most prudent choice.

Since depression inevitably results in social upheaval, you may
wish to "invest" in some areas that are normally outside the realm
of investment discussion. Learn an additional skill in your spare
time, one that will be of use if your current skills become worthless
in a depressionary or chaotic environment. Obtain a residence in an
area that is unlikely to be the target of mob violence or looting.
Move as much money out of the U.S. banking system as you comfortably can. Have some paper currency and a bag of silver coins on
hand for emergency purchases if the banks close. Insure food sup-
plies for what is likely to be a brief period of unavailability of basic

necessities. Investigate alternative countries or continents if the government becomes unbearably oppressive or a serious military conflict appears imminent any time in the years ahead. I also suggest that you arrange to help provide food and/or shelter for local citizens who were unprepared and fall on hard times. It will not only bring personal satisfaction but will make your community a more pleasant place to live.

Taking precautions such as those outlined in this chapter is simply a purchase of an unorthodox type of insurance. Be prepared for the worst and you will find that there is a lot less to worry about. Of utmost practical importance is the fact that if the outlook described in this book is entirely wrong, you will not lose money, but will have suffered merely by making less money (in safe interest-bearing instruments) than those who took risks. If the forecasts do come to pass, and if you arrange your affairs so that you have survived and prospered, you will be in the extreme minority.

Most people are doing the opposite of the preceding advice, as market psychology is positioned perfectly to prevent conventional analysts and their clients from profiting from the trend change that is imminent. In response to confident optimism among economists, many people who still have cash and credit are rushing out to buy property, stocks, junk bonds and businesses, and they are leveraging and extending themselves in the process. Do not fall into that trap. If you have not yet prepared for the depression and are not already stuck (say, in condominiums in New England), the powerful optimism that is now in place at the peak of the current short term business cycle is providing an excellent (and final) opportunity to get as liquid as possible. With the pressure off the economy over the past year or so, you have been given another brief window of opportunity to make final plans for the long term safety of your capital. Use this window of opportunity to your advantage. My job in the early 1980s was to prepare you to make money. My job today is to convince you to protect your assets. As long as the come-hither siren songs of "new Dow highs," "world peace forever," and "soft landing; no recession" continue to beckon, that job is not over.

Ultimately, the decision to act or not to act is yours. *The Elliott Wave Theorist* addressed the same point on May 2, 1983, saying, "As certain as I may be about how conditions will evolve [after the top], my forecasts are hardly infallible. For now, you should concern yourself with whether I am right on the extent of this bull market."

Since my outlook could be wrong, should you wait until the market falls to make up your mind to take action? Well, did you know that, following the recent devaluation of the Mexican peso, three offshore funds that invest in Mexico simply suspended operations for several weeks? If the SEC gives the go-ahead, *any* mutual fund can suspend redemptions, and its investors would simply be locked out. How would *you* like to be told that your investments are frozen, that you cannot get out, that you must sit as the market falls lower month after month? Further, consider this. The stock market rose 250% in just five years, until the 1987 peak. If you were in for that ride, you made a fortune, and you made it fast. Despite all the coverage that stocks enjoy in the press today, the major averages have added only 60% since that high, and they have taken nearly eight years to do it. The lesson is, if you want to get the most out of a market, make sure you are there at the start of the new trend. This necessity is even more applicable to the downside. When gold topped out in 1980, it fell from $850/oz. to $474 in *two months*. So if you say to yourself that you will wait and see if the market proves the outlook in this book correct, fine. Just remember, the early buyer makes the most in a bull market, and the early seller preserves the most in a bear market. By owning high quality yield-bearing instruments in safe currencies now, you may be early, but you will be guaranteed that when stocks, bonds, real estate and the economy finally hit bottom, you will be there with all your purchasing power intact at what is likely to be an even more rewarding opportunity than we had in 1982. Whether the flash point is now or a year from now, the investment landscape years hence will be the opposite of what it is today, and investors who have maintained or increased their purchasing power will be positioned to profit immensely. If you have patiently avoided investing in the stock, bond and property markets until the bargain table is filled with issues and parcels down 80% to 99% from their bull market peaks (stocks and bonds down 100% will not be for sale), you will then be positioned to scoop up the bargains and make a fortune.

CASSANDRA REPLIES

Some people have reacted to the long term opinion compelled by the Wave Principle with the response that it is alarmist and that such a clearly stated forecast for a historic market decline and an economic depression is dangerous. This is an emotional, not an intellectual, response to which I reply, "nonsense." If the market goes up while you are holding interest-bearing cash equivalents in safe currencies, you might make a little less money. So what? On the other hand, forecasting a *boom*, as we did in the late 1970s and early 1980s, carries with it a great responsibility, an understanding of how much damage you can do if you are wrong. The most dangerous statements are made by the *permanent optimists*, the ones who said that silver was going to $100 an ounce (as it dropped over 90%), the ones who said that investing in junk bonds was a good idea (before they crashed), the ones who said that secondary stocks would be the leaders in the 1980s-1990s bull market (while they have suffered their longest period of underperformance in sixty years), the ones who said that real estate was a guaranteed safe long term speculation (before liquidity disappeared and investors became locked in), the nine out of ten economists who said in June 1990 that there was no economic contraction on the horizon (just before the worst contraction in at least eight years), the ones who today say, "the stock market always goes up long term," "secondary stocks will explode on the upside any day," "junk bonds are a bargain," "real estate is a guaranteed safe long term investment," "gold coins will always rise in price," and "there will be no recession," so *"don't* get liquid, *don't* sell your business, *don't* stop building office space, *don't* move money out of the U.S. banking system." These are the truly hazardous forecasts, the ones that, if they are wrong, can *ruin your life.*

In truth, then, it is those who have been counseling a fully invested position in stocks, bonds and real estate over the past four years that bear the risk of being proven irresponsible. Many self-appointed advisors go as far as to mislead people into believing that they are authorities on market behavior when in fact they do not know the first thing about it. These smooth talkers and erudite writers confidently invite investors to take tremendous risk with their hard-earned savings. As a result, many people will soon discover the difference between *saving* and *investing*, a difference that both financial professionals and the media have neglected to explain. *Saving* is placing your money where it will retain its value in safety. *Investing* is placing your money at risk in the hopes of making a profit. A bond fund is *not* a savings account. A stock fund is *not* a savings account. A high yield money market fund is *not* a savings account. At best, every one of these are "investments," and at worst, they are dangerous speculations. Unfortunately, no one is saying so, and *you* will be the victim if you are led to believe otherwise. People in the wrong markets have lost some money already and could lose fortunes in the next few years, yet they are still being told to "hold on" and "buy more." Maybe that conviction will pan out, but what are the human consequences if it does not? If this bear market turns out to be a grizzly, the ones who opted to issue "reassuring" statements with no insight to justify them should be recognized as those whose words were truly dangerous and damaging. I can tell you, it is a wonderful relief to be completely in cash at this juncture. The question is not one of certainty, but one of preparedness and risk. While the negative result of an error of caution will be virtually nil, the risk of betting against it, both financially and otherwise, is incalculable. As it turned out, thankfully, our optimism in the early 1980s proved justified, and was rewarded. How dangerous is inaccurate optimism? An article from October 1991 contained this observation:

> **Forever changed:** The recession has deeply shaken many Americans. A survey by Warwick Baker & Fiore, a New York advertising agency, has found that 20 percent of 1,004 people polled feel they will "never be the same" because of the recession.

This is the effect of unfounded optimism among professional economists upon average people. In that case, the country merely suffered a *recession*. How will unprepared people be affected by a depression? Following bullish economists and investment professionals, businessmen today are once again expanding inventory, buying capital goods, securing long term contracts for lumber, copper and other commodities, and acquiring new businesses. Average investors are putting record amounts of money into stocks and bonds. Everyday people are borrowing to purchase consumer goods. Is it not more prudent to use the current euphoria and "good news" to *sell off* unwanted businesses, *unload* inventory, *sell* futures contracts for commodities, get *out* of stocks and bonds, *pare back* consumer debt, and otherwise prepare for a slowing of economic activity?

Throughout the tidal wave crash, the average citizen will be caught up in events, playing his part without comprehending what is happening because he has been counseled by a legion of optimists, who at this juncture are the true bearers of "gloom and doom." Heeding them will have set him up to be destroyed financially, emotionally and perhaps even physically. At the next major bottom, we will see who has fared best, those who say that a warning is dangerous or the few of us who think that incaution is dangerous.

Remember also that humanity has survived countless crises. As bad as things will get, we are not talking about Armageddon or Doomsday. Expectations for a long period of worldwide depression, economic chaos and ultimately social unrest do not indicate, as some might infer, that one should prepare for a return to the conditions of the Dark Ages. Periods of stagnation or regress are relative, and not only is the one we face at least one degree smaller than the one that produced the Dark Ages, but it is beginning from a much higher base. In other words, bad times are relative. No one will be living in a cave. For the most part, modern life will be maintained; only certain areas of the world will suffer the worst, and if history is any guide, those areas will be rebuilt afterward very quickly. Even if economic conditions deteriorate to the level of the 1930s, most people will get along acceptably well day-to-day. More to the point, *you* can remain perfectly comfortable by taking the right steps along the way. The only people who will be wiped out by the crash are those who participate in it. If you sell your stocks and bonds near the top and buy safe cash equivalents, your net worth will continue to increase despite the general decline in prosperity. There were a lot of prosperous people in the Great Depression, but the majority of them had successfully avoided being victims of the 1929-1932 crash. With the foreknowledge provided by this book, you will be able to avoid an even bigger one.

Good News

Is the forecast in this book depressing, or "bad news?" It is bad news only if you believe that declines in markets and contractions in business are abnormal. It is depressing only if you prefer evading reality to dealing with it. On the other hand, if setbacks, like advancements, are simply a fact of economic life, then to be warned of their approach can only be good news. The bad news is being oblivious and unprepared; the good news is being informed in advance of an impending change in the long term trend of social psychology. Indeed it is a wonderful gift, because while depressions are inevitable, personal bankruptcy and suffering are not. Forewarning gives you time to prepare, to protect yourself by arranging your business and finances accordingly even as times still appear prosperous. If you take the proper actions, you can even put yourself in a position to do something that no fund manager has ever done: make money in a bear market. If you are a fund manager who feels stuck with a forced bullish posture, you can sell your business and let someone else wrestle with the prolonged, tricky, and painful bear market, while you enter a gentlemanly retirement from the world of Wall Street, pursuing your personal passions as you sit out the Grand Supercycle bear. The Wave Principle provides us an advance peek at the probabilities. Accept the gift. Afterward, it is generally too late.

Needless to say, the opinion expressed in this book is far out of favor on Wall Street, not to mention Main Street. Long term forecasts that indicate a change in trend at the right time will never have a widespread acceptance. The reason that such forecasting is dismissed is that by nature, human beings project the future linearly, not cyclically. If you think about the consequences of this trait, you will realize that *the propensity for linear projection is precisely the trait that causes the excesses that produce social cyclicality.* A good deal of study, experience and practice are required to unlearn the natural tendency and adopt the correct orientation. The Wave Principle is a tool for *anticipating* trend changes and events; it does not merely reflect them. By definition, then, an outlook based upon it cannot be popularly accepted until the forecasted trend is well past its center point. When the superbullish *Elliott Wave Principle* was published in 1978, almost nobody bought it. Eight years later, deep into the bull market, tens of thousands of copies were being sold. When this book is published, almost nobody outside *Elliott Wave Theorist* subscribers will buy it. While I would just as soon that my assessment for the next decade be wrong for my family and friends' sake, the dearth of similar opinions among professionals, the public and the media suggests that it is not. Seventeen years later, except for some minor points, I would not change the forecasts in *Elliott Wave Principle.* Ten years from now, I expect to be content with the validity of the essential outlook presented in this book as well.

SOCIAL IMPLICATIONS

While the Wave Principle is the single best method for anticipating the behavior of markets, its value at times goes way beyond even that great benefit. As explained in Chapter 9, the effects that a change in market trend will have on society are not in evidence at the start of the trend. They become intensely manifest by the time of its termination. Is it too early to begin projecting events that will result from the approaching bear market in social mood? To be sure, this book contains dozens of very specific financial forecasts, which are at root social phenomena. Forecasting social events outside that realm, however, is an even more complex and less exact science. Nevertheless, a few observations appear suited to the limited scope of this book.

A long term trend toward a positive social mood always leads to times of peace and political cooperation, such as we enjoy today. An extreme trend change in social mood toward the negative always leads to calamities. The average level of conflict during the bear market will be far greater than it was during the bull market and will lead to periods of turmoil, not just in financial markets, but in society. Indeed, the trends now implied by long term market patterns have *always* produced dramatic social upheaval. The last time a bear market of the currently projected magnitude took place was 1720 to 1784, a period that began with a market crash, ended with the Revolutionary War, and led to a deep and global five-year depression.

The coming trend of negative social psychology will be characterized primarily by polarization between and among various perceived groups, whether political, ideological, religious, geographical, racial or economic. The result will be a net trend toward anger, fear, intolerance, disagreement and exclusion, as opposed to the bull market years, whose net trend has been toward benevolence, confidence, tolerance, agreement and inclusion. Such a sentiment change typically brings conflict in many forms, and evidence of it will be visible in all types of social organizations. Political manifestations will include protectionism in trade matters, a polarized and vocal electorate, separatist movements, xenophobia, citizen-government clashes, the dissolution of old alliances and parties, and the emergence of radical new ones. Tariffs will become popular, regardless of the fact that virtually everyone knows they are dangerous and wrong, because they are a consequence of an increasingly negative psychology involving fear, envy and a misguided attempt at self-defense. Xenophobia will be practiced regardless of people's generally good intentions, because fear and hatred become pervasive in major bear markets regardless of whether or not they are justified. There will also be a danger that governments will impose police-state type controls as a consequence of the bear market. Such periods often end with emotional political oustings, whether by vote, resignation, impeachment, coup or revolution.

The Elliott Wave Theorist said in 1982 that given the outlook for a Cycle degree bull market, which portended an increasingly gentle social sentiment, there would be "no major war for at least ten years." That forecast was as comforting as it was accurate.

By contrast, bear markets of the magnitude projected by this book always lead to at least one major war, if not several wars or protracted warring. Wars are typically the product of "C" waves in bear markets. Though not without perturbation, society weathers "A" waves relatively well. "B" waves make people think the worst has passed, though, and when their hopes are dashed by the "C" wave, they get angry. That is when society becomes its most furious, fearful, nihilistic and exclusionary. The classic result is war.

The next major decline will presumably be wave (A) of a Grand Supercycle, thereby reducing the chances of a world war beginning during the immediately approaching crisis. However, a world war will almost certainly begin during or at the end of wave (C) of the Grand Supercycle, which according to the time analysis in Chapter 5 should terminate in the 2050s. However, it is flatly impossible to make any such timing a *prediction*. The only reliable prediction is that war will occur during or shortly after the "C" wave at the highest degree within whatever correction takes place, whether it is Grand Supercycle wave Four, as I expect, or Supercycle wave II under the milder scenario outlined in Chapter 5. Ironically, under the milder scenario, war will occur sooner, being associated with wave C of II, than if a Grand Supercycle correction unfolds. The compensation will be that it will be less severe.

For whatever reason (perhaps because of society's negative emotional state and, as a result, people's weakened physical state), communicable disease sometimes plays a prominent role in major corrective periods, with some Cycle and Supercycle degree corrections containing epidemics and larger ones pandemics. With war and epidemics possible, the coming crisis will almost certainly pertain not only to property, but to survival. Be sure to stay vigilant. There will be more physical danger in the next fifty-plus years than there was in the last fifty. The most dangerous time socially and politically will be during and for a few years after wave (C), whenever it occurs. One thing is for certain: Several years from now, following the market and watching financial television for the latest stock tip will have become less relevant to the average person's life. The next 10% move in the Dow will be far less important to most people, as their minds will be on other things.

Conflict is always with us, as are joy and harmony. For the most part, human progress and happiness prevail. Throughout even the major corrective periods of history, most people have lived normal and fulfilling lives while an unfortunate few have gotten caught up in the various social maelstroms that such periods produce. The main point of foreknowledge is to be prepared mentally so that you can recognize the geographical centers of physical conflict as they are brewing and act to avoid them if necessary. Forewarning can mean the difference between life and death, which is why this book is important even to non-investors.

With regard to specific upcoming events, junctures such as this in the long term wave structure portend virtually inconceivable social disruptions. In 1929, with the Dow at 381, who would have believed that in less than three years the Dow would fall 89% to 41, that in ten years war and holocaust would begin in Europe, that in twelve years aircraft would attack Pearl Harbor, that in twenty years (at the termination of the wave (IV) bear market in constant dollars), the most populous country in the world, as well as half of Europe, would be taken over by Communists? And who would have believed in 1949 that in forty more years (near the termination of wave V), the Communists would relinquish power and free these same countries? The spirit of each of these actions was consistent with the position of the wave structure at the time. Specifics, however, cannot be forecasted at the outset, only surmised. As the trends develop, more and more specifics can be anticipated, however, and plans can usually be formulated in time to avoid the trouble spots.

Even at this early date, we might speculate on just a few developments that appear likely. For instance, I would be inclined to expect (in no particular order or time frame) that the Middle East and Latin America will destabilize; producing countries will wage a trade war of increasing tariffs; fashionable women will sport floor length skirts and dresses; horror movies will reach new depths of depravity and at least one will win an award; gang and political violence will wax; an epidemic will erupt; articles and seminars will appear on "How to Declare Bankruptcy and Walk Away From Debt"; the U.S. government will make it a crime to send money out of the country and seize property from citizens trying to flee with assets;

militias will declare independence from the U.S. government and clash with federal police; immigration, emigration and foreign travel will be restricted; a nationalistic dictator will take over in Russia; secessionist movements will take place in many countries, including the U.S.; tales of corruption among banking and government officials will surface; new political parties will gain strength and receive press coverage; the U.S. government will abandon the Drug War; one or both of the major political parties will disappear; state and local governments will slash services; North Korea, Cuba, and much of Africa will experience famine; Russia will retire the ruined ruble; a tax revolt will take place; wars will erupt in Asia and the Middle East; the World Bank will fail; a major commodity exchange and a minor stock exchange will fold; the unemployment rate will exceed 30%; several major world powers will become engaged in armed conflict; nihilistic art will become fashionable; there will be a run on the banks and a nationwide closure; Congress will pass laws designed to prevent the stock and bond market debacles that have already occurred; a U.S. president will resign, be impeached, or be rejected for a second term by a landslide vote with record turnout; the Fed will be nationalized; there will be food riots; the U.N. will disband; foreigners will commit terrorist acts on U.S. soil; the U.S. government will adopt numerous police state style controls; radical ideas will be introduced into the political debate; over half the House and nearly one third of the Senate will be thrown out of office in a Congressional election; Social Security, Medicare, workers' compensation, food stamps and minimum wage laws will be repealed, either entirely or to be replaced by a single "national assistance" program; moralists, authoritarians, patriots and libertarians will gain political clout; major international agreements will be broken; several nuclear bombs will be detonated in acts of war; finally, World War III will destroy more lives than all prior wars. The conclusion of this trend of events and social mood will set the base for the next advance, which will produce another glorious period of economic expansion, social well-being, beneficial technological innovation, political freedom, peace, and philosophical and spiritual progress.

THE AFTERMATH

When the king asked the royal philosopher to provide him with a motto that would serve under every circumstance, whether wonderful or devastating, the philosopher, after some thought, replied,

"This, too, shall pass." Rough times, like good times, recur, but they always end. Measured, recurring corrections of prior trends are part of the natural fractal order of things; they have a purpose and are good, or they would not exist. Because human progress takes place in a "three steps forward, two steps back" manner, it is clear that the "two steps back" are required to put psychology and motivation in a condition to support the next geometric rise in material, social and intellectual progress. Corrections may be part of the mechanism of life itself. The very ultimate success of life may depend upon the occasional weeding out of those not intelligent enough to prepare, strong enough to fight, benevolent enough to avoid participating in the destruction of others, or unlucky enough to be in the wrong place at the wrong time.

The Wave Principle shows clearly that the ultimate path of human progress is ever upward; it is merely interrupted by periodic setbacks. At this point in human history, such a period will serve to give the United States, and much of the world, a long time to re-evaluate current economic and political "wisdom" and make the fundamental decisions necessary to bring about the changes that will eventually allow the freer citizens of the world to begin building for a new Grand Supercycle advance.

The magnitude of the coming crash and depression will dwarf any previous such difficulty the country has experienced. The resulting calamity will be the single most important influence on your personal and professional life for the duration. It will affect most things that happen to you, that you decide to do, or that you are forced to do. It will affect your business, your professional and personal relationships with other people, your friends and members of your family. If you are part of society, you are going to have to deal with the coming changes one way or another. The question is, will you deal with them from a position of strength and confidence, or will you react in panic along with everybody else? It is important to come to grips with the implications early. If you get your house in order before the new trend begins, you will be able to avoid much of the damage and, in fact, take advantage of the upcoming historic opportunities by calmly making opportunistic decisions when the time comes.

Someday your grandchildren will ask you about the Great Asset Mania. "What was it *like* when people couldn't get enough stocks and bonds?" "Well," you will reply, "believe it or not, it seemed perfectly normal at the time." Then they will ask you about the statistics.

Were there really more stock mutual funds than there were individual stocks on the NYSE and ASE exchanges *combined*? Did the public actually pour *record amounts* of money into stock mutual funds month after month even though most stocks were barely rising? Did pension funds really put all the assets they were supposed to protect into transportation stocks yielding a record low 1%, industrial stocks yielding a record low 2½%, and illiquid real estate that had risen thousands of percent in just two decades? Did numerous companies actually pass resolutions *forcing* executives to take huge positions in company stock? Did people really pour their savings into junk, municipal and zero-coupon bonds even though the economic recovery after 1991 was one of the weakest ever? Did most professionals really counsel the public that stocks and bonds were a *necessity* in a portfolio and that long term they always went up? And you will say, "Yes."

These closing comments from *Elliott Wave Principle* in 1978 now bear upon the next ten years: "When the fifth wave of the fifth wave tops out, we need not ask why it has done so. Reality, again, will be forced upon us...and the laws of nature will have to be patiently relearned." To which should be added, "at least for a time."

You may take or leave my message, but at least you know one thing: it is unequivocal and, to the extent possible, unhedged. I know what I think, and I know why I think it. As for how things will turn out, we will take another look in a decade or so and see what has happened. The simultaneous dangers and opportunities presented if this outlook plays out will be the kind upon which many fortunes are lost, and a few are built. I wish you success.

> *If you can keep your head when all about you*
> *are losing theirs...*
> *Yours is the Earth and everything that's in it.*

— Rudyard Kipling

APPENDICES

Appendix A

A CAPSULE SUMMARY
OF THE WAVE PRINCIPLE

The Wave Principle is Ralph Nelson Elliott's discovery that social, or crowd, behavior trends and reverses in recognizable patterns. Using stock market data as his main research tool, Elliott isolated thirteen patterns of movement, or "waves," that recur in market price data. He named, defined and illustrated those patterns. He then described how these structures link together to form larger versions of those same patterns, how those in turn link to form identical patterns of the next larger size, and so on. In a nutshell, then, the Wave Principle is a catalog of price patterns and an explanation of where these forms are likely to occur in the overall path of market development.

Pattern Analysis

Until a few years ago, the idea that market movements are patterned was highly controversial, but recent scientific discoveries have established that pattern formation is a fundamental characteristic of complex systems, which include financial markets. Some such systems undergo "punctuated growth," that is, periods of growth alternating with phases of non-growth or decline, building fractally into similar patterns of increasing size. This is precisely the type of pattern identified in market movements by R.N. Elliott some sixty years ago.

The basic pattern Elliott described consists of *impulsive waves* (denoted by numbers) and *corrective waves* (denoted by letters). An impulsive wave is composed of five subwaves and moves in the same direction as the trend of the next larger size. A corrective wave is composed of three subwaves and moves *against* the trend of the next larger size. As Figure A-1 shows, these basic patterns *link* to form five- and three-wave structures of increasingly larger size (larger "degree" in Elliott terminology).

In Figure A-1, the first small sequence is an impulsive wave ending at the peak labeled 1. This pattern signals that the movement of one larger degree is also upward. It additionally signals the start of a three-wave corrective sequence, labeled wave 2.

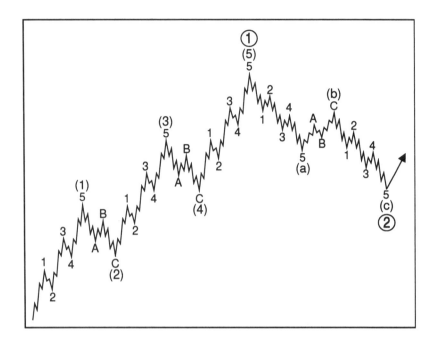

Waves 3, 4 and 5 complete a larger impulsive sequence, labeled wave (1). Exactly as with wave 1, the impulsive structure of wave (1) tells us that the movement at the *next* larger degree is upward and signals the start of a three-wave corrective downtrend of the same degree as wave (1). This correction, wave (2), is followed by waves (3), (4) and (5) to complete an impulsive sequence of the next larger degree, labeled wave ①. Once again, a three-wave correction of the same degree occurs, labeled wave ②. Note that at each "wave one" peak, the implications are the same regardless of the size of the wave. Waves come in degrees, the smaller being the building blocks of the larger. A list of degrees and notations precedes Chapter 2.

Within a corrective wave, waves A and C may be smaller-degree impulsive waves, consisting of five subwaves. This is because they move in the same direction as the next larger trend, i.e., waves (2) and (4) in the illustration. Wave B, however, is always a corrective wave, consisting of three subwaves, because it moves *against* the larger downtrend.

Within impulsive waves, one of the odd-numbered waves (usually wave three) is typically longer than the other two. Most impulsive waves unfold between parallel lines except for fifth waves, which occasionally unfold between converging lines in a form called a "diagonal triangle." Variations in corrective patterns involve repetitions of the three-wave theme, creating more complex structures that are named with such terms as "zigzag," "flat," "triangle" and "double three." Waves two and four typically "alternate" in that they take different forms. These forms and concepts are illustrated just before the start of Chapter 2.

Each type of market pattern has a name and a geometry that is specific and exclusive under certain rules and guidelines, yet variable enough in other aspects to allow for a limited diversity within patterns of the same type. If indeed markets are patterned, and if those patterns have a recognizable geometry, then regardless of the variations allowed, certain relationships in extent and duration are likely to recur. In fact, real world experience shows that they do. The most common and therefore reliable wave relationships are discussed in *Elliott Wave Principle*, by A.J. Frost and Robert Prechter.

Applying the Wave Principle

The goal of any analytical method is to identify market lows suitable for entering positions on the long side (or covering shorts) and market highs suitable for taking profits (or selling short). The Elliott Wave Principle is especially well suited to these functions. Nevertheless, the Wave Principle does not provide *certainty* about any one market outcome; rather, it provides an objective means of assessing the relative *probabilities* of possible future paths for the market. At any time, two or more valid wave interpretations are usually acceptable by the *rules* of the Wave Principle. The rules are highly specific and keep the number of valid alternatives to a minimum. Among the valid alternatives, the analyst will generally regard as preferred the interpretation that satisfies the largest number of *guidelines* and will accord top alternate status to the interpretation satisfying the next largest number of guidelines, and so on.

Alternate interpretations are extremely important. They are not "bad" or rejected wave interpretations. Rather, they are valid interpretations that are accorded a lower probability than the preferred count. They are an essential aspect of trading with the Wave Principle, because in the event that the market fails to follow the preferred scenario, the top alternate count becomes the investor's backup plan.

Fibonacci Relationships

One of Elliott's most significant discoveries is that the number of waves that exist in the stock market's patterns reflects the Fibonacci sequence of numbers (1, 1, 2, 3, 5, 8, 13, 21, 34, etc.), an additive sequence that nature employs in many processes of growth and decay, expansion and contraction, progress and regress. The sequence is governed by the Fibonacci ratio, which is .618 or ϕ (phi), the only number when divided into 1 equals itself plus 1, i.e., 1.618. ϕ is (after the first few numbers) the ratio between adjacent terms in not only the Fibonacci sequence, but in any additive sequence that derives from adding two successive terms to get the next, which is why nature employs it so ubiquitously in growth patterns. Alternate terms in such sequences are related by ϕ^2, or .382, whose inverse is 2.618. Elliott's observation that markets unfold in sequences of five and three waves led inescapably to the conclusion that bear markets, bull markets and complete cycles produce a Fibonacci number of subwaves that follow the entire sequence, as illustrated in Figure A-2. Because Fibonacci ratios appear throughout the price and time structure of the stock market, they apparently govern its progress.

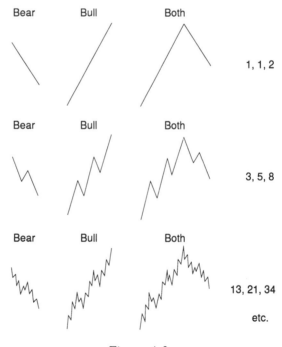

Figure A-2

What the Wave Principle says, then, is that mankind's progress (of which the stock market is a popularly determined valuation) does not occur in a straight line, does not occur randomly, and does not occur cyclically. Rather, progress takes place in a "three steps forward, two steps back" fashion, a form that nature prefers. As a corollary, the Wave Principle reveals that periods of setback in fact are a requisite for social (and perhaps even individual) progress.

Implications

A long term forecast for the stock market provides insight into the potential changes in social psychology and even the occurrence of resulting events. Since the Wave Principle reflects social mood change, it has not been surprising to discover, with preliminary data, that the trends of popular culture that also reflect mood change move in concert with the ebb and flow of aggregate stock prices. Popular tastes in entertainment, self-expression and political representation all reflect changing social moods and appear to be in harmony with the trends revealed more precisely by stock market data. At one-sided extremes of mood expression, changes in cultural trends can be forecasted.

On a philosophical level, the Wave Principle suggests that the nature of mankind has within it the seeds of social change. As an example simply stated, prosperity ultimately breeds reactionism, while adversity eventually breeds a desire to achieve and succeed. The social mood is always in flux at all degrees of trend, moving toward one of two polar opposites in every conceivable area, from a preference for heroic symbols to a preference for antiheroes, from joy and love of life to cynicism, from a desire to build and produce to a desire to destroy. Most important to individuals, portfolio managers and investment corporations is that the Wave Principle indicates in advance the relative *magnitude* of the next period of social progress or regress.

Living in harmony with those trends can make the difference between success and failure in financial affairs. As the Easterners say, "Follow the Way." As the Westerners say, "Don't fight the tape." In order to heed these nuggets of advice, however, it is necessary to know what is the Way, and which way the tape. There is no better method for answering that question than the Wave Principle.

To obtain a full understanding of the Wave Principle including the terms and patterns, please read *Elliott Wave Principle* by A.J. Frost and Robert Prechter.

GLOSSARY OF ELLIOTT WAVE TERMS

Alternation (guideline of) - If wave two is a sharp correction, wave four will usually be a sideways correction, and vice versa.

Apex - Intersection of the two boundary lines of a contracting triangle.

Corrective wave - A three wave pattern, or combination of three wave patterns, that moves in the opposite direction of the trend of one larger degree.

Diagonal Triangle (Ending) - A wedge shaped pattern containing overlap that occurs only in fifth or C waves. Subdivides 3-3-3-3-3.

Diagonal Triangle (Leading) - A wedge shaped pattern containing overlap that occurs only in first or A waves. Subdivides 5-3-5-3-5.

Double Three - Combination of two simple sideways corrective patterns, labeled W and Y, separated by a corrective wave labeled X.

Double Zigzag - Combination of two zigzags, labeled W and Y, separated by a corrective wave labeled X.

Equality (guideline of) - In a five-wave sequence, when wave three is the longest, waves five and one tend to be equal in price length.

Expanded Flat - Flat correction in which wave B enters new price territory relative to the preceding impulse wave.

Failure - See Truncated Fifth.

Flat - Sideways correction labeled A-B-C. Subdivides 3-3-5.

Impulse Wave - A five wave pattern that subdivides 5-3-5-3-5 and contains no overlap.

Impulsive Wave - A five wave pattern that makes progress, i.e., any impulse or diagonal triangle.

Irregular Flat - See Expanded Flat.

One-two, one-two - The initial development in a five wave pattern, just prior to acceleration at the center of wave three.

Overlap - The entrance by wave four into the price territory of wave one. Not permitted in impulse waves.

Previous Fourth Wave - The fourth wave within the preceding impulse wave of the same degree. Corrective patterns typically terminate in this area.

Sharp Correction - Any corrective pattern that does not contain a price extreme meeting or exceeding that of the ending level of the prior impulse wave; alternates with sideways correction.

Sideways Correction - Any corrective pattern that contains a price extreme meeting or exceeding that of the prior impulse wave; alternates with sharp correction.

Third of a Third - Powerful middle section within an impulse wave.

Thrust - Impulsive wave following completion of a triangle.

Triangle (contracting, ascending or descending) - Corrective pattern, subdividing 3-3-3-3-3 and labeled a-b-c-d-e. Occurs as a fourth, B or Y wave. Trendlines converge as pattern progresses.

Triangle (expanding) - Same as other triangles but trendlines diverge as pattern progresses.

Triple Three - Combination of three simple sideways corrective patterns labeled W, Y and Z, each separated by a corrective wave labeled X.

Triple Zigzag - Combination of three zigzags, labeled W, Y and Z, each separated by a corrective wave labeled X.

Truncated Fifth - The fifth wave in an impulsive pattern that fails to exceed the price extreme of the third wave.

Zigzag - Sharp correction, labeled A-B-C. Subdivides 5-3-5.

THE MESSAGE FROM FIXED TIME CYCLES

Time forecasting (as opposed to recognizing an important juncture as it is occurring) is the most difficult analytical task using the currently known tools of the Wave Principle. While time analysis provides specific possibilities, they become high or low *probabilities* only when each suggested time relationship is actually approached.

Until the time length of patterns can be more accurately forecast, I feel compelled by the challenge of the puzzle to apply any and all tools that have some applicability to the time forecasting problem. The main one of these is fixed-time cycles. Stock market history reveals a tendency for prices to bottom at regular intervals, with advances in between.

Unfortunately, cycles are inherently unreliable. As countless analysts have observed, cyclic market behavior is subject to changes in emphasis, shifts in length, and even disappearance. Cycle enthusiasts are at a loss to explain these repeated disappointments, although some have devised methods for dealing with them that are quite inventive and often useful in practical application.

The reason for the difficulty is that cycles are not the essence behind the market's behavior. Market behavior is based upon chaotic processes, which are perfectly patterned, yet not perfectly regular. Upon occasion, times of prolonged regular periodicity arise as a by-product. As an example outside the realm of time, you may have noticed that computer generated fractal artworks often contain, in the midst of a chaotic tapestry, a perfect oval or other such form. That form is a *by-product* of the process, not the generator of the process. The same thing is true of market cycles: They are a by-product of the process, not the generator. While chaotic processes show regular forms for brief times, they then disappear, like a bubble in boiling water. Because the market is a chaotic process, its precise repetitions are similarly temporary.

For this reason, expecting fixed periodicities to repeat is a bit like playing Russian Roulette. We know that the cycle will disappear someday. Yet we also know that until that day comes, it can repeat many times with remarkable precision. A classic example is the four-year cycle that held fast from 1954 until 1982 (see Figure 2-5 for reference), producing seven revolutions marking eight market bottoms. Had an observer recognized that cycle in 1962, he could have amassed a fortune over the next two decades on the basis of that one observation alone. However, in 1986, the falling portion of the cycle failed to provide a bear market, and in 1987, its rising portion failed to prevent the biggest two-week crash since 1929.

Elliott Wave Principle demonstrated the fundamentality of the Wave Principle relative to cycles by actually forecasting the demise of the four-year cycle. Because wave V was expected to behave more like wave I than wave III (since wave III was the extension), the authors made this forecast:

> The current wave V, then, should be a simpler structure [than wave III] with shorter cycle lengths, and could provide for the sudden contraction of the popular four-year cycle to more like three and a half years.

In fact, a 3-year cycle, beginning in 1975 and with lows in 1978, 1981, 1984, 1987 and 1990 held sway from that point forward, whereas the 4-year cycle bottom due in 1986 was hardly discernible. Even the 3-year cycle may now have disappeared, since there was no discernible bottom in 1993. Since the stock market today is shifting from an advancing Grand Supercycle to a declining one, even very long term cycles, which are the focus of this chapter, are at risk of termination. Indeed, given my best efforts using the cyclic method of time forecasting, I have experienced over the years at least as many failures as successes. Then why undertake the analysis?

The value of these exercises is not so much precise prediction, but extra knowledge that can be weighed against market behavior *when the indicated times arrive*. In the context presented here, this knowledge is understood as being tentative and less reliable than the form and price forecasts based upon Elliott Wave analysis. Nevertheless, it will increase in utility if, as the forecasted times are approached, the market is behaving in such a way as to indicate the high probability of a low in the making, i.e., with price patterns, momentum indicators and investor sentiment all commensurate with a projected cyclic bottom.

THE IDEALIZED KONDRATIEFF CYCLE

Known by the ancient Israelites, identified by the Mayas of Central America centuries ago, and rediscovered in the 1920s by economist Nikolai Kondratieff of Russia, the Kondratieff cycle is a repetitive pattern of financial and economic behavior that lasts on average approximately 54 years. That this length is close to a Fibonacci 55 years may or may not be coincidence.

The cycle is of such duration and strength that its observers have concluded all kinds of things about its presumed cause, involving theories of factory capacity utilization, generation-by-generation experience with excessive debt or lack thereof, etc. However, there is no difference between the operation of this cycle and any other. Its size associates it with certain phenomena, such as inflation and deflation, the rise and fall of wholesale prices, the expansion and contraction of production, and the expansion of credit followed by debt liquidation, that would not have time to result from a cycle lasting merely weeks. The associated phenomena may appear causal, but they are actually results of patterns of mass psychological change as reflected by the cycle. There are many cycles smaller and larger than the Kondratieff cycle. Does the 3-week cycle have anything to do with inventories and debt? If not, then why should the 54-year cycle be fundamentally different? As I see it, all cycles result from the natural workings of social psychology.

A study of the past five Kondratieff cycles reveals that the progression of financial events through each one is the same, although the timing of the events within the cycles varies. From the trough, an economic expansion takes place. It is accompanied by monetary stability or mild inflation, and rising capital markets. After a couple of decades, inflation accelerates, causing the price of physical goods to rise. Capital markets go sideways or down during this period, falling substantially in inflation-adjusted terms. After a decade or so, the end of the period of high inflation is signaled by a sharp recession in business activity. Following the recession is a period called the "plateau," a decade or so of disinflation or mild deflation during which time the value of capital markets rises dramatically while the economy expands again. That period is followed by a severe deflation that causes the prices of capital markets as well as physical goods to fall. This fall brings on a depression in business activity. Debt liquidation takes place over several years, and the economy "resets" for the next cycle. The idealized Kondratieff cycle is depicted in Figure B-1.

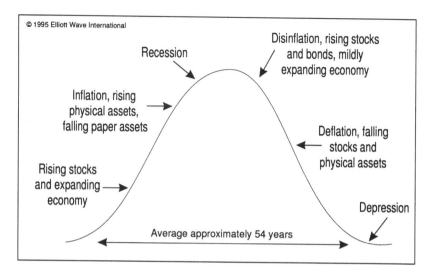

Figure B-1

Analytical History

Elliott Wave Principle showed an idealized diagram of the Kondratieff cycle and concluded as follows:

> As we interpret the Kondratieff cycle, we have now reached another plateau, having had a trough war (World War II), a peak war (Vietnam), and a primary recession (1974-75). This plateau should again be accompanied by relatively prosperous times and a strong bull market in stocks. The economy should [then] collapse in the mid-1980s, and be followed by three or four years of severe depression and a long period of deflation through to the trough year 2000.

Unfortunately, A.J. Frost and I had taken the original version of Figure B-2 from Kondratieff cycle experts at face value. As we later realized, those experts had little confidence in the cycle's precision, as their diagram showed the previous low in the late 1930s, a scant 40 years after the preceding trough of 1896. The depression of the 1930s appeared to most interpreters as the defining factor, even though it made the preceding cycle too short. Their error stemmed from the classic error of all conventional analysts, which is to assume that events cause cycles rather than understanding that cycles prompt events. As a result, their analysis was off by a decade, and our time forecast suffered as a result.

Despite this error, our Kondratieff cycle study was indispensable in supporting the Elliott Wave case that a stock market boom lay directly ahead. Even being off by a decade could not disrupt the inescapable conclusion that no depression was imminent. On October 5, 1981, at the bottom of a big slide in stock prices, when worry was widespread, *The Elliott Wave Theorist* said:

> I do *not* subscribe to the idea that the Kondratieff cycle turn to the downside has been made. My work overwhelmingly supports the idea that [the stock market] is in for a huge move to the upside *right now*, indicating a period of several years of *extremely high liquidity* (reflation) and a recovery in the economy. And what better way to start upward than to have the opinion of the public at its highest level of bearishness since the 1974 Cycle wave low?

That was ten months before the great liftoff. *The Elliott Wave Theorist* repeatedly countered "killer wave" arguments until the stock market boom could no longer be denied. No killer wave occurred, of course, and today the very idea has long been forgotten, just when it truly pertains.

The behavior of monetary conditions and the economy provided both initial confusion and the final answer to the question of the Kondratieff cycle's true position. The double peaks in inflation in 1974 and 1980 and the double recessions of 1974-1975 and 1980-1982 produced a complex transition from the inflationary period to the plateau period. The resumption of the rise of gold and silver prices in the latter half of the 1970s and their subsequent reversal in 1980 suddenly made it clear that the assumption that the previous Kondratieff cycle had bottomed in the 1930s and peaked in the mid-1970s was wrong.

As *The Elliott Wave Theorist* later put it, "The charts and dates make it absolutely clear that the Kondratieff cycle's inflationary peak was 1980-1981, *not* 1974 as many analysts still insist." Deep within the recession of 1982, *The Elliott Wave Theorist* quickly came to the proper conclusion, that the Kondratieff cycle's post-inflation recession was in progress or ending, and that there was a strong probability that finally, "the plateau has just begun." The November issue of that year added, "A Kondratieff plateau period fits here like a glove. The last plateau period lasted from 1921 to 1929, and the market went crazy."

The April 1983 Special Report (which is reprinted in its entirety in Appendix A of *Elliott Wave Principle*) corrected the timing
error and showed the "Economic K-Wave" (see Figure 3-2) as having begun in 1949, 53 years after the preceding bottom, as it should
have. That was the year that Supercycle wave IV ended in the CPI-
adjusted Dow, which is important in displaying the current cycle
because of the disengagement in the twentieth century of the U.S.
dollar from any concrete anchor.

Although the debt liquidation phase of the last cycle ended in
1948/1949, that was not the most *severe* point of debt liquidation
because the Elliott Wave pattern for Cycle wave IV was a triangle
(see Figure 3-2), which produced an early low in prices even though
the cycle was still in effect. Wave A into 1932 was the most severe,
and wave C into 1942 was the next most severe. The recession of
1948-1949 was simply a mopping up at the end of the cycle. This
analysis correctly placed the entire cycle seven to seventeen years
beyond the position that others had assumed. Thus, it had become
clear by 1982 that the cycle was following its classic time schedule,
if not a classic profile at its trough and peak. The result was that
the plateau was due to carry not to "the early 1980s," but to the
early *1990s*. Figure B-2 is the idealized diagram shown in *Elliott
Wave Principle*, with the appropriate corrections, noted in boxes,
added to the last cycle.

Analysis

The reason that a discussion of the Kondratieff cycle appears
warranted for this book is that the current cycle has followed the
typical script fairly closely. From 1949 came two decades of rising
stock prices and economic expansion, with a background of monetary stability involving mild inflation. Then came a decade of
accelerating inflation and falling paper asset markets. The end of
this period was signaled by the sharp recession in business activity
of 1980-1982, which squelched the inflation. The next event due was
the plateau, which has unfolded in textbook fashion. Disinflation
has reigned throughout, producing "relatively prosperous times, and
a strong bull market in stocks," exactly as *Elliott Wave Principle*
had forecasted. Note that our description was for "relatively" prosperous times, not broadly prosperous ones. Accordingly, the economy
has expanded substantially, yet without the robustness of the first
phase of the cycle in the 1950s and 1960s. The plateau period al-

As produced in *Elliott Wave Principle* from another source, with later dates corrected in boxes.

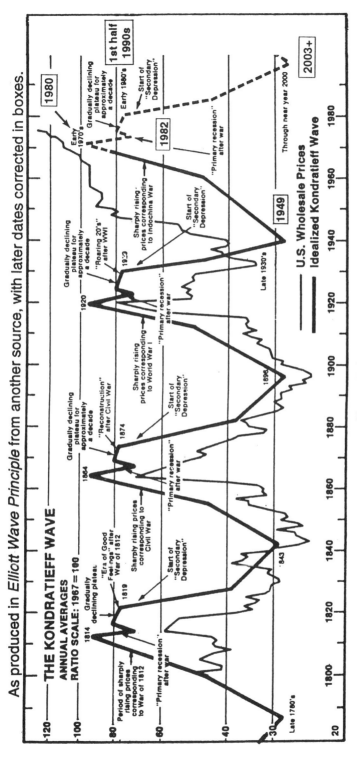

Figure B-2

ways supports a *selective* prosperity during the transition from inflation to deflation, since the sectors of the economy that benefit
from inflation, such as farms and oil companies, find themselves in
a relatively depressed state. The prosperity in a plateau is built
largely on a rise in the value of investments, a fragile base and one
that allows for the swift transition to depression when those values
collapse in a wave of deflation. Because the plateau phase began in
1982, a typical duration would have it ending in the early to mid-
1990s. That is where we are today. The next phase is the last one in
the cycle: deflation, debt liquidation and depression, just as occurred
in the 1840s-1850s, the 1890s, and the 1930s-1940s. Figure B-3 shows
how inflation-adjusted stock prices have fit into the last one and a
half cycles.

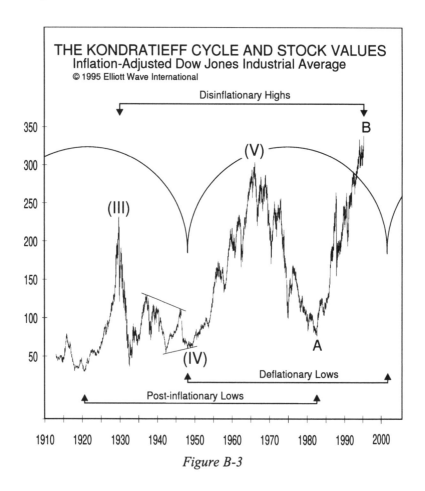

Figure B-3

Confirmation From Momentum

The technical aspects of the stock market advance from 1982 fit the theory that the Kondratieff cycle is operating. Figure 3-2 showed that the forecasted Cycle wave V bull market was to occur during the *declining* portion of the Kondratieff cycle, just as did the Cycle wave V bull market of the 1920s. A stock market advance against a declining cycle is usually thin in terms of the net daily advance-decline figures, which this one certainly has been, as illustrated in Figure 6-7. This fact confirms my long-standing interpretation of the position of the cycle.

In a similar vein, the price performance of the market often indicates the position of a cycle within *larger* cycles. Examine Figure 3-3 again and observe the dramatic lessening of long term upside progress dating back to 1929. This slowdown implies that a cycle even larger than the Kondratieff has been pointing down for a number of decades. Chapter 6 demonstrates that upside progress has continued to slow in the past eight years, and the past four years as well. Thus, the declining upside momentum of stock prices at various scales dates from as far back as 1929 and from as recently as 1966, 1987 and every year since 1991. This condition conforms to the thesis that numerous cycles, including the Kondratieff, are topping.

Outlook

The assessment under the Wave Principle that a Grand Supercycle is ending places the next bear market in the class of the 1722-1784 experience, which involved *two* Kondratieff cycle lows. The expected duration of the impending bear market, as discussed in Chapter 5, could mean that as many as *three* Kondratieff cycle lows will occur within it. This forecast will focus only on the first one, as it will be hard enough to forecast. Possible dates for later lows are discussed briefly in Chapter 5 and at the end of this section.

As of 1995, the Kondratieff cycle is now in position to cause, as *Elliott Wave Principle* put it, "three or four years of severe depression and a long period of deflation." This is a good time to mention that because of that deflation, the final years of a Kondratieff economic cycle constitute the only time that falling interest rates are not reliably bullish for stocks and the economy. From 1929 to 1933, rates mostly fell, yet stocks and economic activity fell right along with them. Interest rates on safe (actually safe, not simply labeled "guaranteed" or "insured") debt, rare as it will be in this cycle, will likewise fall as the desire for business loans recedes. Any such signs of falling interest rates should not be interpreted as bullish, as they would be during the first half of a Kondratieff cycle.

When will the final phase of the current cycle end? A dozen years ago, after figuring out the proper position of the cycle, *The Elliott Wave Theorist* projected the next bottom as follows: "Based on its previous low in 1896, the most recent Kondratieff cycle bottom...may have occurred as late as 1949, which places the next bottom around **2003**." Figure B-3 shows the projected Kondratieff cycle into that year.

How reliable is this timing projection? Most economists dismiss cycles altogether and appear particularly to relish denying the existence of the Kondratieff cycle. I take a strong position on the opposite side. While the time length for the Kondratieff cycle is usually cited as "50 to 60 years, averaging about 54 years in length," the record of stock prices reveals that this cycle has recently been quite precise. As you can see by Figure B-4, price lows occurred in 1896, **53** years before 1949, and in 1842, **54** years before 1896, and (possibly) 1788, **54** years before 1842. Sparse data indicates that the latter date could have been any of several years between 1778 and 1788 (see discussion in Chapter 2). The cycle that occurred in the 1700s in British stock prices appears to have been longer, at **62**

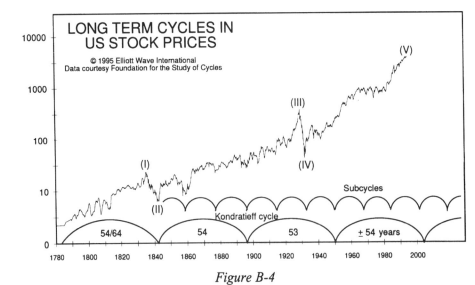

Figure B-4

years, lasting from 1722 to 1784. The answer, then, is that if the
cycle is still operating, our timing projection should be fairly reliable. The earliest likely year for a bottom is **2002**, the best fit is
2003, and a match of the longest cycle on record would place the low
as far out as **2011**.

Figures B-5 through B-9 display the five most recent Kondratieff cycles in terms of stock prices, along with the dominant subcycle.
(The data, courtesy of the Foundation for the Study of Cycles, is
plotted in logarithms.) Let's examine the various end-of-cycle resolutions to see if we can develop a price projection for the end of the
current cycle.

The mildest late-cycle stock market decline bottomed in 1896
and brought stock prices down 46%. It is unlikely that the next Kondratieff cycle decline will be so mild. First, that decline ended a
correction of only Cycle degree within a Supercycle *third* wave, the
most powerful part of the larger advance. The current situation will
resolve with a bear market of at least Supercycle degree, quite a
different situation. What's more, the drop into 1896 was the only
decline among the last three that began from a level well below the
long term Elliott Wave resistance line connecting the highs of 1835
and 1929 (see Figure 2-1). The lack of corresponding overvaluation
reduced the downside potential. Once again, today's situation is completely different, as the market is actually *above* the long term
trendline for the first time ever. Thus, there is every reason to bet
against the occurrence of a mild decline.

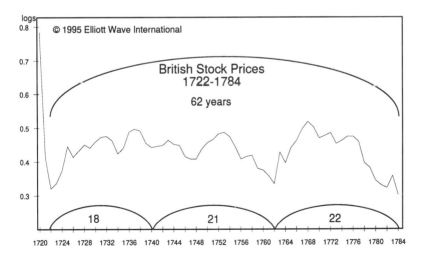

Figure B-5

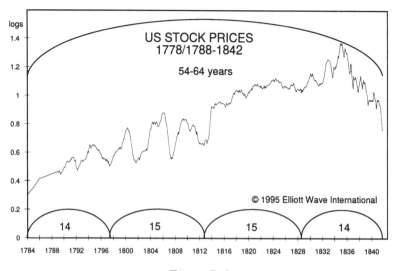

Figure B-6

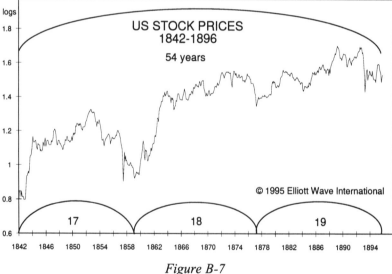

Figure B-7

In more typical final resolutions, the end-of-cycle declines bottoming in 1784, 1842 and 1932 brought stock prices down 98%, 78% and 89%, respectively. Certainly the upcoming fall will reflect one of these. Which one?

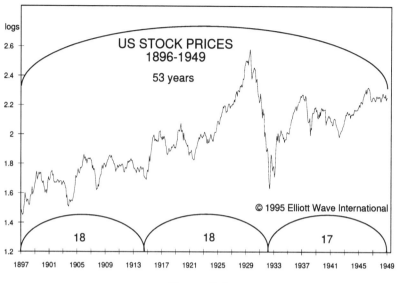

Figure B-8

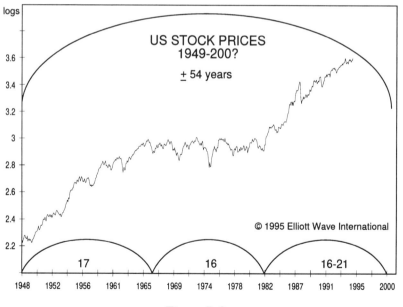

Figure B-9

The deepest decline of the past three centuries was the one that ended in 1722 after a decline of 98% for the average stock in two years. (Figure B-5 depicts a 66% decline, but that relates only to the annual daily averages of the few issues that survived.) This was the only decline of the five that was associated with the start of a Grand Supercycle bear market, which is exactly what the stock market faces today. While the first wave of the Grand Supercycle need not be as severe as that one, it is possible, for the first time in nearly three centuries, to say that it *could* be that severe. At minimum, the Kondratieff cycle assures that the bull market from 1982, which is taking place after the idealized peak of the cycle, is doomed to complete retracement. In all these regards, then, the Wave Principle and the Kondratieff cycle are in complete agreement.

The only time that stocks fell early in the cycle was 1929-1932, a collapse that mitigated the severity of the final years of correction. The current cycle is emphatically *not* following that pattern but the more common pattern of continued high stock prices until the last few years. Of exceptional importance, then, is the fact that in the past two hundred years, each time the stock market made new highs near the end of the Kondratieff cycle, the final years witnessed a powerful downside resolution. The Kondratieff cycle today is in its 46th year and should have only eight years remaining in it. Time is running out for stock prices to pay the piper named Kondratieff.

Even if the stock market were to continue rising through the rest of the decade, that feat by itself would not contraindicate this book's conclusion about the position of the Kondratieff cycle. In fact, the worst decline of all, from 1720 to 1722, occurred at the end of the cycle in which stock prices held up the longest.

The next three Kondratieff cycle lows are due ideally in 2003, 2057 and 2111. As described in Chapter 5, these three times (which will be adjusted, if necessary, based upon the actual time of each preceding low) should roughly coincide with Supercycle degree lows within the Grand Supercycle bear market.

THE 16-20 YEAR CYCLE

The Kondratieff cycle appears to subdivide into harmonic subcycles ranging from 14 to 22 years long, as illustrated in Figures B-5 through B-9. The range of the past 150 years has been a narrower and therefore more reliable band of 16-19 years. The last three Kondratieff cycles saw subcycle lows in 1842, 1859, 1877, 1896, 1914,

1932, 1949, 1966 and 1982. As an important aside, the bottoming of this cycle in October 1966 explains why some stocks (secondary stocks in 1968 and blue chips in 1973) made new highs during the first seven years of the Cycle wave IV correction.

The 16-20-year cycle currently in progress is now 13 years old and is due to bottom in 1998-2002. As the April 1983 Special Report noted in support of this conclusion, "The very regular recurrence of turning points at 16.6-16.9-year intervals (see the bottom of Figure 3-2) projects 1999 for the next turning point." The projected low in 2003 for the larger Kondratieff cycle could force a longer subcycle this time, as noted in Figure B-9.

As that chart suggests, the stock market is at the end of both the Kondratieff cycle and its third harmonic subcycle, suspended high in the air like a cartoon character that has run off a cliff but has yet to realize it. Those who after 1987 wanted a "second chance" to sell at good prices are getting it. With the new bullish mood, however, few are acting.

THE BENNER-FIBONACCI CYCLE

Elliott Wave Principle presented a unique timing device based upon Samuel Benner's cyclic discoveries but modified to fit the behavior of the stock market. It projected a high in 1983, a major low in 1987, and a high in 1991. The 1983 high in the S&P 500 preceded a year-long 16% drop in the averages and marked the peak in one-year upside momentum for the 1980s' bull market and the end of relative strength for secondary stocks. The crash in 1987, of course, fit the projection for a major low due that year. The cycle high that was due in 1991 produced a peak in the upside rate of change, just as did 1983.

Now let's update these cycles. As you can see by the schematic in Figure B-10, the next cycle low is due in 1995. This projection precisely fits the most powerfully indicated Fibonacci year of the decade, but other indications call for a *high* in 1995. There is a precedent for this coincidence. The last time that Fibonacci time counts pointed to a high (see Chapter 4) in the same year that the Benner-Fibonacci cycle pointed to a low was *1987*. The result was both a high *and* a low, with an intervening crash of record proportion. The identical setup this year implies a crash for 1995. The difference is that the expected top this year is three degrees larger than the Primary degree top of 1987, so any crash might be correspondingly larger. This potential is irrelevant both to the overall analysis and

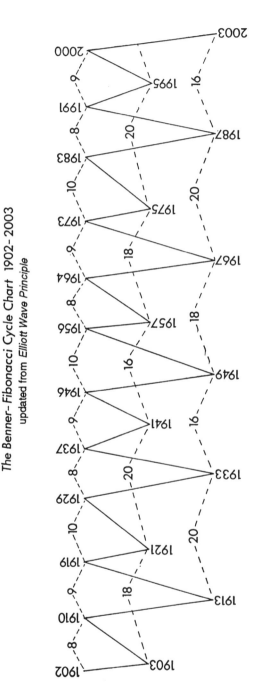

The Benner-Fibonacci Cycle Chart 1902-2003
updated from *Elliott Wave Principle*

Figure B-10

PEAKS: 8-9-10, repeat. TROUGHS:16-18-20,repeat. MAJOR TROUGHS:16-18-20,repeat.

to most investment strategies, but it is certainly a potential that speculators might wish to note. Finally, as Figure B-10 reiterates, the next major bottom for the Kondratieff cycle is due in 2003.

THE DECENNIAL PATTERN

The Decennial Pattern, first described by Edgar Lawrence Smith in the 1920s, is a detailed depiction of the ten-year cycle. The fact that the pattern reflects an Elliott Wave adds credence to its validity. Figure B-11 was first shown in *Elliott Wave Principle* in 1978. *The Elliott Wave Theorist* found the Decennial Pattern of great value in the 1980s in helping project a bullish outlook from mid-1984 to mid-1987. Notice how perfectly the 1980s fit into the historical pattern, producing a major bottom in the "2" year, a pullback into the middle of the "4" year, a peak in the third quarter of the "7" year, a crash into the fourth quarter of the "7" year, an advance into the "9" year, and a correction into the "0" year.

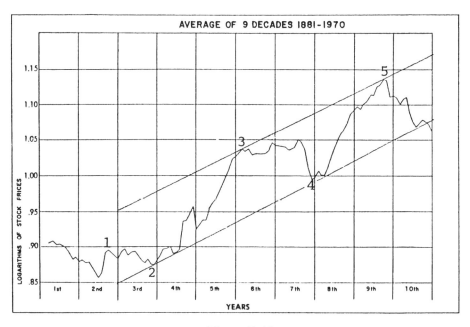

Figure B-11

So far, however, the 1990s have diverged completely from the typical profile, rising in the "1", "2" and "3" years and going sideways in the "4" year. One reason might be the renewed popularity of the pattern. The Decennial Pattern has recently enjoyed some publicity, primarily because it calls for powerful gains throughout 1995, 1996 and most of 1997. However, the divergence from the norm in the past four years places the generally expected outcome powerfully in doubt. With so many cycles pointing lower, this cycle is at risk of failure. The strongest correlation of the Decennial Pattern with other cycles discussed in this appendix is in the low due in the "2" through "4" years of the *next* decade, when so many other cycles are due to bottom.

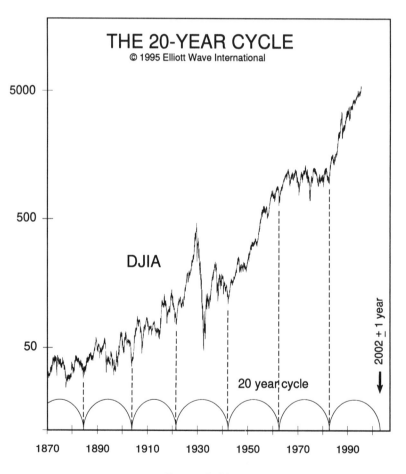

Figure B-12

THE 20-YEAR CYCLE

The 20-year cycle reflects the dramatic stock market lows of 1884, 1903, 1921, 1942, 1962 and 1982, as shown in Figure B-12. This cycle projects another low in the year 2002, coinciding with the outlook from the Kondratieff cycle.

THE 8- AND 12-YEAR CYCLES IN SECONDARY STOCKS

For most of this century, secondary stocks have exploded upward every eight and twelve years. The length of time that each advance carries depends upon the position of the stock market in its long term Elliott Wave structure. Take a look at Figure B-13, which shows the ratio of S&P's Low Priced Stock Index to its High Grade Stock Index and depicts the 8- and 12-year cycles underneath. The ideal years for 8-year cycle lows, with the actual dates in parentheses if different, are: 1934(33), 1942, 1950(49), 1958(57), 1966, 1974, 1982 and 1990. These dates coincide with the beginnings of soaring relative strength in secondary stocks. The 12-year cycle is less reliable but coincides well with the remaining lows.

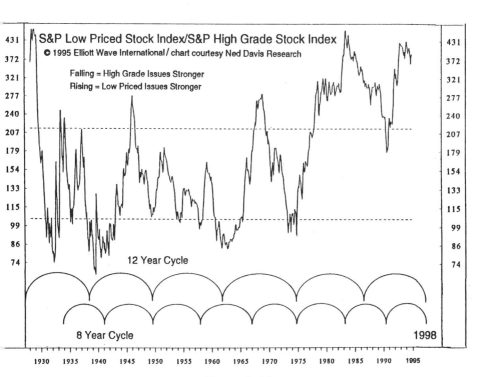

Figure B-13

Both the 8- *and* 12-year cycles point down into 1998. Notice that 1998 will be the first time in twenty-four years that the 8- and 12-year cycles will bottom together. The two prior times were 1974 and 1950 (1949), two of the most depressed lows of this century. With only three years remaining in the cycle, the losses should be severe; no stocks will be spared in the selloff that lies directly ahead. Accordingly, 1998 should mark a deep low for both blue chips and secondaries.

The irony, of course, is that market observers have taken the long bull market in broad stock indexes as a sign that everything is safe and bullish in the stock market. A cyclic viewpoint yields the opposite conclusion. So does a study of relative valuation. As you can see by Figure B-13, the peak in 1983 marked a relative valuation for secondaries equivalent to that of 1928. After the drop into 1990, the 8-year cycle has brought the ratio back to a near-record relative valuation. From this perspective as well, there is a long way to fall.

THE 4-YEAR CYCLE

Though of only mild influence in 1986 and 1994, the 4-year cycle has remained the most reliable rhythm in stock prices, having been in continuous operation for four decades, since 1954. As with all cycles, each time it turns up, the stock market typically reaches a peak rate of change quickly, then spends the rest of the cycle in a state of momentum dissipation. From the cycle's latest bottom in late 1994, the 10-week rate of change on the NYSE index has registered its lowest peak in the 40-year history of the cycle, an exceptionally weak 7.2%. As a comparison, the overbought condition following the 1982 low was a very bullish 33.7%. The 24-week rate of change shows the same thing, as shown by this list of overbought levels achieved in the months immediately following the first ten 4-year cycle lows: 1954: **17.9%**; 1958: **17.5%**; 1962: **26.1%**; 1966: **24.2%**; 1970: **27.5%**; 1974: **38.2%**; 1978: **11.7%**; 1982: **39.2%**; 1986: **27.6%**; 1990: **25.1%**. Can you see a big difference in the early 1995 estimated figure of **14%** (based on trend extrapolation and "drop-off" figures), shown in Figure B-14? By these readings, this 4-year cycle has so far generated the second-weakest advance of any 4-year cycle upturn on record. The last time this cycle had approximately as weak an upturn was 1978, which led to four years of zero progress, and that was within a Cycle degree bull market. The current signal is almost certainly indicating the approach of a bear market.

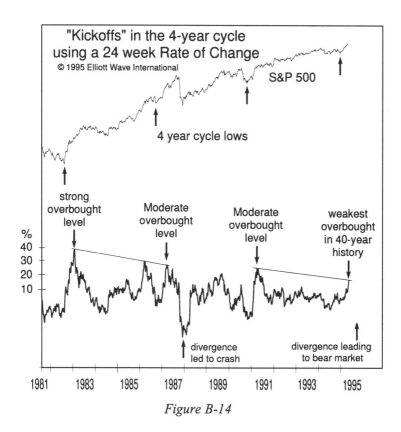

Figure B-14

This weak overbought condition here in the second quarter of 1995 also confirms our conclusion that longer term cycles, such as the 8-, 12- and 20-year rhythms, are exerting powerful downside pressure, dampening the effect of the 4-year cycle. If the longer cycles were up, the shorter one would be expected to exert upside pressure for another two years. However, with other cycles down, there remains every reason to believe that this 4-year cycle will be "left-hand translated" and create a market top early in the cycle.

THE NEXT MAJOR STOCK MARKET BOTTOM

The next 4- and 8-year cycle lows are due in 1998. The next 12-year cycle low is due in 1998. The next 16-to-20-year cycle low is due in 1998-2002. The 16.6-16.9-year turning point cycle is due in 1999. The next 18-year cycle low is due in 2000. The next 20-year cycle low is due in 2002. The next Decennial Pattern low is due in 2002-2004. The Kondratieff/Benner cycle low is due in 2003. The next

4-year cycle is due to bottom in 2004. Thus, regardless of whether the stock market tops out in 1995, cycles strongly suggest a major low in the **1998-2004** period.

AN 11-YEAR CYCLE IN BONDS

Bonds' most consistent time cycle supports the case for a low early in the next decade. As Figure B-15 reveals, a reliable 11-year cycle bottomed in 1981. It was less pronounced in 1992, so it may be fading. Its next low is due in 2003, in close agreement with the Fibonacci time projection of **8** years to 2001 shown in Figure 12-11, and the *same* year that stocks are due to bottom. These projections suggest an ideal scenario of a major bottom in bonds in 2001 and a "test" of the bottom (i.e., a higher low) in 2003, coinciding with a final bottom in stocks. While the uncertainty of this cycle's continuing validity is such that we might not rely on any forecast based upon it, it is good enough that *if* bonds follow this scenario into 2003, they should be considered a buy.

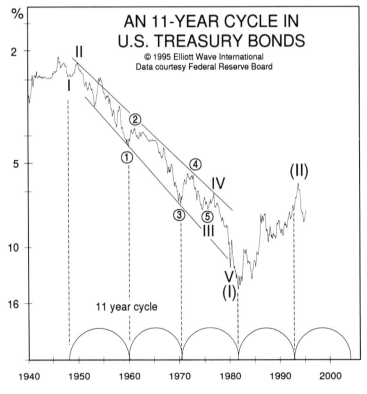

Figure B-15

ILLUSTRATIONS IN
At the Crest of the Tidal Wave,
UPDATED WITH FIGURES AVAILABLE
THROUGH JUNE 1997

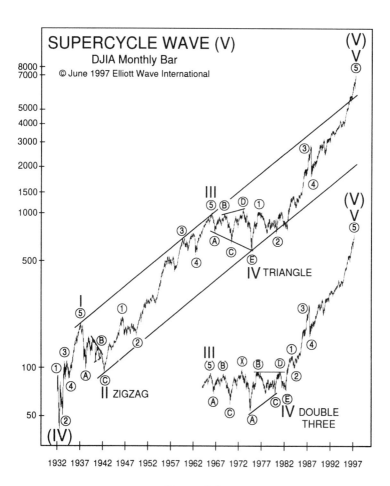

Figure 2-5

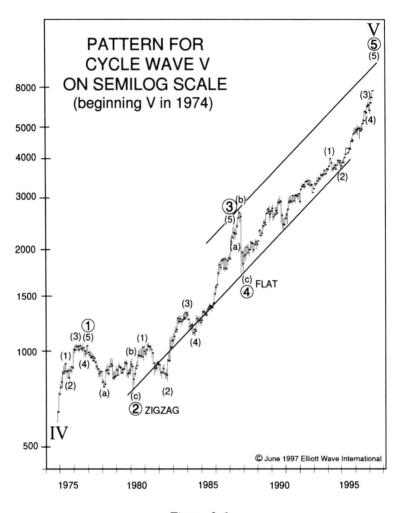

Figure 2-6

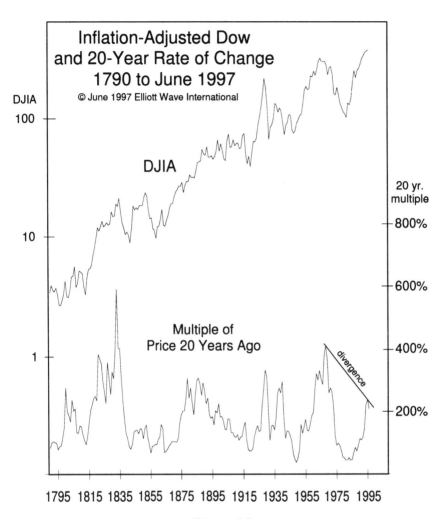

Figure 6-2

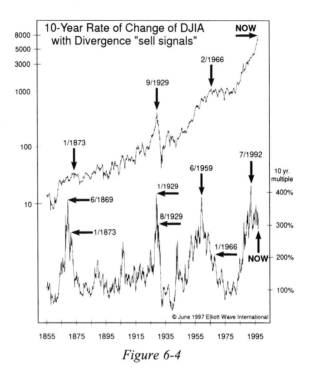

Figure 6-4

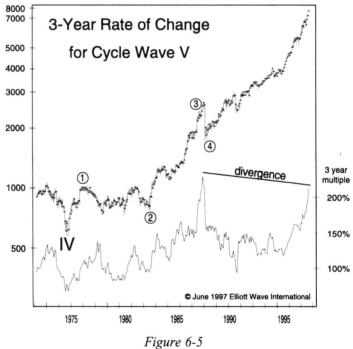

Figure 6-5

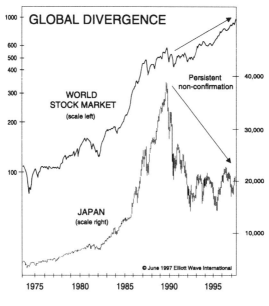

Figure 6-6

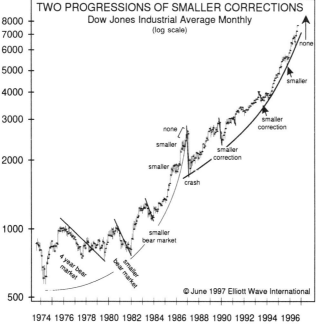

Figure 6-11

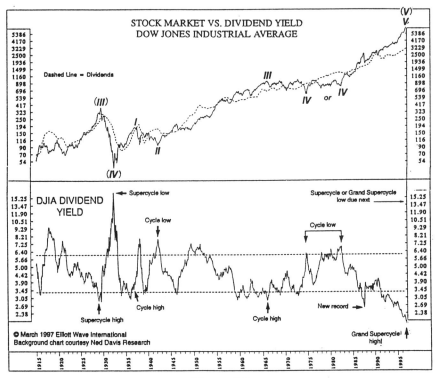

Figure 7-2

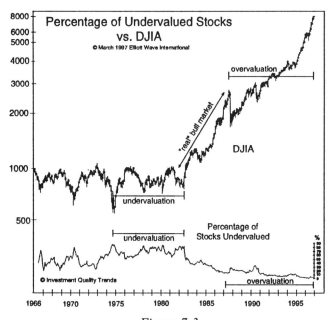

Figure 7-3

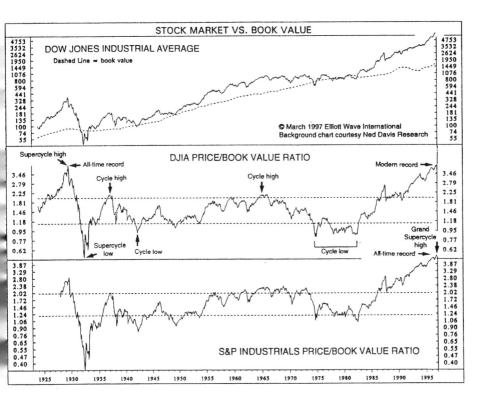

Figure 7-4

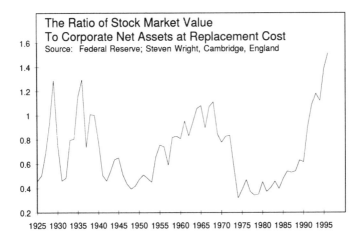

Figure 7-4a

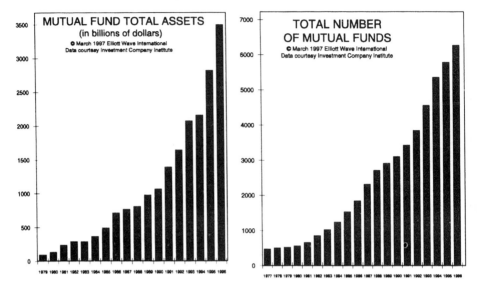

Figure 8-1

Figure 8-2

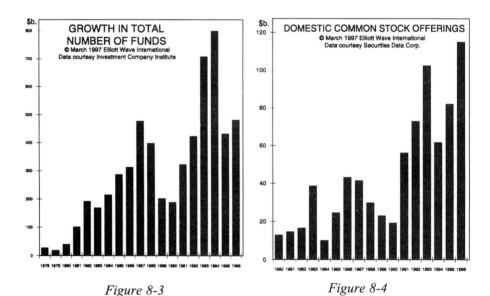

Figure 8-3

Figure 8-4

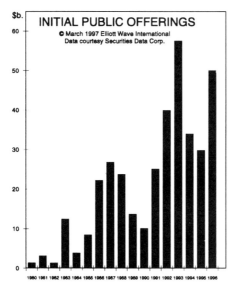

Figure 8-5

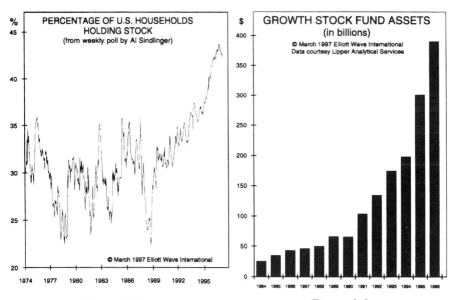

Figure 8-7   *Figure 8-8*

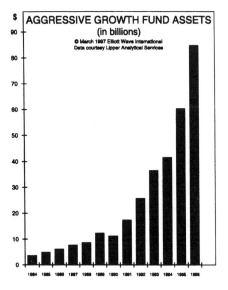

Figure 8-9

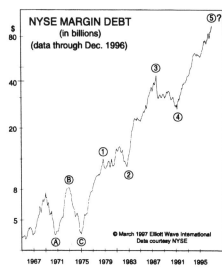

Figure 8-10

Figure 8-11

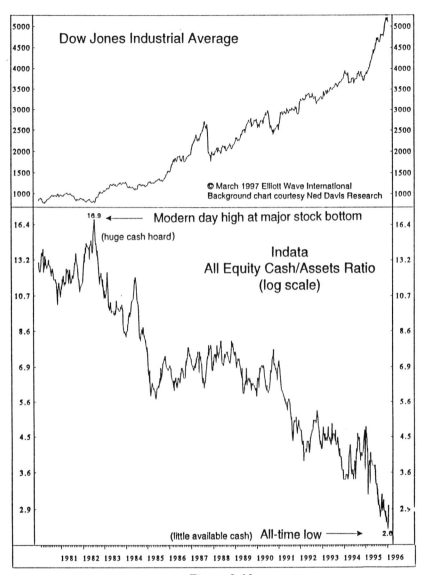

Figure 8-12

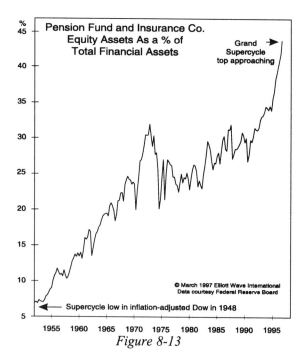

Figure 8-13

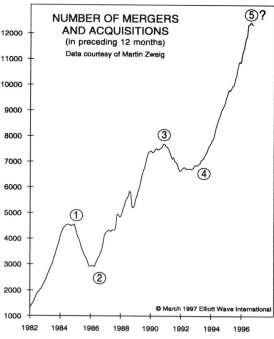

Figure 8-14

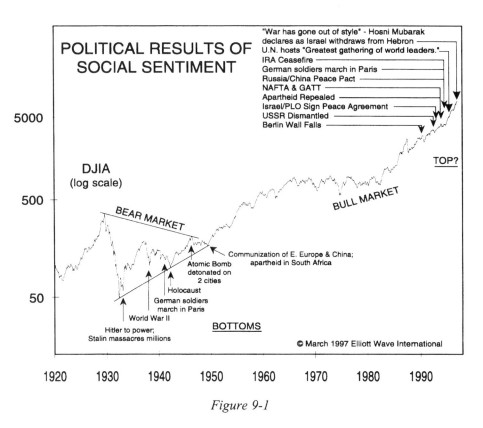

Figure 9-1

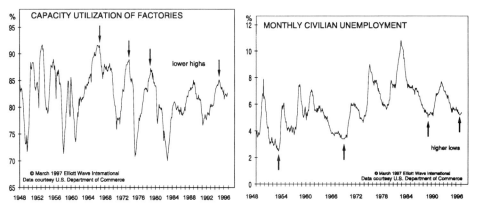

Figure 10-4   *Figure 10-5*

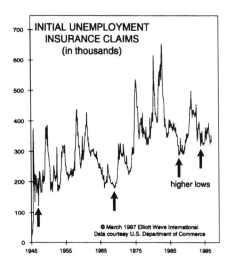

Figure 10-6

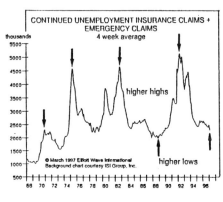

Figure 10-7

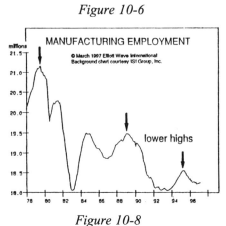

Figure 10-8

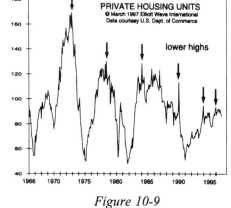

Figure 10-9

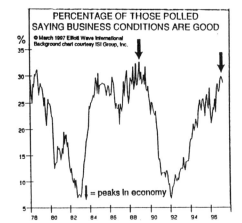

Figure 10-10

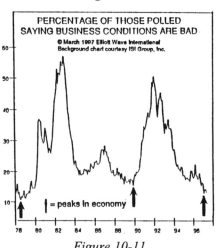

Figure 10-11

Figure 10-12

Figure 10-13

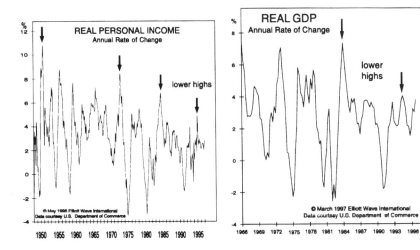

Figure 10-14

Figure 10-15

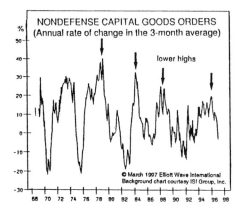

Figure 10-16

Figure 10-17

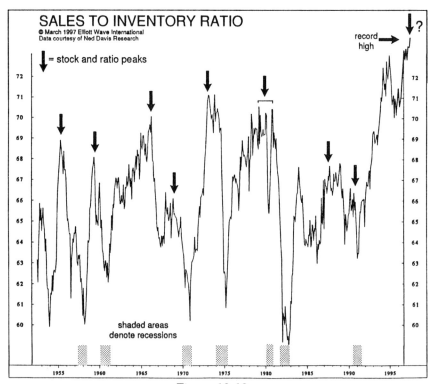

Figure 10-18

Figure 10-28

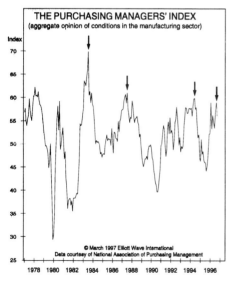

Figure 10-29

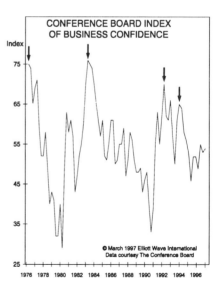

Figure 10-30

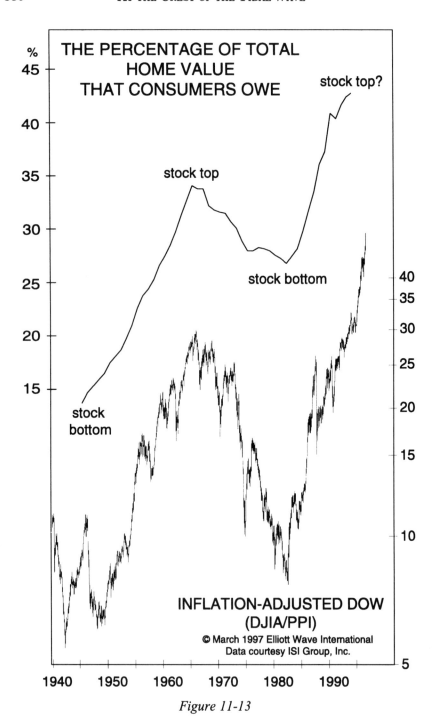

Figure 11-13

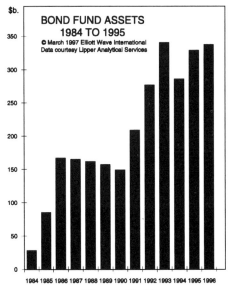

Figure 13-12

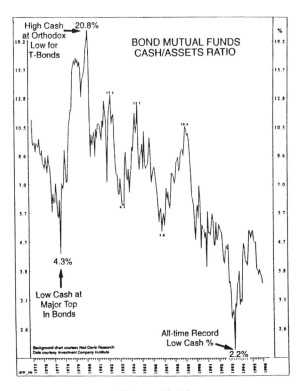

Figure 13-13

USEFUL SERVICES

A number of firms in addition to Elliott Wave International provide services that are suited to turbulent times and provide value by reaching beyond the conventional wisdom. I highly regard all of these services, but as I lack omniscience about their futures, none can be guaranteed. It will be your job to assess their value (or lack thereof) to you. Needless to say, there are additional analysts and services for whom I have the utmost respect and whose opinions I value highly. However, many of those are substantially oriented to stock selection, which while valuable in most market environments, may be incompatible with the upcoming one. Listings are alphabetical.

MARKET TIMING AND ANALYSIS PUBLICATIONS

Boom, Gloom & Doom Report
Marc Faber Ltd.
Rm 2705 New World Tower
16-18 Queens Rd. Central
HONG KONG
852-2-801-5410
Editor: Marc Faber

Cycles Magazine
Foundation for the Study of Cycles
900 West Valley Road
Suite 502
Wayne, PA 19087
610-995-2120
Editor: Richard Mogey

The Dines Report
PO Box 22
Belvedere, CA 94920
800-845-8259
Editor: James Dines

Dow Theory Letters
PO Box 1759
LaJolla, CA 92038
619-454-0481
Editor: Richard Russell

Grant's Interest Rate Observer
30 Wall Street
New York, NY 10005
212-809-7994
Editor: James Grant

InvesTech
2472 Birch Glen
Whitefish, MT 59937
406-862-7777
Editor: James Stack

Ned Davis Research
600 Bird Bay Dr.
Venice FL 34292
941-484-6107
(data and chart services for
institutional clients)
President: Ned Davis

Stockmarket Cycles
PO Box 6873
Santa Rosa, CA 95406-0873
707-579-8444
Editor: Peter Eliades

Market Timing and Analysis Publications, continued...

Universal Economics
Legg Mason Wood Walker
600 Thimble Shoals Blvd. #110
Newport News, VA 23606-2526
804-873-3300
Editor: Paul Montgomery

Weiss Research
4176 Burns Rd.
Palm Beach Gardens, FL 33410
561-627-3300
Publications Editor: Martin Weiss

The Wellington Letter
66 Queen St., Ste 3801
Honolulu, HI 96813
808-545-2243
Editor: Bert Dohmen

SOCIAL OBSERVATIONS

Early Warning Report
Box 1616PR
Rocklin, CA 95677
916-632-2501
Editor: Rick Maybury

The Ron Paul Report
PO Box 602
Lake Jackson, TX 77566
409-265-6403
Editor: Ron Paul

Strategic Investment
Agora Financial Publishing
824 E. Baltimore St.
Baltimore, MD 21202-4799
800-433-1528
Editor: James Dale Davidson

MAVERICK ECONOMISTS

A. Gary Schilling & Co.
500 Morris Ave.
Springfield, NJ 07081
201-467-0070

ISI Group
717 Fifth Ave.
New York, NY 10022
212-446-6475

Jerome Levy Economics Institute
69 S. Moger Ave.
Mount Kisco, NY 10549
914-666-0641

Sindlinger & Co.
405 Osborne Lane
Wallingford, PA 19086
610-565-0247

GOLD AND SILVER DEALERS

Hancock & Harwell
Suite 310
3155 Roswell Rd.
Atlanta, GA 30305
800-995-6566
Robert L. Harwell and Jack Hancock

Investment Rarities Inc.
7850 Metro Parkway #106
Minneapolis, MN 55425-1521
800-328-1860 or 612-853-0700
James Cook

Jefferson Coin & Bullion Inc.
2400 Jefferson Hwy.
Suite 600
Jefferson, LA 70121
504-837-3033
President: James U. Blanchard III
Publication: *Gold Newsletter*

U.S. Gold & Silver Investments
PO Box 19435
Portland, OR 97280
503-624-4816
Larry Heim

DEFENSIVE MONEY MANAGEMENT WITH THE ELLIOTT WAVE OUTLOOK IN MIND

FX 500 Limited
930 Tahoe Blvd., Suite 802
Incline Village, NV 89451-9436
714-499-6063
Contact: Don Evans
($500,000 minimum)

Growth Stock Outlook, Inc.
Box 15381
Chevy Chase, MD 20815
301-654-5205
Manager: Charles Allmon
Publication: *Growth Stock Outlook*
($175,000 minimum)

Whittacat Consulting Associates
International
146 John St.
PO Box 747
Bracebridge, Ontario P1L 1R8
CANADA
416-762-2330; 800-638-5760
Contact: Mark Edward Workman
($2m. minimum)

Zulauf Asset Management AG
Grafenauweg 4
CH-6300 Zug
SWITZERLAND
(From US dial 011) 41-42-23 46 33
Fax: 41-42-23 46 34
Manager: Felix Zulauf
($3m. USD minimum)

INTERNATIONAL WEALTH PRESERVATION STRATEGIES AND SERVICES

SafeWealth Ltd. &
Globacor (Consultants) Ltd.
PO Box 1995-A, Windsor
Berkshire, SL4 5LL
UNITED KINGDOM
800-462-5943 and
(From US dial 011) 44-1753-554-461
Fax: 44-1753-554-642
or
7B Pleasant Boulevard, Box 970-A
Toronto, Ontario M4T 1K2
CANADA
Contact: Jean-Pierre Louvet or
Douglas P. Scott
Publication: *The Capital Preservation Strategist Consultancy Report*

Index

T

The Wall Street Journal 19, 116, 119, 120, 123, 124, 125, 129, 137, 138, 155, 161, 178, 241, 272, 273
third wave 42, 68, 73, 84, 87, 95, 122, 123, 124, 183, 184, 197, 254, 278, 310, 321
Third World 165, 231, 234
trade war 166, 229, 300
Treasury bills (T-bills) 99, 111, 119, 149, 150, 164, 239, 245, 246, 254, 280, 281
Treasury bonds 145, 149, 245, 248, 250, 251, 257, 266
triangles 32, 35, 42, 57, 61, 62, 64, 65, 67, 81, 245, 248, 249, 250, 307, 310, 316

U

U.S. dollar 38, 41, 48, 107, 116, 143, 166, 184, 198, 240, 241, 243, 244, 286, 316
U.S. government 48, 121, 229, 289, 301
urgent selling 103, 104

V

valuation 29, 39, 49, 106-117, 184, 197, 228, 292, 321, 330
Value Line index 30, 270, 280
volatility 100, 101, 102, 287

W

Wall of Worry 118, 171, 173
war 13, 18, 28, 29, 30, 47, 57, 126, 128, 166, 178, 179, 180, 213, 215, 229, 298, 299, 300, 301, 314
War of 1812 28, 47
Weiss, Geraldine 112
World Stock Index 14
World War I 28, 47, 179
World War II 28, 47, 179, 215, 301

X

xenophobia 298

Y

Yeltsin 179

Z

zero coupon bonds 268, 272
zigzags 27, 33, 34, 56, 57, 62, 67, 73, 248, 250, 252, 254, 307, 310
Zulus 13, 16

When is it right to judge an investment book a "classic"?

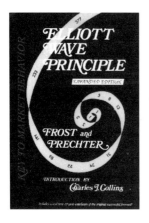

Two decades is long enough to judge whether investors deem a book about an investment method a "classic," and surely the jury is in on this one: *Elliott Wave Principle* has been published in **seven** languages, and continues to sell thousands of copies every year.

If you don't yet own a copy of this perennial best-seller — or if you own an earlier edition — now is the time to read the book that reintroduced the Wave Principle to the world.

Elliott Wave Principle *presents a remarkable theory to the world in over 200 pages of captivating detail. This hardback edition contains newly expanded and clarified chapters explaining even more precisely the principles, rules and guidelines of wave analysis.*

You will even read how the authors applied "Elliott" at the start of the great bull market that has pierced its horns into the history books.

This is the definitive work.

There are many books about "successful investing." Yet none of them — not one — offers you a method more successful than what you will learn from *Elliott Wave Principle — Key to Market Behavior.*

Surf the Elliott Wave International Website

- **FREE** Course on the Elliott Wave Principle

- **FREE** Message Board with Bob Prechter

- Information on *Elliott Wave International's* Products and Services

www.elliottwave.com

Preview of our Monthly Publications

You can receive one issue of our monthly financial publications — FREE! Choose the publication you want, described below, and we'll rush you the current issue.

The Elliott Wave Theorist

The world-renowned market publication and vehicle for the monthly forecasts that earned Robert Prechter the title, "Guru of the Decade." Includes stocks, bonds, and precious metals, plus social, monetary and cultural trends. (10-12 pp.)

Currency Market Perspective

All major cash and futures markets and cross rates receive in-depth analysis each month, complete with detailed Elliott Wave charts. The editor also covers the political and economic trends that are important to the currency markets. (10-12 pp.)

Global Market Perspective

The combined effort of eight experienced wave analysts (including Robert Prechter) who forecast the price movement of all the major global financial markets — equities, interest rates, currencies, precious metals and energy as well as social and cultural trends. (100+ pp.)

World Commodity Perspective

Comprehensive coverage includes the CRB, Grains, Meats, Softs and Industrials. Lots of charts, forecasts and Elliott Wave analysis, plus insights of an editor dedicated to these specialty markets. (10-12 pp.)

This offer is available only from ***Elliott Wave International***. To receive your **FREE** issue — simply copy or cut out the order form on the back of this page and mail it or fax it to:

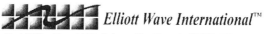 *Elliott Wave International*™

Post Office Box 1618, Gainesville, Georgia 30503, USA
or fax it to: 770-536-2514

For more information call: 800-336-1618 or 770-536-0309